The Economic Report of the ~~President~~ People

Economic Report of the ~~President~~ PEOPLE

Center for Popular Economics

SOUTH END PRESS **BOSTON**

First edition
Editing, typsetting, layout by South End Press, USA
Manufactured in the USA
Cover by Lydia Sargent

Library of Congress Cataloguing in Publication Data
Main entry under title:

The Economic report of the people!

    The crossed out word "President" appears in the title before the word
"people."
    Includes bibliographical references and index.
    1. United States—Economic conditions—1981-
2. United States—Economic policy—1981-
3. Supply-side economics—United States. 4. Debts,
External—Developing countries. I. Center for Popular
Economics (U.S.)
HC106.8.E29 1986   330.973'0927   85-30342
ISBN 0-89608-316-0
ISBN 0-89608-315-2 (pbk.)

SOUTH END PRESS   116 St Botolph St   Boston MA 02115

This book is dedicated to the thousands of community and union activists who have participated in our summer institutes and workshops over the past seven years.

Their dedication to economic justice and their grassroots achievements continue to strengthen our commitment to people before profits.

Acknowledgements

This project was made possible by the generous support of the Field Foundation, the Presbyterian Church (U.S.A.), the United Church of Christ, Board of Homeland Ministries, and the Economics and Democratic Values Project.
Many people served as consultants to this project. We would like to thank: Peter Alexander, University of Massachusetts, Amherst; Gar Alperovitz, National Center for Economic Alternatives; Teresa Amott, Women for Economic Justice, Wellesley College; Masoto Aoki, University of Massachusetts, Amherst; Thomas Asher, Discount Foundation; Judy Ashkanaz; Harriet Barlow, Blue Mountain Center; Harold Baron, Office of the Mayor, Chicago, Illinois; Richard Barnet, Institute for Policy Studies; Randall Bartlett, Smith College; Janis Barry, Fordham University; Nanette Berg, University of Massachusetts, Amherst; Peter Bohmer, Pennsylvania State University; Bob Borasage, Institute for Policy Studies; Susan B. Carter, Smith College; John Cavanagh, Institute for Policy Studies; Josh Cohen, Massachusetts Institute for Technology; Miriam Colon, Boone & Young & Associates; Joe Conason, *The Village Voice*; James Crotty, University of Massachusetts, Amherst; Nancy Folbre, University of Massachusetts, Amherst; Jetta Fraser, University of Massachusetts, Amherst; Herbert Gintis, University of Massachusetts, Amherst; Michael Goldhaber, Institute for Policy Studies; David Gordon, New School for Social Research; Lucy Gorham, House Subcommittee on Inter-Governmental Relations; Peter Gottschalk, Bowdoin College; Juliet Graham, University of Massachusetts, Amherst; Robert Greenstein, Center for Budget and Policy Priorities; Terianne Falcone, University of Massachusetts, Amherst; Andre Gunder Frank, Institute for Policy Studies; Nancy Gutman, University of Massachusetts, Amherst; Chester Hartman, Institute for Policy Studies; Heidi Hartmann, National Academy of Science; Peter Hayes, University of California, Berkeley; Curtis Haynes, University of Massachusetts, Amherst; Roger Hickey, Economic Policy Institute; Naka Ishii, Nautilus Pacific Research; Aylette Jenness, The Children's Museum, Boston; Charles Jeszeck, Service Employees International Union; Joseph Keesecker, Presbyterian Hunger Program; Robert Kuttner, *The New Republic*; Frances Moore Lappé, Institute for Food and Development Policy;

Rochelle Lefkowitz, Fenton Communications; Steve Max, Midwest Academy; S. M. Miller, Boston University; Phillip Newell, Presbyterian Church in the U.S.A.; Richard Parker, Richard Parker Associates; Frances Fox Piven, Graduate Center, City University of New York; Robert Pollin, University of California, Riverside; Lee Price, U.S. House of Representatives Economic Stabilization Committee; Michael Reich, University of California, Berkeley; Shoshana Rihn; Judy Robinson, University of Massachusetts, Amherst; Joel Rogers, Rutgers University; Clara Rodriguez, Fordham University; Miriam Smalhout, Institute for Policy Studies; Elaine Sorensen, University of Massachusetts, Amherst; Greg Speeter, Center for Organizational & Community Development; Jim Stormes, University of Massachusetts, Amherst; Sue Thrasher, Highlander Center; Andres Torres, New School for Social Research; David Vail, Bowdoin College; Howard Wachtel, American University; Joy Wallens, Paragraphics; Herbert White, United Church of Christ; Meg Worcester, Words and Music; Brenda Wyss, University of Massachusetts, Amherst.

We would also like to thank South End Press for their excellent and timely production efforts, Shoshana Rihn for compiling the index, and all the members of the Center for Popular Economics for their support and inspiration.

The Center for Popular Economics also thanks all the foundations and individuals, who over the years have enabled us to work with so many activists and popular economists across the U.S. and Canada: A Territory Resource; Bread and Roses Community Fund; Circle Fund; Discount Foundation; The Domestic and Foreign Missionary Society of the Protestant Episcopal Church in the U.S.A.; Evergreen Fund; W. H. & C. Bernstein Ferry; Fund for Tomorrow, Inc.; Funding Exchange/National Community Funds; Haymarket Peoples Fund; Holy Cross Fathers; Max and Anna Levinson Foundation; The Limantour Fund; Peace Development Fund; Public Concern Foundation; PBP Foundation; Shalan Foundation; The Sunflower Foundation; The Fairtree Foundation; Twenty-first Century Foundation; Windom Fund; Women's Opportunity Giving Fund of the Presbyterian Church in the U.S.A.; The Youth Project.

Table of Contents

Authors and Editors

Editors:

LYUBA ZARSKY is the general editor and project coordinator of the *Economic Report of the People* and co-authored Chapters 1 and 2. She is the co-author of *American Lake: Nuclear Peril in the Pacific* (Penguin 1986) and *500 Mile Island: The Political Economy of Nuclear Power in the Philippines* (Pacific Research 1979), as well as articles in *Mother Jones, Le Monde Diplomatique*, and elsewhere. She is a doctoral candidate in Economics at the University of Massachusetts, Amherst and a specialist in international economic and security relations. She is currently researching Japanese trade penetration in external markets and economic integration in the Pacific Basin.

SAMUEL BOWLES is the general editor of the *Economic Report of the People* and co-author of Chapters 1 and 2. He is Professor of Economics at the University of Massachusetts at Amherst, and received his Ph.D. from Harvard University. He has also taught economics at Harvard and the University of Havana and is co-author of *Beyond the Wasteland: A Democratic Alternative to Economic Decline* (Anchor/Doubleday, 1983), *Understanding Capitalism: Competition, Command, and Change in the U.S. Economy* (Harper and Row, 1984), and *Democracy and Capitalism: Property, Community, and the Contradictions of Modern Social Thought* (Basic Books, 1986).

SUSAN ELLS is the editorial and production consultant for the *Economic Report of the People*. She is Director of Development for the Center for Popular Economics and a reporter for *The Brattleboro Reformer* (Brattleboro, Vermont). She is a graduate of the Fletcher School, Tufts University, former manager of affirmative action for Polaroid Corporation and founding President of the Women's Technical Institute, Boston. She is a research fellow with the World Development Institute at Boston University and has published in *In These Times, Management Review* and *Society and Innovation*.

Authors:

ELAINE McCRATE is the primary author of Chapter 3. She is Assistant Professor of Economics at the University of Vermont. She is currently conducting research on the distribution of income in the U.S. and the economic influences on the changing structure of black and white families since 1955. She has worked in the Women's Movement since 1972.

EDWIN MELENDEZ is the primary author of Chapter 4. He holds a Ph.D. in Economics from the University of Massachusetts and teaches economics and Puerto Rican studies at Fordham University. He is formerly a labor organizer and activist in the student and socialist movements within Puerto Rico. His current research interests include imperialism and economic development. He is the author of a major econometric model of the Puerto Rican economy in the post-World War II era.

RANDY ALBELDA is the co-author of Chapter 5. She is an Assistant Professor of Economics at Hobart and William Smith Colleges in Geneva, New York and earned her Ph.D. in Economics from the University of Massachusetts in 1983. Her primary interests include labor economics and the political economy of race and gender. She is a co-editor of *Alternatives to Economic Orthodoxy: A Reader in Political Economy* and has published in *Socialist Review, Review of Radical Political Economics*, and *Industrial and Labor Relations Review*. Her current research projects include a study on the impact of comparable worth by race and job segment, and the demand for women workers in the United States since World War II.

JUNE LAPIDUS is the co-author of Chapter 5. She is a doctoral candidate in Economics at the University of Massachusetts and has taught Women's Studies at the State University of New York, Buffalo. She has published in *Feminist Studies* and specializes in the structure of labor markets and the role of women in the economy.

MARC KITCHEL was a researcher for Chapter 6. He is a doctoral candidate in Economics at the University of Massachusetts and specializes in labor economics and the restructuring of the U.S. economy.

MARY JO HILLIARD was a researcher for Chapter 6. She is a doctoral candidate in Economics at the University of Massachusetts doing research on labor economics in industrialized and developing countries.

DIANE FLAHERTY is the primary author of Chapter 7. She is Associate Professor of Economics at the University of Massachusetts and holds a Ph.D. in Economics from New York University. Her teaching and research interests include the economies of Eastern European nations and the political economy of health care. She has taught at Barnard College, Cambridge University, and Columbia University.

GERALD EPSTEIN is the primary author of Chapter 8. He received his Ph.D. in Economics from Princeton University, and now teaches at the New School for Social Research. He is co-author of *Trading Partners: A Democratic Approach to International Trade and Finance* (South End Press, forthcoming) and author of "The Triple Debt Crisis" (*World Policy Journal*, Fall 1985). He has taught at Williams College and Princeton University. His research interests include international banking and the role of financial institutions and central banks as they affect inflation, unemployment and the distribution of income. He testified recently before the U.S. House Committee on Banking concerning the accountability of the Federal Reserve System.

TOM RIDDELL is the primary author of Chapter 9. He is Assistant Professor of Economics at Smith College and holds a Ph.D. in Economics from American University. His research interests include the economics of militarism and public policy analyses. He has recently completed an econometric study of the relationship between military spending, military intervention and international economic relations, and an assessment of the relationship between military spending and employment. He is a co-author of the popular introductory textbook *Economics: A Tool for Understanding Society* (Addison-Wesley—3rd edition to be published in 1986).

DAVID KOTZ is the primary author of Chapter 10. He is Associate Professor of Economics at the University of Massachusetts and holds a Ph.D. from the University of California at Berkeley. His current teaching and research interests include the structure of American industry, economic crises, and the ownership and control of large corporations. He is a member of the Massachusetts Teachers Association and the author of *Bank Control of Large Corporations* (University of California Press, 1978). He has recently presented Congressional testimony concerning financial deregulation and the banking system of the U.S. and has lectured in the People's Republic of China on macroeconomic problems and the industrial structure of the U.S. economy.

MANUEL PASTOR is the primary author of Chapter 11. He is Assistant Professor of Economics at Occidental College. His current research focuses on the role of the International Monetary Fund in Latin America. His teaching interests include international finance and the political economy of underdevelopment. He has traveled widely in Latin America as a Fulbright scholar.

JULIET B. SCHOR is the primary author of Chapter 12 and the author of Chapter 13. She is Assistant Professor of Economics at Harvard University, and has taught at Williams College and Barnard College, and was a Research Fellow at the Brookings Institution. She is the co-author, with Gerald Epstein, of *Trading Partners: A Democratic Approach to International Trade and Finance* (South End Press, forthcoming). Her research interests include labor markets, social welfare expenditures, and political economic theory.

Center for Popular Economics

The Center For Popular Economics was founded in 1979 to train public interest, community, women's, labor, religious and third world groups in economic concepts and issues.

The Center's workshops, Summer Institute and publications demystify economics and give social change advocates an integrated overview of current economic issues. With the Center's help, individuals increase their self-confidence to use economic ideas and arguments to further their organization's strategies and goals.

Staff economists include faculty members and graduate students at the University of Massachusetts-Amherst; and faculty members at Smith College; Harvard University; Fordham University; the University of Vermont; Hobart and William Smith Colleges; New School for Social Research; Occidental College; University of Texas, Canisius College and SUNY-Purchase.

Center programs include a Summer Institute in popular economics, short-term seminars and workshops and a speaker's bureau. The Center's second book, *Bottom Lines: A Critic's Guide to the U.S. Economy* is forthcoming from Pantheon, New York.

For more information on the Center's programs, write: Center for Popular Economics, Box 785, Amherst, MA 01004 or call (413) 545-0743.

Figures

Part I
The Economics of Reaction

1 The Carrot and the Stick

Each year, the Presidentially-appointed Council of Economic Advisors assesses the health of the U.S. economy in the *Economic Report of the President.* Not surprisingly, the team installed by Ronald Reagan has found consistently that his "free market" policies have been just what the doctor ordered for the ailing economy. This *Report* offers another diagnosis, one based on placing a stethoscope nearer to the lives of ordinary Americans.

The recent revival of free market orthodoxy represents a deliberate attempt to dismantle the economic order which emerged from the Great Depression and the Second World War. When the post-World War II economic boom ended in the early 1970s, conservative economists and business interests mounted an attack on the legacy of the New Deal and the Great Society. Since 1979, the architects of a new age of economic reaction—at the Federal Reserve System, in conservative think tanks, and since 1981 in the Oval Office—have set themselves to the task of turning back the clock to an earlier economic order. This new/old order aims to fundamentally alter the post-New Deal relationship between government and the economy and between employers, employees and unions. It also aims to reassert the dominant U.S. role in the rest of the world.

But the old-time religion of the free market has not delivered the goods. Its sole success has been a pyrrhic victory over inflation, one for which the American people are paying dearly. And they will continue to pay for years to come. Nor has it reversed the long-term rise in the level of unemployment, sagging productivity, or lack of improvement in living standards. Rather, as we will show in the pages which follow, the new conservative orthodoxy has left a path of economic indebtedness and social division.

Economies, we are told, run on the basis of a carrot and stick. A combination of incentives and threats is what makes any economy tick. The question is: who gets the carrot and who gets the stick?

3

Under today's conservative economics, corporations and the wealthy are offered the carrot and everyone else gets the stick. Its underlying analysis of our economic ills appears to be that the rich are not doing their part for the economy because they have too little money, and the rest of us are not doing our part because we have too much.

But most Americans—61% in 1985—think that the distribution of money and wealth in the U.S. is not fair and favor closing the gap.[1] Yet criticism of conservative economics has been stalled because its proponents have argued that it is promoting economic recovery and longer-term prosperity. The short-term sacrifices are worth it, they claim, because all of us will prosper in the end.

This report disputes that view. It argues that conservative economics has not only clubbed a vast majority of Americans, widening economic disparities; it has also failed to reverse the underlying decline in U.S. economic performance. Relying on the club, it has mortgaged the future, steering the economy toward a risky, uncertain, highly-indebted existence of sluggish growth and high unemployment. Conservative economics should be supplanted not only because it is unfair and undemocratic but also because it is ineffective and risky.

These are unconventional views. But they can be supported by facts and analysis, as we do in this report. Our economic views are relatively uncommon not because they are implausible but because they do not serve the interests of those who have benefited most handsomely under the conservative regime. The report points clearly toward an alternative policy approach, which we call democratic economics—an approach the wealthy and powerful would prefer to ignore.

The alternative to stick and carrot policies is participation: a new economic order based on fair and democratic policies which directly raise living standards and improve the quality of life, provide economic security, and promote corporate and government accountability.

The economic logic of a new democratic order is simple: it makes more economic sense to go with the American grain than to go against it. Democratic economics would stimulate high productivity growth and rapid innovation through high wages, a key to U.S. prosperity since the nineteenth century. It would allow the economy to shift out of industries which are no longer productive, competitive, or socially desirable—without decimating communities and lowering the standard of living—by guaranteeing the right to a job and giving workers a say in economic decisions. It would stimulate investment and enhance financial stability by maintaining low interest rates and increasing popular control of the Federal Reserve System. By increasing popular stakes and participation in the economy, democratic economics would reduce the enormous costs required to enforce a regime which most people think is unfair.

The Costs of the "Big Stick"

Since 1979, national economic policies have been a patchwork of monetarist tight money, supply-side tax cuts and a military Keynesian strategy which uses burgeoning weapons expenditures to prop up demand for goods and services. The overall strategy is sometimes called "Reaganomics" in recognition of its most articulate spokesman and most thoroughgoing executor. But its inception dates back to the second half of the Carter administration, especially the appointment of Paul Volcker as head of the Federal Reserve in 1979. We call the overall strategy conservative economics or economic orthodoxy.

The strategy is loosely unified by a commitment to three principles:

— a trickle-down philosophy which believes that putting money into the hands of the rich and into the coffers of big business is the key to economic success;

— a "guns but not butter" perspective on national priorities which advocates paring away social and human development programs while expanding military procurements to buttress an aggressive foreign policy;

— an ultra "free market" rhetoric which argues that government attempts to structure the economy hurt the efficiency and fairness of the market. In reality, of course, the rhetoric is applied selectively. With lucrative military contracts, bank bailouts, and a deliberately overvalued dollar, the Reagan administration has played a major role in determining which industries and communities thrive—and which are abandoned to the slash-and-burn logic of "free market" competition.

There is also a racial logic—if not intent—to the conservative economic gameplan: blacks and other people of color have disproportionately borne the brunt of high levels of unemployment, the gutting of Fair Employment Practices enforcement and of the Civil Rights Commission, and cuts in social programs.

How well an economic strategy works depends in important measure on how people respond to it. Though often described in textbooks as a well-oiled machine of interacting parts, the economy is made up of people. Each brings to the economy some combination of working skills and property; each expects to be able to dispose of their skills or their property in such a way as to acquire the goods and services which make up their livelihood.

The multitude of economic interactions must be organized by some system of motivation, co-ordination, direction and control. Two problems of motivation and control are paramount in a capitalist economy. First, private businesses and the wealthy must somehow be induced to invest and create jobs, devoting a substantial portion of their incomes not to their own consumption but to the expansion of the productive capacities of the nation. Second, workers must somehow be induced to provide labor: to work hard for wages which leave a surplus for their employer.

For the business owner, the positive incentive to invest is the expected return on the investment. The threat is that failing to invest may mean falling behind in the competition with other businesses, and eventually going out of business. For the worker, the carrot which induces hard work and long hours is a higher wage, more consumption and greater economic security. The stick is the financial and social distress of unemployment.

The effects of the conservative economic policies enacted since the late 1970s make it quite clear who got the carrot and who got the stick. According to the *Economic Report of the President, 1985*:

— before-tax profits and interest grew 3.6% per year between 1979 and 1984 (correcting for inflation);

— real wages of non-supervisory workers, outside of agriculture, fell by 5% between 1979 and 1984;

— small businesses failed at record rates: while 13% more businesses were formed in 1983 than in 1979, over four times as many businesses failed in 1983 than in 1979; the average failed business was small, owning about half a million dollars of assets;

— net farm income (adjusted for inflation) fell by 36% between 1979 and 1984 (first three quarters); while the food prices paid by consumers continued to climb, the prices paid to farmers for their crops over this period rose by less than a quarter as much as the prices paid for farm inputs.

Did the carrot for big business and the stick for small business, farmers, workers, and the unemployed work? It obviously paid off in a larger share of the pie for the well-to-do. In 1984, the latest year for which complete data are available, the richest 5% of all families received 16% of all income—more than in any year in the past two decades.[2] But what about the pie? Did the trickle-down strategy induce investment and a sustained recovery from the doldrums of the 1970s? Did some of the pay-off trickle down to middle income and lower income people?

While it is too early to offer a definitive judgment, the record thus far is one of more failures than successes: notably, the growth of the gross national product between 1979 and 1985 was lower than in any completed business cycle since the Second World War.[3] And many of the apparent economic successes, we will show, are the precarious and unsustainable result of living on borrowed time.

The disappointing results of the conservative carrot-stick strategy are not entirely the fault of the policy architects. Increasing levels of competition from other countries and the depressed condition of the world economy are both cause and partial effect of poor U.S. economic performance over the last five years.

Nonetheless, there is an overriding flaw in the conservative economic gameplan: it relies on an extraordinarily costly approach to solving our economic problems.

The cost of conservative economics is perhaps best illustrated by its approach to fighting inflation: contrary to the monetarist claims, the war against inflation was not won quickly with a swift surgical strike. Rather than stopping inflation in its tracks and leaving the economy unscathed, monetarist tight money policies initiated in 1979 bogged down the U.S. economy for three and a half years in the early 1980s—the longest and deepest recession since the 1930s.

The underlying logic—that the unemployment generated as a result of tight money policies would discipline labor and drive down wages—worked, but it worked slowly. Eventually, two digit levels of unemployment reduced real wages and consumer spending power enough to put a damper on prices. Similarly, the overvalued dollar invited unprecedented levels of imports and thus competition from non-U.S. firms, further reducing domestic prices. But the cost was far greater than even the Keynesian critics of monetarism had imagined.

The economic cost of idle factories and unemployment which are the result of conservative economics is staggering. As we show in Chapter 8, the price tag in terms of lost output attributable to monetarist-induced slow economic growth compared to a high employment alternative, comes to over one and half trillion dollars. This is more than the dollar cost to the U.S. of the First World War, the Korean War and the Vietnam War combined, all measured in today's dollars. It is almost as large as the cost of World War II.[4]

Supply-Side Constraints

If the stick strategy represented by monetarism, remilitarization, and supply-side tax cuts has gained the support of many economists, it has done so by default. The main contending carrot strategy is the widely criticized Keynesian economic model.

Writing at the height of the Great Depression, John Maynard Keynes argued that the expansion of government services and income redistribution to the less well-to-do would lift the economy to higher levels of output by stimulating the level of demand for goods and services. Paradoxically but plausibly, he argued that as long as there are unemployed workers ready to work and idle factories ready to fire up, stimulating total demand can raise both consumption and investment at the same time. Not only would wages and government services increase but profits as well. In today's terms, the Keynesian model might be termed trickle-up economics.

Few businessmen would dispute Keynes' point: selling all that one can produce is always a problem in a capitalist economy. The more money there is in the hands of people who will spend it, the better is the selling environment. But Keynesian economics focused on demand to the neglect of production and supply.

The economists who came to be called supply-siders made just this point: not only the amount of demand, but what is produced and how it is produced are problems which must be addressed by economic policy. While their criticism of the Keynesian solution to economic problems was on target, the supply-siders erred in identifying the government—over-regulation and over-taxation—as the culprit of supply-side problems.

After six years of sluggish economic growth and high levels of idle capacity and unemployment, the Keynesian model again looks appealing. There can be little doubt, for example, that substantial budget deficits significantly bolstered total demand for goods and services during the era of conservative economics.

But Keynesian economics is no more adequate today than in the late 1970s. The problems which beset the U.S. economy today go considerably beyond the persistent shortfall between total demand for goods and services and total productive capacity. The U.S. economy today faces severe supply-side problems, including:

— an outmoded, hierarchical system of control of work on the shop floor and in the office which invites resistance and absenteeism and discourages productive effort;

— discrimination against people because of their race, age, sex, or sexual preference, which amounts not only to an unconscionable social injustice but also a massive waste of talent and skill;

— the increasingly costly and ominous degradation of the environment by profit-seeking firms;

— a financial system and an approach to business management which rewards speculation and the fast buck instead of productive long-term investment, thereby diverting corporate attention away from the real problems of productivity;

— the systematic disregard for the future productivity of the economy measured by reduced support for education, environmental protection, child care, and basic research and development;

— the misallocation of resources towards a burgeoning military sector of the economy.

None of these supply-side problems can be addressed through deregulation, "unleashing the profit motive," "letting the market do its work," or other orthodox prescriptions. Indeed, as we show throughout this report, structural economic problems are in major part the result of the normal workings of the market and the pursuit of profits.

If Keynesian economic policy erred in ignoring supply-side problems, conservative economic policy erred more seriously still, for it actively fostered demand side problems, while misreading and posing false solutions to supply-side problems. Yet the conservative brand of carrots for the rich and sticks for the rest has apparently earned grudging acceptance simply because it is seen as the only show in town.

It need not be. A new beginning in economic policy must start from the fundamental importance of people in the economic system. People are important because our development as people ought to be the end of economic activity, and the production of goods and services the means. The economy should be for people. But taking people seriously is important for two other reasons as well.

First, labor is uncontestably the most important input into the economy, accounting for about three quarters of the value of all inputs. An increase in the quality or effectiveness of the workforce have considerably larger overall effect than a similar improvement in the quality of equipment.

Second, people's reaction to economic systems and economic policies is a key to their success or failure. Economic policies which secure the loyalty, enthusiasm and commitment of most people will have lower enforcement costs and a higher chance of success than policies which invite resistance and contempt.

The past six years of conservative economic orthodoxy has demonstrated a dangerous disregard for people as actors in the productive processes of today and the future. To develop an alternative—which we begin in our concluding section—will require rethinking of basic economic categories, assumptions and facts. We hope that this report will be a contribution in this task.

Footnotes

1. B. Bearak & R. E. Myer, "America and Its Poor," Part IV, *LA Times*, August 3, 1985.
2. U.S. Census Bureau, Current Population Reports, *Money Income of Families, Households, and Persons*, P-60 Series, various years.
3. *Economic Report of the President*, 1985, Table B2, p. 234. The figures refer to real (corrected for inflation) gross national product.
4. Dollar costs of wars are from *Statistical Abstract of the U.S., 1985*, p. 338, and refer to original incremental direct costs.

2 False Pessimism

The conservative economic orthodoxy has promoted a widespread sense that democratic and fair economic initiatives—however desirable they may be in the abstract—fly in the face of economic or political realities. Indeed, economists are fond of telling politicians what they cannot do. Many public officials have learned the lessons of the "dismal science" so well that they have taken up the task of explaining why it is that policies to promote fairness and democracy in the United States are contrary to the laws of economics.

Many of these obstacles to a more fair and democratic economic life, however, are more imaginary than real: in some cases they are simply fictions created out of whole cloth. We refer to them as the six "Why Our Hands Are Tied Myths;" they appear as our rogues gallery of economic misinformation in Figure 2.1.

Myth Number 1: Full Employment Is Impossible in Today's High-Technology Global Economy

While new labor-saving technologies and imported goods displace workers in the impacted sectors of the economy, it does not follow that full employment is impossible: neither technology nor the amount of imports determine the total number of jobs available in the U.S. economy. The pace and pattern of technical change and the evolution of international economic relationships create serious problems of adjustment which any sensible economic policy must address. But they do not place the guarantee of the right to a job beyond our reach.

The number of jobs depends on employers' demands for labor, which in turn depends on two things: the level of demand for goods and services; and how much labor is needed to produce the goods and

Figure 2.1
Why Our Hands Are Tied: Six Myths

Myth Number 1. Full employment is impossible in today's high technology global economy
Myth Number 2. We cannot increase wages because high wages have already priced the U.S. out of world markets
Myth Number 3. We cannot accelerate economic growth without inviting an outburst of inflation
Myth Number 4. We cannot increase consumption because growth of the U.S. economy is constrained by too low savings
Myth Number 5. Eliminating the budget deficit must be the top priority; otherwise, interest rates will remain excessive
Myth Number 6. The voters will not support a progressive reordering of economic priorities

services demanded. The introduction of new technologies tends to have a simultaneous, contradictory effect: it expands the demand for goods and services but does so by reducing the time (and therefore the cost) it takes to produce them. On balance, rapid increases in labor productivity have been associated with an abundance of jobs, rather than high unemployment:

— from 1959 to 1969, labor productivity grew at a strong 2.8% per annum, total output grew at 4.1% annually and unemployment fell from 5.3% to 3.4%. From 1969 to 1984, labor productivity growth slowed to 1.5% annually. The rate of output growth slowed even more, to 1.4% annually, and the demand for labor languished, with unemployment rising from 3.4% to 7.4%;[1]

— among the advanced industrial nations during the entire post World War II period, rapid increases in labor productivity in manufacturing have been associated with low unemployment rates in countries as different as Japan, Sweden, Italy and Austria.[2]

International trade, like technical change, is as likely to create jobs as to destroy them. Exports create jobs as surely as imports displace them. When imports are not offset by exports, the overall result is unemployment. This will certainly be the case when the value of the dollar is kept artificially high by the policies of the Federal Reserve System. The high dollar depresses exports and attracts imports, displacing or destroying jobs in the United States. But the culprit is not international trade but the policies which produced the inflated value of the dollar.

The number of jobs in an economy, in short, depends more on the overall economic policy and priorities of the government, which strongly affect the level of demand, than on either imports or technology. The level of unemployment is largely not an economic fact of life. Unemployment is a political choice. Today's political leaders have chosen to promote or at least to tolerate a record high level.[3]

Myth Number 2: We Cannot Increase Wages Because Excessive Wages Have Already Priced the U.S. Out of World Markets

The ability of U.S. companies to compete in world markets depends primarily on three things: the productivity and wages of U.S. labor, and the value of the dollar. The first two influence the dollar cost of U.S.-produced goods. The value of the dollar determines how many francs or yen a prospective foreign buyer will have to pay to obtain the U.S. dollars necessary to buy U.S.-produced goods. To blame high wages for the ballooning trade deficit is misplaced for two reasons.

First, the overvalued dollar has been, by far, the main thing blunting the competitive edge of U.S. producers. A calculation by the U.S. Bureau of Labor Statistics makes this clear.[4] We will compare the competitive position of the U.S. and France, countries which have followed diametrically opposed economic strategies. Similar calculations could easily be made—with similar results—for most of our trading partners.

Between 1980 and 1984, money wages in the manufacturing sector of the French economy rose by two-thirds, compared to less than a third for the U.S. This should have resulted in a U.S. gain of one-third *vis-a-vis* competition with France. In fact, the more rapid productivity growth in France made up some of this difference, but had the value of the dollar *not* risen, the U.S. still would have ended up with a 27% improvement in its competitive position. However, the rise in the value of the dollar more than wiped out the potential gains: between 1980 and 1984 the U.S. competitive position compared to France—indicated by labor costs measured in U.S. dollars per unit of output—deteriorated by 45%. As a result, U.S.-produced goods were almost prohibitively expensive to the French buyer, and French imports to the U.S. became bargains too good to refuse—as many wine connoisseurs have discovered.

Second, as the comparison with France suggests, rapid wage growth and rapid productivity growth often go together. Similarly, sluggish wage growth and the productivity doldrums are often associated, for three reasons: first, low wages inhibit technological innovation; second, low wages do not inspire a greater work effort; and third, low wages generally mean less demand for goods and services, retarding investment and technical change.

When Henry Ford offered his workers the unheard-of-sum of $5 a day in the early part of this century, he was expressing a common-sense truth which orthodox economists often forget: high wages contribute to productivity.

The complex relationship between wages and productivity cannot be fully resolved here. The most relevant question, however, can be answered without a doubt: do rapid wage increases doom a country to being left behind in the competition for world markets?

The answer is no. Over the period 1956 to 1983, countries with rapid wage increases—Japan, the Netherlands, Italy, and others—have done far better in international competition than countries with slow wage growth—the U.S. and the United Kingdom (see Figure 2.2).

Figure 2.2
Must Wages Fall to Promote Exports?

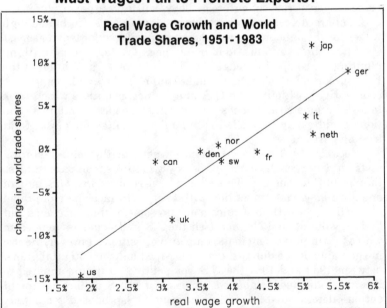

Source: OECD, **National Accounts**, (Paris, various years) and U.S. Bureau of Labor Statistics, unpublished data on wages in manufacturing.

Myth Number 3: We Cannot Accelerate Economic Growth Without Inviting an Outburst of Inflation

There is no doubt that the U.S. economy remains highly prone to inflation. But recent low levels of inflation are not evidence of a sound victory over rapid inflation. Rather, they are the result of high levels of unemployment in the 1980s which has dampened wage increases, as well as the increase in competition from imports which has kept the lid on prices.

Although rapid inflation lurks in the wings, the way to keep it off center stage is not to retard the rate of economic growth. There is a demand and a supply side of prices and inflation. The orthodox way to fight inflation is to find a way of holding down demand for goods and services—preferably by reducing wages and government social programs. But there is obviously another way: to expand the supply of goods and services to meet the demand.

Whatever their promises, there can be little doubt that the inflation-fighting policies of conservative economists have not solved the supply-side problem.

After five years of deliberately retarding economic growth, monetary authorities continue to worry about reigniting inflation when the unemployment rate drops toward 7%—a rate higher than any recession *trough* prior to 1975. In short, the long-term solution to the problem of inflation—the restructuring of the economy to ensure stable and rapid growth—is as far from being achieved today as it was when Paul Volcker took over the Federal Reserve System in 1979 and decided to put the U.S. economy through the wringer.

The problem is more serious than it may appear. The massive flood of imports has allowed the U.S. economy to live beyond its means for a number of years, providing the economy with goods and services for which we do not have to pay with an equivalent value of exports. The result is that the supply side of the inflation picture has been temporarily brightened by hocking the future. Eventually we will repay the debt by exporting more than we import over some sustained period of time. When that happens, the availability of goods and services will be less than the amount we are actually producing.

The burden of these eventual repayments will not loom large if the economy finds a solution to its productivity impasse. But if it remains mired in economic stagnation, the prospect of a further bout of high inflation seems unavoidable.

As in the case of savings and investment, orthodox economics has reversed the causality: inflation is not the result of rapid economic growth, it is the result of economic stagnation. Rapid growth is not the problem; it is a necessary part of the solution.

Myth Number 4: We Cannot Increase Consumption Because the Growth of the U.S. Economy Is Constrained by Too Low Savings

This belt-tightening logic is used to justify not only lower wages and cuts in public social programs but also to justify tax give-aways which channel a larger share of income into the pockets of the well-to-do. Reduced consumption, it is claimed, will increase savings and accelerate investment, which depends on the amount of savings.

The "less consumption means more investment" myth is sometimes presented as simply the law of arithmetic. But it is just another example of economic misinformation based on a mistaken theory of what determines savings and what determines investment.

Contrary to orthodox economics, saving is the offspring of investment, not the other way around. Saving is the result of a healthy economy, not its cause. Equally important, investment does not wait for saving. If the conditions are right, investment will take place, often financed by borrowing either domestically or from abroad. The result of an expansion of investment is generally an expansion of savings.

Private saving is made up of personal saving and business saving. Businesses save when they make high profits and choose not to pay them out as dividends. High profits depend on a high level of demand for the goods and services they produce; and this in turn is fostered by high—not low—levels of consumption.

People save when they feel well off. They feel well off when their standard of living is rising. When their standard of living is falling or stagnant, people often borrow rather than save in an attempt to maintain their former living standards. The depressed levels of the personal savings ratio since the mid 1970s—reaching an all-time low in 1985—are the result of high levels of unemployment and the slowdown and even reversal in the growth of living standards.[5]

The way to increase savings is to put everybody who wants a job to work at decent wages. Cutting wages so as to cut consumption—or slashing publicly financed forms of consumption such as food stamps—is likely to continue the enforced stagnation of the U.S. economy. Growth in the economy depends on growth in demand for goods and services—and consumption is by far the largest component of this demand. Stagnation of the economy will continue to depress savings. Orthodox economic policies, in short, have created rather than solved the savings problem.

The flaw in the orthodox reasoning is what we call the zero-sum illusion. If all available economic inputs were fully used and used well, and if no international flows of investment could take place, then it would indeed be true that to get more investment would require less consumption, just as in the "guns vs. butter" trade-off in economics textbooks. But with one worker in ten either out of work or too discouraged to look for work, and with a fifth of our industrial capacity idle, can anyone really believe that increasing the production of machinery, factory construction and the like, requires a reduction in the amount of food, clothing, and schooling that is produced?

Myth Number 5: Eliminating the Budget Deficit Must be the Top Priority; Otherwise, Interest Rates Will Remain Excessive

Everyone agrees that the budget deficit must be reduced. But few reasons are given, aside from platitudes about fiscal responsiblity more germane to a household than to a nation. The reason heard most often—that high budget deficits generate high interest rates—is perfectly logical: government deficits mean more borrowing by the government, and more borrowing should tend to push up interest rates. But the "deficits cause high interest rates" theory does not square with the facts, as we show in Chapter 9.

Among orthodox economists and conservative policymakers, the commitment to cut the budget deficit is based more on a desire to cut social programs than on any well-founded economic reasoning. And high interest rates are more the result of deliberate tight money policies than high levels of government spending.

There are good reasons to reduce the budget deficit. Chief among them is the method of financing large deficits: the payment of large interest payments to the wealthy holders of the public debt. Financing the deficit further tilts the already distorted spending priorities of the government towards the rich—a kind of "Robin Hood in Reverse" welfare state.

But there are dangers in trying to cut the budget deficit in a highly recession-prone economy which is operating far below capacity. The fact that the government is now spending much more than it receives from taxes is a major prop for the economy's total demand for goods and services already sagging under the effects of stagnant real wages and growing import competition. Withdrawing this prop, given the existing weak economy, would certainly plunge the economy into a serious recession.

As long as attention remains riveted on cutting the deficit, little progress is likely to be made in giving the U.S. economy more than symptomatic relief. The budget deficit—like the low rate of savings—is not *the* economic problem, it is not even the *cause* of the economic problem. But it is likely to persist as long as the reigning orthodoxy insists that limping economic growth, regressive taxation, military expansionism, and high levels of unemployment are just what the doctor ordered.

Myth Number 6: The Voters Will Not Support a Progressive Reordering of Economic Priorities

Everyone wants to cut waste in government, and nobody wants to provide public support to able-bodied loafers who could be doing productive work. Everyone wants the nation defended against external attack.

Until recently, many assumed that this meant that the majority of Americans supported cuts in social service and income support programs and applauded the massive military buildup underway since the late 1970s. Recent polls make it clear that this is decidedly not the case.

Nearly 60% of those polled by the *Los Angeles Times* in August 1985, for example, thought that the government should spend more money on poverty programs.[6] In 1,525 interviews conducted by the Gallup polling organization in April 1985:[7]

— 87% of those asked opposed "cuts in entitlement programs such as social security, medicare, and the like"; 9% approved of these cuts;

— 66% approved cuts in defense spending, while 28% opposed them;

— 55% opposed cuts in "government spending for social programs"; among blacks 79% were opposed, among women 63% were opposed; 39% supported these cuts (16% of blacks, 31% of women).

It is time to ring down the curtain on the reign of economic misinformation and political pessimism.

Footnotes

1. Here, as in most of our comparisons over a period of time, we refer to years which were business cycle peaks (or nearly so, in the case of 1984). We have used the year in which the unemployment rate reaches a cyclical minimum to identify business cycle peaks. All data

from the *Economic Report of the President*, 1985. Labor productivity growth refers to the non-farm business sector (p. 278); output growth refers to constant dollar gross national product (p. 234); and unemployment is for all workers (p. 271).

2. U.S. Department of Labor, "International Comparisons of Manufacturing Productivity and Labor Cost Trends," USDL 85-230, June 10, 1985, and *Handbook of Labor Statistics* December, 1983.

3. On the economic feasibility of full employment see Juliet B. Schor, Testimony to the U.S. House Committee on Labor and Education, Sub-Committee on Employment Opportunities, September 4, 1985.

4. U.S. Department of Labor, *op. cit.*

5. The personal savings ratio is personal savings divided by personal disposable income. Commerce Department data reported in the *Wall Street Journal*, September 20, 1985, indicate a personal savings ratio of 2.8% in August, the lowest monthly figure since the government began reporting this series in 1959.

6. B. Bearak and R. E. Myer, "America and Its Poor." Part IV, *LA Times*, August 3, 1985.

7. Gallup Report, Number 237, June, 1985.

Part II
Winners and Losers

Preface

The fundamental question facing American voters, claimed presidential candidate Ronald Reagan in 1980, is: "Are you better off now than you were four years ago?" If the question is asked after six years of conservative economics, the answer is a resounding "no." Conservative economic policies, beginning with Jimmy Carter's appointment of Paul Volcker as head of the Federal Reserve, have not improved the American standard of living. Instead, they have widened the income gap between poor and middle income people, and the rich. Indeed, the very rich have been the only beneficiaries of the conservative program: by 1984, the wealthiest 20% of the U.S. population captured an astounding 43% of all national income—the highest proportion on record.

The conservative strategy has also widened the economic and social divisions between people of color and whites, women and men, union and non-union workers, farmers and consumers.

For people of color, conservative policies have meant a reversal of economic gains made in the 1960s and 1970s and an attempt to resurrect the racist social order of the 1950s.

For women, conservative economics has meant that the promise of economic equality with men remains a pipedream. Conservative attacks on government social spending have also slashed public income support to the families for which women are increasingly solely responsible.

For workers and farmers, conservative policies have brought attacks on living standards, political power, and a way of life.

The legacy of conservative economics, in short, will be the deepening and widening of social and economic conflicts based on wealth, race, gender, and occupation. Far from improving the economic lot of the majority, conservative economics has benefited only the wealthy—and promoted an embittered and deeply divided America.

3 Is It Trickling Down?

Thirty-five years old and divorced, Mary worked a full-time sales job in a Philadelphia department store to support herself and her two sons. At the minimum wage, her take-home pay came to $520 per month—below the poverty line. Until the fall of 1981, Mary received a $169 monthly check from the Aid to Families with Dependent Children program. But on October 1, 1981, the welfare check stopped coming. Like 400,000 other poor working parents, Mary became ineligible for assistance under the Reagan administration's budget reforms. Along with her check, Mary's family lost its health insurance under the Medicaid program.[1]

On March 30, 1984, a mock funeral procession gathered in South Chicago. Composed of steelworkers, many with over twenty-five years of experience in the South Works of U.S. Steel, the procession marked the shutdown of the plant. The neighbors of these workers, laid off when Wisconsin Steel shut down four years earlier, had few words of encouragement to offer them. One of them, a black man in his forties, had gone on to perform odd jobs—installing bathtubs and fixing gutters. Another, a Chicano in his fifties, subsequently spent his days looking for aluminum cans and flattening them out. According to a recent Census Bureau survey, over half of the workers who had been dislocated in the steel industry between 1979 and 1983 were still unemployed in January 1984. Those re-employed earned on average only 60% of their former pay.[2]

The gap between America's rich and poor is growing wider. According to the U.S. Census Bureau:

— the poorest *two-fifths* of the population received only 15.7% of the total national income in 1984—less than in any year since data were initiated in 1947, and less than the richest 5%. The wealthiest fifth captured almost 43% of all income, the highest proportion on record;[3]

— the income gap between people of color and whites widened between 1979 and 1984. While the per capita household income of whites stayed the same, it fell by 3% for blacks and by 8% for Latinos;[4]

— poverty rates among children under eighteen years old rose from 16% in 1979 to 21% in 1984. Over half the children in families with a female head of household lived in poverty in 1984.[5]

Today's increasing income inequality is the result of long-term structural changes—especially the shift from manufacturing to services and the erosion of marriage as a social institution. But unlike government policies in the 1960s and 1970s, conservative economic policies since 1979 have not attempted to counter these social and economic trends by redistributing income toward the poor. Indeed, conservative policies have halted improvements in average U.S. living standards and increased income disparities between people of color and whites, children and adults, rich and poor.

Social Dissolution

The United States is currently undergoing a major breakdown in its system of distributing and redistributing income. Of a scale reminiscent of the Great Depression, this breakdown stems from three developments.

First, the social institution of marriage is eroding. An unprecedented growth in the number of households maintained by women has undermined the most effective system of redistributing income from one person to another in the U.S.—the married-couple family. While more women have entered the labor force in the post-war economy, they and their children have in general not made up in earned income what they lost in shared income with men. Women's wages remain considerably lower than those of men, and women remain largely ghettoized in low-paying clerical and service jobs (see Chapter 5).

Second, the U.S. economy has suffered a long-term decline in its overall performance. Pre-dating the Volcker-Reagan strategy of conscious "trickle-down" policies, economic decline precipitated the downward slide in incomes and heightened pre-existing trends towards greater inequality. Some of this decline is directly associated with economic stagnation between 1973-1979: gains in real wages and growth in the real per capita value of most government transfers ground to a halt in the 1970s.

These trends are associated with the rapid growth of service industries throughout the post-war period. With fast food establishments at one end and financial services at the other, the service sector is often characterized by lower wages, less full-time work, bigger wage gaps between workers, and less union protection than manufacturing industries.

The third development contributing to income stagnation and inequality has been the deliberate application of conservative economic policy since 1979. Macroeconomic policy and changes in the tax and transfer systems under Volcker and Reagan, have not improved living standards. According to the best available evidence, these policies actually reduced disposable income for 60% of the people. The real winners were the richest 20% (see Figures 3.1 and 3.2).

Throughout the 1970s, government redistribution programs softened the impacts of the economic crisis and the revolution in family structure. Sub-employment and rising unemployment were offset by rising government transfers. But the public income-maintenance system was ill-prepared to wage full-scale war against the poverty and inequality resulting from the shortfall of job opportunities and the demise of the male breadwinner family. For one thing, the distribution of benefits was uneven: the primary beneficiaries were not the unemployed or single parents with children but the elderly. In the 1980s, poor economic performance and high unemployment, coupled with massive retrenchment in the government's earlier commitment to redistribute income toward the bottom, fueled the explosion of poverty and inequality.

Figure 3.1
The Poor Get Poorer

Distribution of Family Money Income, Selected Years 1973-1984

Income Quintile	Share of Total Aggregate Income (%)			Change: 1979-1984
	1973	1979	1984	
Poorest 20%	5.5	5.2	4.7	− 0.5
Middle income:				
Second 20%	11.9	11.6	11.0	− 0.6
Third 20%	17.5	17.5	17.0	− 0.5
Fourth 20%	24.0	24.1	24.4	0.3
Richest 20%	41.1	41.7	42.9	1.2

Source: U.S. Bureau of the Census, Current Population Reports, *Money Income of Families, Households, and Persons in the United States*, P-60 Series, No. 146, Table 17, and No. 149, Table 4.

Figure 3.2
The Rich Get Richer

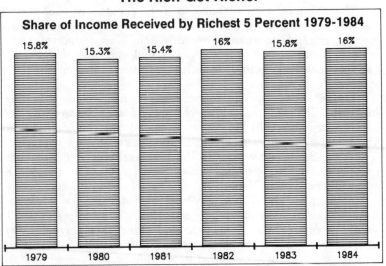

Share of Income Received by Richest 5 Percent 1979-1984

1979	1980	1981	1982	1983	1984
15.8%	15.3%	15.4%	16%	15.8%	16%

Source: U.S. Census Bureau, **Current Population Survey**, P-60 Series.

Income Stagnation and Inequality

Free market economists claim that the market is the cure for the problem of economic inequality. They point to the post-1982 recovery as a signal of renewed progress for the majority of U.S. citizens. The new economic orthodoxy, conservatives assert, has ushered in an era of growing economic opportunity for all Americans. By eliminating "nonessential" and "ineffective" government programs, Washington claims to have provided the necessary incentive for people to work, save and invest: to be productive, and to be rewarded for it.

In reality, conservative economics has slowed the improvement of U.S. living standards. Adjusted for inflation, U.S. after-tax income per capita grew only 1.8% per year from 1979 to 1984. This was a substantial decrease from average annual growth rates of 2.7% between 1959 and 1969; and it was virtually no improvement over growth rates of 1.7% between 1973 and 1979.[6]

After-tax income figures are not available by race, but the Census Bureau provides a measure of pre-tax income per household member. These figures show that the income of whites remained virtually unchanged. Blacks and Latinos, however, were doing significantly worse in real terms in 1984 than they were in 1979. Pre-tax per capita household income for blacks fell by 3%, while for Latinos the decrease was 8%.[7]

The civilian unemployment rate averaged over 7% in 1984 and the first three quarters of 1985. This is higher than the level of unemployment in any previous cyclical peak since the Great Depression. Workers of color were hit especially hard: with unemployment at 14%, one out of seven black workers over twenty years of age was officially counted as unemployed in 1984.[8] And this official unemployment rate actually underestimates the number of people without jobs because it does not include people who have simply given up looking for jobs, or people who are involuntarily employed part-time.

Conservative economics also reversed progress towards closing income disparities between the rich and poor. The gap between the incomes of rich and poor U.S. families narrowed substantially in the twenty years between the late 1940s and the late 1960s; it then widened gradually over the 1970s. In the 1980s, it exploded.[9] By 1984, the percentage share of aggregate family income received by the most affluent 5% of families had risen to 16%, its highest level since 1961. The richest 20% also gained, while the share of the poorest 20% fell to 4.7%.[10]

Meanwhile, the super-rich maintained their privileged position. In 1983, 2% of all families who owned financial assets such as savings and government bonds held over half of such assets; the top 10% held 86% of the assets.[11] Because information on asset ownership is one of the best-kept secrets in the U.S. economy—data is only available sporadically—it is not possible to determine precisely how the fortunes of the very wealthy have changed over the last few decades. But we can conclude that a tiny minority of families continues to own and ultimately control the lion's share of non-labor economic resources.

The human misery of declining or stagnating income cannot be measured quantitatively. But a few key indicators, such as home ownership, poverty rates, and infant mortality rates, present evidence of staggering costs. Home ownership rates among families and "unrelated individuals" fell from 65% in 1977 to 60% in 1983.[12] Among people of color, the rate fell a staggering 12% from 52% to 40%.[13] According to the National Association of Realtors, the income needed to qualify for a home ownership loan has outstripped the median income of the population as a whole since 1978.[14]

Fading American hopes are also reflected in the rise in the number of people living in poverty. After 1978, poverty rates increased among young men, prime-age men, female-headed households, children, whites, blacks, and Latinos. Poverty rates increased at a particularly rapid clip from 1980 to 1983. Economic expansion in 1984 reduced the official poverty rate slightly; but the 1984 rate was still one-quarter higher than in 1979, after the late 1970s business cycle expansion, and one-third higher than in 1973, after the expansion of the early 1970s (see Figure 3.3).[15]

One of the most poignant and widely accepted indicators of the standard of living is the infant mortality rate. This rate has declined rapidly over the years in the U.S. and in other economically developed

Figure 3.3
Government Programs Reduce Poverty

Poverty Rates With and Without Government Transfers, 1960-1984

Year	Pre-transfer poverty incidence (%)	Official (post-transfer) poverty incidence (%)	% Reduction in poverty incidence due to transfers
1960	— —	20.2	— —
1961	— —	21.9	— —
1962	— —	21.0	— —
1963	— —	19.5	— —
1964	— —	19.0	— —
1965	21.3	17.3	4.0
1966	— —	15.7	— —
1967	19.4	14.3	5.1
1968	18.2	12.8	5.4
1969	17.7	12.1	5.6
1970	18.8	12.6	6.2
1971	19.6	12.5	7.1
1972	19.2	11.9	7.3
1973	19.0	11.1	7.9
1974	20.3	11.2	9.1
1975	22.0	12.3	9.7
1976	21.0	11.8	9.2
1977	21.0	11.6	9.4
1978	20.2	11.4	8.8
1979	20.5	11.7	8.8
1980	21.9	13.0	8.9
1981	23.1	14.0	9.1
1982	24.0	15.0	9.0
1983	24.2	15.3	8.9
1984	— —	14.4	— —

Source: Sheldon Danziger and Peter Gottschalk, "The Poverty of Losing Ground," *Challenge*, May-June 1985, p. 34.

1983 and 1984 figures from U.S. Census Bureau, Current Population Survey, P-60 Series, 1985.

countries. But in 1984, according to provisional data, the U.S. infant mortality rate decline slowed to a barely perceptible crawl.[16] Some analysts attribute this disturbing setback to cuts in federal funding for programs for pregnant women, young children, and mothers of young children.[17]

In some areas within the U.S., infant mortality rates actually rose during the early 1980s. According to a 1985 study of the rural poor, aggregate infant mortality rates in the eighty-five poorest rural counties rose significantly between 1981 and 1983. This gap in infant mortality rates between the rural poor and the rest of the nation grew by a dramatic 39% in these two years.[18] Furthermore, the gap between black and white infant mortality rates grew by 4% from 1982 to 1983. Black infants died at nearly double the rate of white infants in 1983.[19]

Some observers attribute regional and racial discrepancies in the rate of infant death to high rates of unemployment. For example, after a thirty year decline, the infant mortality rate in Michigan rose by 3% between 1980-1981. For 37 consecutive months during that period, Michigan suffered double digit unemployment. Particularly hard hit were Flint and Pontiac counties, where the unemployment rate was over 26% in December 1982. The rate of infant deaths in each of these two counties was twice the state average.[20]

Are Baby-Boomers to Blame?

Some economists argue that the apparent deterioration in the U.S. standard of living is primarily the result of the large influx of baby boomers into the labor force in the 1970s. According to this view, the entry-level earnings of the baby boomers—lower, more unequal, and less steady than those of more experienced workers—have distorted the trends in measured income patterns. If these workers are on the lower end of the same seniority and age-based wage track as older workers, then aggregate trends towards declining incomes and greater inequality will be reversed as they grow older.

There is no doubt that the age shift of the labor force has affected measures of living standards and inequality. But the youthfulness of the labor force does not explain the trends.

The spiralling unemployment of recent years, for example, cannot be attributed primarily to an increase in the number of young workers, or in new entrants to the labor force. Labor economist Michael Podgursky concluded that while the greater number of young workers pushed up the unemployment rate after 1969, this effect has since declined. Between 1975 and 1982, over half of the increase in the unemployment rate was accounted for by prime-age men (25-54); prime-age women accounted for about one-fourth.[21]

Furthermore, greater income inequality is not just a baby-boom phenomenon. Poverty economists Peter Gottschalk and Michael Dooley found that inequality in earnings has been rising within all age groups of working men, even after controlling for the level of education, experience, and unemployment.[22]

Rather than a younger labor force, income trends can be better explained by examining the interaction of structural changes in the family, economy, and government.

Family Revolution

The major demographic backdrop for the trend toward increasing inequality is the increase in non-traditional, non-male-headed families. In 1955, 9.0% of white families and 20.7% of families of color were headed by women. By 1984, 12.6% of white families and 43.1% of black families were comprised of women and their depndents.[23]

Historically, poverty rates for female-headed families have been high. At their lowest in 1979, one in five white and one in two black female-headed families remained in poverty. The recent increase in the number of families maintained by women means that more people now live below the poverty level (see Figure 3.4). And the greater likelihood that a female-headed family will be black gives the "feminization of poverty" a distinctly racial dimension.[24]

The disproportionate risk of poverty among female-headed families stems from four enduring structural characteristics of the

Figure 3.4
More Americans Are Poor

Percent of Persons Below the Poverty Level, 1959-1984				
Year	White	Black	Latino	All children under 18 yrs
1967	11.0	39.3	— —	16.3
1968	10.0	34.7	— —	15.3
1969	9.5	32.2	— —	13.8
1970	9.9	33.5	— —	14.9
1971	9.9	32.5	— —	15.1
1972	9.0	33.3	— —	14.9
1973	8.4	31.4	21.9	14.2
1974	8.6	30.3	23.0	15.1
1975	9.7	31.3	26.9	16.8
1976	9.1	31.1	24.7	15.8
1977	8.9	31.3	22.4	16.0
1978	8.7	30.6	21.6	15.7
1979	9.0	31.0	21.8	16.0
1980	10.2	32.5	25.7	17.9
1981	11.1	34.2	26.5	19.5
1982	12.0	35.6	29.9	21.3
1983	12.2	35.7	28.1	21.8
1984	11.5	33.8	28.4	21.0

Source: U.S. Census Bureau, **Current Population Reports.** "Characteristics of the Population Below the Poverty Level: 1983," Series, no. 147, issued February, 1985; 1983 revised and 1984 figures are from P-60 no. 149, "Advanced Report; Characteristics of the Population Below the Poverty Level, 1985."

economy and of families. First, while far more jobs are available to women than there used to be, the likelihood of being employed (particularly in full-time jobs) is still lower for women than men. Second, while there has been some recent improvement in the ratio of white female to white male wages, and substantial improvement in the female-male wage ratio for blacks, women's wages remain considerably lower than men's. Third, single and divorced mothers continue to shoulder the primary responsibility for their children, stretching the ability of women's incomes to meet needs, and reducing the ability of women to work for pay. Finally, female-headed families are disproportionately black or Latino, and face not only sexual but also racial discrimination.

Widespread female poverty has persisted despite some employment gains by women relative to men. Indeed, it is possible to argue that the "feminization of poverty" is due to the fact that new economic opportunities reduced many women's economic dependence on men, diminishing their need to marry as a way to claim part of a husband's income.[25] The growth of even low-wage job opportunities for women, especially the growth of female-dominated clerical and service occupations, enabled many women to leave or postpone marriage. Three-fifths of the 23 million new jobs created in the economy from 1970 to 1984 went to women.[26]

The recent increase in the number of poor women who are not married is due in important measure simply to the increasing numbers of single women, rather than to an increase in the prevalence of poverty among this group. Over the 1970s, the poverty rate among both black and white female-headed families actually fell slightly.[27]

Economic losses among men starting in the 1970s also made the offer of marriage one which many women could afford to turn down. One study found that between 1976 and 1984, the median inflation-adjusted income of white males fell by 22%.[28] Men have accounted for a greater proportion of the surge in unemployment than women, even as their share of the labor force has declined.[29] Although female-headed families have always made up a disproportionate number of the poor, their rate of poverty increased only 10% from 1978-1983. In male-headed households, the rate of poverty rose 50%.[30]

Poverty was "feminized," in short, not because of an increasing rate of poverty *among* unmarried women, but largely because the *number* of unmarried women increased—while women's income, despite some improvement, remained low relative to men's. Furthermore, childrearing remains the nearly exclusive responsibility of women: in 1984, nine out of ten children not in married-couple families resided in families headed by females rather than males.[31]

As traditions fade, the family is increasingly doing without its principal source of funds—men. And the government has not made up much of the difference.

Economic Dislocation

The American dream—an upwardly mobile couple in their comfortable home and new car—is fading. Its demise is due at least as much to structural economic changes as it is to the erosion of the traditional family. The final tally is not in, but a growing body of evidence suggests that opportunities for secure, well-paid, full-time employment are shrinking.

The real wage of the American worker is falling. Between 1973 and 1979, the average real wage of non-agricultural production workers in the private sector fell by 4.4%. Between 1979 and 1984, real wages fell even more—by 5.7%.[32] Whatever the economic benefits of the Reagan-Volcker assault on inflation, they have not yet shown up in real wage gains.

Structural unemployment is also on the rise. Using data collected by Dun and Bradstreet, economists Barry Bluestone and Bennett Harrison found that "runaway shops, shutdowns, and permanent physical cutbacks may have cost the country as many as 38 million jobs."[33] (The number of jobs lost to cutbacks short of closure is difficult to determine. According to Bluestone and Harrison, more than 32 million jobs were lost as a direct result of plant, store, and office shutdowns, plus runaway shops.) Economist Candee Harris found that, due to plant closures alone, an average of 800,000 jobs were lost annually from 1978-1982 in manufacturing facilities with 100 or more employees.[34]

This dislocation of workers has continued under the Reagan administration. There were 5.1 million displaced workers in January 1984—workers with at least three years of experience—who had lost their jobs between 1979 and 1983 because of plant closings, relocations, slack work, or the cancellation of positions or shifts.[35]

Among these displaced workers, the median duration of unemployment was six months.[36] About one-third had not received any unemployment compensation; one-half of those who did had exhausted their benefits by 1984. At least one-half of those re-employed were earning less than they had in their old jobs.[37]

Estimates of long-term earnings losses among permanently displaced prime-age men vary by industry. In 1978, former auto, steel, meatpacking, aerospace, and flat glass workers had lost one-sixth of their income six years after the initial job loss.[38] A 1985 study of displaced steelworkers found that 61% of laid-off production workers who found new jobs were re-employed as laborers or in service sector industries.[39] The loss in income was apparent in changes in the former steelworkers' educational plans for their children: 21% had to withdraw or were unable to enroll their children in college.[40]

The job problem goes beyond the absolute lack of employment opportunity stemming from the persistence of high unemployment rates. The structure of jobs also appears to be heavily implicated in the growth of inequality. One study found that between 1958 and 1977, the distribution of income from work among men with some earnings became more unequal.[41] Another study concluded that male earnings' inequality grew by 2% annually over this period.[42] For women, inequality changed little during this time. But because of greater differences among women in the number of hours worked for pay, inequality among women was greater than among men.[43]

There is a good *prima facie* case that a long-term shift of employment from manufacturing and agriculture to sales and services is causing the widening gap between workers' incomes. In 1977, income inequality—as measured by the Gini Coefficient—was higher than the all-industry average for male wage and salary workers in retail trade, business service, personal service, and professional service industries. For male workers in the relatively highly unionized sectors—mining, construction, manufacturing, transportation, communications, and public utilities—wage inequality was lower than in other industries (except public administration). Similar patterns were evident among women: income inequality among women wage and salary earners in retail trade, business service, and personal service industries was high. For women wage and salary workers in mining, construction, manufacturing, transportation, communications, and public utilities, the disparities were among the lowest.[44]

Highly unequal in terms of workers' pay, the service industries are the fastest growing in the United States. The service sector (including trade, finance, insurance, real estate, services and government) accounted for 56.7% of total U.S. employment in 1940. By 1960, the figure had jumped to 62.3% and then to 71.5% in 1980. In contrast, goods-producing employment (including mining, manufacturing, and construction) shrank from 43.3% in 1940, to 37.7% in 1960, and then to 28.5% in 1980.[45]

The shift of employment from manufacturing to service industries is the result of long-term social and economic trends. Repeated in nearly all advanced industrialized countries, the shift reflects increased affluence: as people get richer, they tend to spend more on services.[46] And as more women have entered the labor force, market demand for services formerly provided inside the home has skyrocketed.

The structural shift also reflects the long-term decline in the international competitiveness of U.S. manufacturing. The U.S. share of world trade in manufactured goods dropped steadily from 25% in 1953 to 15.6% in 1979.[47] While deterioration in the U.S. trade position pre-dates conservative economics, the high value of the dollar generated by the Volcker-Reagan strategy has decimated U.S. exports, driving many workers out of manufacturing and into service sector jobs.

Government Retrenchment

Trends toward larger numbers of female-headed households, lower pay, higher unemployment and greater earnings inequality were well established before the onset of economic orthodoxy in the late 1970s. These trends, however, were substantially blunted by the structure of taxes and transfers during the 1970s.[48]

While *pre*-tax income inequality rose between 1974 and 1980, the inequality of incomes *after* taxes fell somewhat.[49] Even more important than taxes was the public transfer system. Government payments and in-kind transfers as a percentage of (post-transfer) income in 1980 ranged from 158% for families in the lowest 10% of the income distribution, to 3% for the highest 10% in 1980.[50]

Transfers also maintained a ceiling in the 1970s on the rising levels of poverty which were being produced by the changing structure of the economy and the family. In 1970, the fraction of people whose incomes would be classified as poor in the absence of government transfers began to rise. From 1969-1974, the so-called pre-transfer poverty rate rose. However, total cash and in-kind government transfers per household rose as well. As a result, the post-transfer poverty rate fell by over 10% (see Figure 3.3).[51]

The same structural trends in the economy and the family persisted into the early 1980s. But under the reign of conservative economics, the government exacerbated rather than softened their impact. Federal policy changes after 1980 apparently lowered average disposable income from what it would have been in the absence of the Reagan-Volcker initiative.

Researchers Marilyn Moon and Isabel Sawhill at the Urban Institute compared the outcome of trickle-down economic policy with simulated outcomes of likely alternatives.[52] Their benchmark alternative policy scenario was not a liberal wish-list—it included a continuing high level of unemployment, for example, and policies which would reduce the relative incomes of the poor. But it did embody less military spending, greater domestic spending, fewer tax cuts, and a more expansive monetary policy than the policies of the Reagan administration. The simulation indicated that real disposable family income would have increased by 4.0%, compared to an actual increase of 3.5%. They concluded that Reagan-Volcker policies may be said to have reduced incomes by .5% (see Figure 3.5).

The disappointing growth of *average* incomes is the good news. The bad news is that the free-market experiment contributed dramatically to widening income gaps. Under Reagan-Volcker policies, the rich got substantially richer and the poor much poorer, even in addition to the increasing inequality the market was producing on its own. Moon and Sawhill concluded that the poorest 20% of U.S. families would have lost 3.5% of their 1980 income under the hypo-

Figure 3.5
Conservative Economics Fuels Poverty

**Contribution of Reagan Policies to
Changes in the Level and Distribution
of Real Disposable Family Income, 1980-1984
(1982 dollars)**

	Income Quintile				
	Bottom	Second	Third	Fourth	Top	All Families
Percentage change since 1980	− 7.6	− 1.7	0.9	3.4	8.7	3.5
Percentage change since 1980 under alternative policy scenario	− 3.5	1.3	2.6	4.0	7.1	4.0
Difference attributable to Reagan policies	− 4.1	− 3.0	− 1.7	− 0.6	1.6	− 0.5

Source: Marilyn Moon and Isabel Sawhill, "Family Incomes: Gainers and Losers," in J.L. Palmer and I. Sawhill, Ed., *The Reagan Record, An Assessment of America's Domestic Frontier,* copyright 1984 by the Urban Institute, Washington D.C., p. 329. Reprinted with permission from Ballinger Publishing Company.

thetical alternative policy; the next-to-the-bottom 20% would have gained only 1.3%. Under the Reagan-Volcker policies, both groups were net losers: the bottom 20% in reality lost 7.6%, while the next-poorest 20% lost 1.7% (see Figure 3.5). Only the very top 20% of all families were net gainers under the first Reagan administration. Their incomes would have increased by 7.1% anyway—but the Reagan-Volcker program gave them even more: their actual incomes increased 8.7%.

Married-couple families experienced small increases in disposable incomes over these years, although the simulation indicated that Reagan-Volcker policies reduced these gains from what they otherwise would have been, particularly for one-earner families. Female-headed and black families bore the brunt of the losses. Black families on average would have gained .5% under the alternative policy scenario, but the policy changes left them with a 2.1% decline. Female-headed families, which would have otherwise experienced a .5% loss, instead contended with a 3.3% loss.

Can We Do Better?

The explicit logic behind supply-side economics—and some corporate reindustrialization schemes as well—is that slow growth or actual reductions in the standard of living are necessary in the short run to reignite the engine of economic growth. Likewise, they argue, equality may be a morally desirable goal but it has conflicted head on with efficiency, and thus with a nation's ability to improve the livelihood of its people. Inequality is believed necessary to motivate work effort, innovation, risk-taking, and saving, all of which make an economy grow. Hard workers, innovators, risk-takers and savers must get more than others to ensure their continuing contribution to growth. Free market economics further contends that any institution which meddles with the market mechanism, especially government, impairs the economy's long-run ability to eliminate poverty and enhance general well-being.

But the free market experiment, according to the best available evidence, left the bottom 80% of the population significantly worse off. Researchers at the Wisconsin Institute for Research on Poverty concluded that even with an improbable decade of sustained annual growth with no recessions, no further program cuts, and a miraculous halt in long established trends toward inequality, it would still take over a decade to reduce the poverty rate to its 1979 level.[53]

Conservative economics, with its carrot for the rich and the stick for the rest, simply has not trickled down the benefits. The vast majority of people are no better off than they were in 1979. Barring a change in economic policy, they are likely to be worse off and deeply divided in the years to come.

Footnotes

Chapter Three

1. *Wall Street Journal*, "Reagan Team Weighs Impact of Welfare Cuts on Working Parents," October 21, 1981, p. 1; George E. Peterson, "Federalism and the States," in John L. Palmer and Isabel V. Sawhill, Eds., *The Reagan Record*, The Urban Institute, Ballinger, Cambridge, 1984, p. 232, U.S. Census Bureau, Current Population Reports, *Consumer Income*, P-60 Series.

2. James Fallows, "America's Changing Economic Landscape," *Atlantic*; March 1985, and Paul O. Flaim and Ellen Sehgal, "Displaced Workers of 1979-1983: How Well Have They Fared?" *Monthly Labor Review*, Vol. 108, No. 6, 1985, pp. 3-16.

3. U.S. Census Bureau, Current Population Reports, *Money Income of Families, Households and Persons in the United States*," P-60 Series, 1983 and advance 1984 reports.

4. *Ibid.*, 1980-1984. 1984 figures from P-60 Series, No. 149, Table 13 and P-20 Series, No. 398, Table 24.

5. U.S. Census Bureau, Current Population Reports, *Characteristics of the Population Below the Poverty Level: 1983*, P-60 Series, No. 147, issued February, 1985; and P-60 No. 149.

6. *Economic Report of the President*, 1985, Table B-24.

7. White pre-tax per capita household income fell from $10,783 in 1979 to $10,370 in 1984 in constant 1984 dollars; for blacks, income fell from $6215 to $5769; for Latinos, from $6215 to $5769. U.S. Census Bureau, *Money Income of Families, Households and Persons in the United States*, P-60 Series, 1980-1984. 1984 figures from P-60 Series, No. 149, Table 13 and P-20 Series, No. 398, Table 24.

8. The unemployment rate for blacks aged 20 and over was 14.3% for men and 13.5% for women in 1984. *Economic Report of the President*, 1985, Table B-35, p. 273.

9. The Federal Reserve's survey of consumer finances, which includes unrelated individuals as well as families, shows comparable aggregate trends.

10. U.S. Census Bureau, P-60 Series, 1983 and advance 1984; and *Federal Reserve Bulletin*, 1984.

11. *Federal Reserve Bulletin*, "Survey of Consumer Finances, 1983: A Second Report," December, 1984, pp. 863-64. Financial assets are checking, savings, NOW and money market accounts, certificates of deposit, IRA or Keogh accounts, savings bonds, stocks, bonds, nontaxable holdings, and trusts. Financial assets do not include property and businesses.

12. "Unrelated individuals" is the Census Bureau's category of people not living with relatives or living in institutions.

13. *Federal Reserve Bulletin*, "Survey of Consumer Finances, 1983," September 1984, pp. 679-692.

14. *Washington Post*, September 8, 1984; U.S. Census Bureau, Current Population Reports, "Money Income and Poverty Status of Families and Persons in the United States in 1984," P-60 Series, Number 149, 1985, Table B.

15. In 1984 the poverty rate was 23% higher than in 1979 and 30% higher than in 1973.

16. In 1983, the infant mortality rate declined by 2.6% from the 1982 rate. Between 1972 and 1982, the annual average rate of decline was 4.6%. See Mickey Leland, "For America's Poorest, Infant Mor-

tality Is Up," *The New York Times*, October 24, 1985.

17. C. Arden Miller, "Infant Mortality in the U.S.," *Scientific American*, July 1985, pp. 31-37.

18. Mickey Leland, *op. cit.*

19. The 1983 rate for whites was 9.7 for each 1000 live births; for blacks the rate was 19.2 per 1000. *Ibid.*

20. C. Arden Miller et al., "The World Economic Crisis and the Children: United States Case Study," *International Journal of Health Services*, Vol. 15, No. 1, 1985, p. 127.

21. Prime-age men's share of the unemployment rate was 56.7% and prime-age women's was 23.6% from 1975-1982 (cyclical troughs). Moreover, involuntary job loss increased unemployment rates between 1969 and 1982, while voluntary quits made a declining contribution to unemployment, and labor force entrants had a basically constant effect on unemployment over this period. Michael Podgursky, "Sources of Secular Increases In the Unemployment Rate, 1969-1982," *Monthly Labor Review*, July 1984.

22. Dooley and Gottschalk asserted that "a decline in the trend toward greater inequality within education-experience categories is not strongly confirmed by the data for men with more than 10 years of experience." Michael Dooley and Peter Gottschalk, "Does A Younger Male Labor Force Mean Greater Earnings Inequality?," *Monthly Labor Review*, November 1982, p. 43. In a later study, Dooley and Gottschalk found that the proportion of men with weekly earnings below $231 (in 1984 prices) rose from 12.3% in 1969 to 13.4% in 1973 and to 15.2% in 1978, the last year for which their data are available. See "The Increasing Proportion of Men With Low Earnings in the United States," *Demography*, Vol 2, No. 1, February 1985, pp. 25-34.

23. U.S. Census Bureau, 1984, *op. cit.*, P-20 series, table on female family heads, no husband present.

24. U.S. Census Bureau, 1984, *op. cit.*, and *Economic Report of the President*, 1985.

25. Elaine McCrate, "The Growth of Nonmarriage Among U.S. Women: An Unanswered Question for the New Family Economics and an Alternative," Mimeo, University of Massachusetts, 1984, p. 2.

26. Sara Kuhn and Barry Bluestone, "Economic Restructuring and the Female Labor Market; The Impact of Industrial Change on Women," paper presented to the Conference on Women and Structural Transformation: The Crisis of Work and Family Life, Rutgers University, November 1983.

27. *Economic Report of the President*, 1985, p. 264.

28. The fall was from $21,175 in 1976 to $16,467 in 1984. Lester C. Thurow, "Average White Male No Longer Leads the March to Prosperity," *Los Angeles Times*, October 20, 1985.

29. Michael Podgursky, "Sources of Secular Increases in the

Unemployment Rate, 1969-1982," *Monthly Labor Review*, July 1984, pp. 19-25.

30. U.S. Census Bureau, Current Population Reports, Consumer Income Series, P-60 Series, 1984.

31. U.S. Census Bureau, Current Population Reports, Household and Family Characteristics, P-20 Series, 1985.

32. Average gross hourly earnings, total private non-agricultural labor force, *Economic Report of the President*, 1985, p. 276.

33. Barry Bluestone and Bennett Harrison, *The Deindustrialization of America*, Basic Books, New York, 1982, p. 26.

34. Candee S. Harris, "Plant Closings: The Magnitude of the Problem." Working Paper #13, Business MicroData Project, The Brookings Institution, Washington, D.C., June 1985.

35. Flaim and Sehgal, *op. cit.*

36. This figure actually understates the length of time without work because many workers surveyed were still unemployed in January 1984.

37. Flaim and Sehgal, *op. cit.*

38. Louis Jacobson, "Earnings Losses of Workers Displaced From Manufacturing Industries," in W. C. Dewald, Ed. *The Impact of International Trade and Investment on Employment*, U.S. Department of Labor, Bureau of International Affairs, Government Printing Office, 1978.

39. Steelworkers Research Project, *Chicago Steelworkers: The Cost of Unemployment*, Local 65, United Steelworkers of America, 1985, p. 16.

40. *Ibid.*, p. 22.

41. Peter Henle and Paul Ryscavage, "The Distribution of Earned Income Among Men and Women, 1958-1977," *Monthly Labor Review*, April 1980, pp. 3-10. The last year for which information is available is 1977.

42. Robert D. Plotnick, "Trends in Male Earnings Inequality," *Southern Economic Journal*, January 1982, pp. 724-732.

43. Henle and Ryscavage, *op cit*. Neither of these studies included workers with no earnings at all. However, Dooley and Gottschalk (*op. cit.*, 1982) found that the proportion of men with zero earnings increased from 1967-1978, even within groups having the same education and experience.

44. Henle and Ryscavage, *op. cit.* The Gini Coefficient is derived from a simple graph which ranks families from poorest to richest on the horizontal axis, then plots the cumulative percentage of income held by each percent of families. Thus, if income distribution is perfectly equal, the bottom 2% of families will have 2% of all income, the bottom 50% will have 50% of all income, etc., and the curve is on a 45-degree line from the lower left-hand corner to the upper right-hand corner. If, instead, the bottom 5% of families have 2% of all income, and

the bottom 50% have 25%, then the curve will be bowed downward. The Gini Coefficient measures the gap between the 45-degree line and the actual income distribution, relative to the size of the triangle below the diagonal line. If income distribution is perfectly equal, the coefficient is equal to zero; if distribution is perfectly unequal, the coefficient equals one. A lower gini coefficient means greater equality.

45. Direct production employment in key manufacturing industries is declining absolutely as well as relatively. Sara Kuhn and Barry Bluestone estimated that total production employment in manufacturing fell 5% from 1973-1980. Ten key industries lost 1.3 million jobs from 1973-1982. In the 1983-1984 recovery, 29 of the 74 major manufacturing sectors continued to decline, while 28 others had 1984 employment levels significantly below 1978 levels. These industries, which provide almost 75% of manufacturing employment, lost 1.9 million jobs since the 1983-1985 recovery began. Kuhn and Bluestone, *op. cit.*

46. For data on other developed economies, see *Labor Force Statistics 1958-1979*, OECD, 1981 and *Yearbook of Labour Statistics*, ILO, 1980, 1982.

47. Jack Carlson and Hugh Graham, *The Economic Importance of Exports to the United States*, Center for Strategic and International Studies, Georgetown University, Washington, D.C., 1980, p. 20.

48. Joseph A. Pechman and Mark J. Mazur, "The Rich, the Poor, and the Taxes They Pay: An Update," Brookings General Series Reprint 409, The Brookings Institution, Washington, D.C., 1985, p. 34.

49. Susan Weller Burch,"Recent Changes in the Income and Tax Distribution," Working Paper Number 45, Board of Governors of the Federal Reserve System, April, 1985.

50. Pechman and Mazur, *op. cit.* In arriving at these figures, Pechman and Mazur assumed that there was no shifting of taxes.

51. Sheldon Danziger and Peter Gottschalk, "The Poverty of Losing Ground," *Challenge*, May-June 1985, pp. 32-38, and "Macroeconomic Conditions, Income Transfers, and the Trend in Poverty," in D. Lee Bawden, Ed. *The Social Contract Revisited*, Washington, D.C., 1984.

52. Marilyn Moon and Isabel Sawhill, "Family Incomes: Gainers and Losers," in Palmer and Sawhill, Eds., *op. cit.*, p. 329.

53. Danziger and Gottschalk, in Bawden, Ed., *op. cit.*

4 Divided America

In 1963, Martin Luther King's dream of a multi-racial society of free and equal citizens electrified millions of Americans. In the decade which followed, black Americans and other people of color made significant political and economic progress.[1] But as the twenty-fifth anniversary of King's catalyzing vision approaches, the United States is moving not nearer but further from making his dream a reality.

Economic, social, and political reversals for people of color began in the late 1970s. They are the result of trends that pre-date the Reagan era, particularly the dissolution of the civil rights movement, the end of the postwar economic expansion, and the persistence of racist ideologies.

But conservative economic strategies—including an assault on the public sector and the use of unemployment to discipline labor—have dramatically accelerated the economic decline of people of color. Furthermore, conservative rhetoric has heightened a dog-eat-dog ideology which holds that people of color can advance only at the expense of whites. As Rosalyn Carter put it, the conservative reign has made white America comfortable with its prejudices.

In short, while progress toward racial equality slowed before 1981, the Reagan administration has played a critical role in worsening the economic position of people of color. As a result, race relations have deteriorated and the U.S. is becoming a nation ever more deeply divided among itself.

The New Age of Reaction

From the mid-1960s to the mid-1970s, people of color made significant economic gains relative to whites. Since the late 1970s, however, and especially since the advent of the Reagan administration, the trend toward economic gains for people of color has been reversed. Indeed, the Reagan administration has attempted to dismantle the institutional structure put into place in the 1960s and 1970s to combat racial economic discrimination.

The current period of racial reaction parallels an earlier period of American history marked by growing racism and racial division. After 1877, a reaction set in against the major political and economic advances blacks had made in the decade and a half following the emancipation of the slaves. Termed the Black Reconstruction by the historian W. E. B. DuBois, blacks made significant gains in land ownership, voting rights, and political power. The reaction reversed most of these gains, triggering policies and sentiments which disenfranchised black voters, increased violence against blacks and intensified the economic exploitation of black workers.

Commentators on the current scene, such as economist Michael Reich of the University of California at Berkeley, have warned of a repetition of this tragic pattern. Noting the gains in employment and occupational mobility achieved between the end of the Second World War and the mid-1970s, he observes:[2]

> In the 1980s, many of these indices show signs of worsening. And under Reagan, the political direction of the Federal Government on racial matters is once again reversing. The second Reconstruction has clearly ended and we are already well into a second Era of Reaction.

The reaction goes far beyond the economy and touches virtually all aspects of our society:

— the composition of the judicial system, which had progressed towards racial parity during the late 1970s, turned towards racial exclusion in the 1980s. Twenty-one percent of Jimmy Carter's appointments to District Courts were black, Latino or Asian; only 7% of Ronald Reagan's first term appointments were people of color;[3]

— the proportion of students entering medical school who are black declined over the past decade, despite the fact that black applications to medical school increased and the test scores by black applicants improved more rapidly than those of whites. According to a recent study, the acceptance rate for black applicants fell from 43% to 40% between 1974 and 1983, while the acceptance rate for whites rose from 35% to 50%. The study's co-author, Dr. Steven Shea of Columbia's College of Physicians and Surgeons, concluded: "I think there's been a general shift in the social climate, and the importance of achieving equality for minorities has diminished on the national agenda;"[4]

— according to linguists, white and black English are becoming increasingly dissimilar. University of Pennsylvania Professor William Labov, author of a 1985 study of "black English vernacular," concludes that ordinary communication between whites and blacks is becoming increasingly difficult. According to Labov, the divergence of language reflects increasing racial segregation and social isolation;[5]

— fewer blacks and Latinos are enrolling in colleges. Between 1976 and 1983, the percentage of black high school graduates enrolling in college declined from 33.5% to 27%. The Latino percentage went down from 35.8% to 31.4%. For whites, the figure remained unchanged at 33%.[6]

Less easily measured has been the amplification of racial ideologies of white supremacy. These racist ideologies often build on such touchstones of conservative rhetoric as the belief in the biological determination of economic success and the closely associated notion that in a market society, those who are less successful have only their own moral or genetic inferiority to blame.

The Reagan administration, in short, has not only attempted to restore an economic order reminiscent of the days of Harding and Coolidge; it has also helped to reconstruct and consolidate a *racial* order which had been challenged by the social movements and economic trends of the 1960s and early 1970s. Some of this shoring up of the racial order in America is the result of long-term economic and ideological trends. But much of the new Age of Reaction has been catalyzed by economic and social policies whose effects, if not intent, can only be called racist.

The Reversal of a Decade of Economic Gains for People of Color

Political pressure and economic trends improved the relative living standards of people of color between 1965 and 1975. After remaining fairly constant over the whole post-war period, the median income of families of color jumped from 55% to 65% of the white level. Women of color made especially rapid income gains. Unemployment among all people of color dipped from 2 to 1.8 times that of whites (see Figure 4.1).

During the 1970s, many economists and others heralded the imminent end of racial discrimination. They claimed that racial gains were the result of long-term historical trends which were built into the very structure of liberal and capitalist America. The *Economic Report of the President, 1974*, signed by Richard Nixon, hailed the "long run narrowing of the racial income difference." The *Report* attributed the gains to the joint effects of growing racial tolerance and a capitalist economic system in which competition forces cost-conscious businesses to hire the most qualified and productive workers at the lowest price—regardless of race.[7]

Trends since 1974 do not support this assessment, however, and cast doubt on the positive role played by the capitalist system in promoting racial equality and harmony. Almost all indices of the relative economic status of people of color were worse in 1984 than in 1975 (see Figure 4.1). In some cases, the decline is not large enough to represent a credible trend. But the impression is unmistakable that progress towards racial equality has stopped.

Figure 4.1
A Reversal of Gains

Post-War Trends in the Relative Economic Status of People of Color						
	1945	1955	1965	1975	1983	1984
Ratio of Non-White to White Median Family Income	.56	.55	.55	.65	——	.62
Ratio of Black to White Median Family Income	——	——	.54	.61	——	.56
Ratio of Non-White to White Individual Median Incomes:						
Male	——	.53	.54	.63	.63	——
Female	——	.54	.73	.92	.90	——
Ratio of Non-White to White Unemployment Rate	——	2.2	2.0	1.8	——	2.2

Sources: Michael Reich, "Postwar Racial Income Differences: Trends and Theories," Rows 1-3, Unpublished Mss., University of California at Berkeley, 1985; Row 4, *Economic Report of the President, 1985, p. 271.*

Pennsylvania State University economist Peter Bohmer attempted to discern whether racial economic progress had indeed stopped or if the statistics reflected only changes in the business cycle, especially the severe recession of the early 1980s. In a detailed statistical study, he found there was no improvement in the relative earnings of men of color to white men in the private sector since 1975. This followed a strong upward trend in earlier years. Bohmer found a downward trend for workers in the public sector, however, as well as for public and private sector workers taken as a whole. Similar results were obtained for women workers.[8]

Does the Market Promote Racial Equality?

Contrary to conservative claims, the labor market clearly has not promoted racial equality in the last decade. But even the improvements before 1975 should not have prompted the congratulatory attitude adopted in Nixon's *Economic Report*, for they stemmed not from market forces but from two quite particular and time-bound events.

First, much of the gains in the incomes of black men relative to white men is the result of the black migration out of the agricultural South and into the industrial North during the 1950s and 1960s. As a result, the composition of black male employment changed dramatically. In 1950, nearly a quarter of employed black men held jobs in agriculture. Another quarter were employed as laborers. By 1970, less than 4% worked in agriculture and only 16% as laborers. Instead, black men moved into jobs primarily as operators and craft and clerical workers in the higher-paying industrial sector.[9]

While the migration boosted black male income, the relative position of black men worsened in the Northeast. Indeed, in both the Northeast and Midwest, the ratio of the income of "non-white" to white men was lower in 1983 than it was in 1953. While relative gains were made in the South and West between 1953 and 1975, all four regions showed a marked decline or no improvement between 1975 and 1983 (see Figure 4.2).[10]

A second factor which raised the economic standing of people of color relative to whites was the gain made by women of color. In 1955, "non-white" full-time female workers earned 54% of what white female workers earned. By 1965, the ratio had jumped to 73%. It peaked at 92% in 1975 and dropped to 90% in 1983 (see Figure 4.1). While all women continue to earn substantially less than men, this improvement for "non-white" women helped to narrow the earnings gap between whites and people of color (see Chapter 5).

Like those for black men, gains for black women stemmed primarily from changes in their occupational structure. Black women

Figure 4.2
Income Gaps are Growing Wider

Ratio of Non-White to White
Male Median Income by Region, 1953-1983

	Northeast	Midwest	South	West
1953	.75	.75	.42	.68
1965	.69	.75	.47	.74
1975	.75	.77	.56	.80
1983	.67	.61	.56	.78

Source: Michael Reich, "Postwar Racial Income Differences: Trends and Theories," University of California, Berkeley, 1985, based on U.S. Census Bureau, *Current Population Reports,* various years.

were drawn from work in private households to jobs in the service sector, especially government employment, or as clerical workers. Over 42% of employed black women worked in private households in 1950. By 1980, the figure had fallen to 5%.[11]

Improvements in the relative incomes of people of color, in short, were spurred not by the workings of the labor market but by migration and by expansion of the public sector. Perhaps more important, the data on relative incomes mask what can only be called an on-going disaster on the jobs front. People of color have suffered disproportionately high and growing rates of unemployment. Between 1954 and 1984, the percent of white adults holding a job rose from 55% to 60%. Among people of color, the number fell from 58% to 54% (see Figure 4.3).

Since the mid-1970s, the employment picture for both whites and people of color has worsened considerably. Unemployment has been consistently higher than any time during the entire post-war period and it has been disproportionately higher for black men and black women. In the second quarter of 1985, barely one half of all black families had a full-time employee among its members; of the remainder, well over a quarter had no member working for pay at all.[12] For Hispanic families the situation was slightly better: two of three families had at least one full-time employee.

Since the late 1970s, there has been a growing gap in the unemployment rates of black men and women relative to white men and women. Between 1959 and 1974, black male unemployment was 2.22 times that of whites; between 1976-1984, it grew to 2.4 times that of whites. The absolute spread between the two rates swelled from 5.1

Figure 4.3
Growing Joblessness
**Employment to Population Ratio,
White and "Black and Other"**

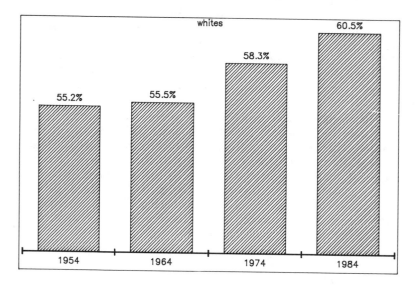

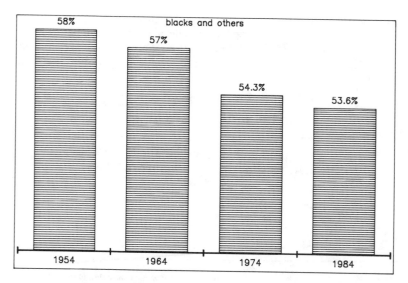

Source: **Economic Report of the President,** 1985, p 270.

percentage points to 8.8 percentage points. For women, the corresponding unemployment ratio rose from 1.93 to 2.18 and the gap between the rates rose from 5.0 percentage points to 8.2 percentage points.[13]

According to Bohmer's econometric estimates, only about half of the recent erosion in the employment picture for black men and a quarter of that for black women can be explained by the generally weaker employment situation for all workers. The remainder, concludes Bohmer, is "caused by the further deterioration of the relation between black and white unemployment—higher rates of black unemployment than previously for the same rate of white unemployment."[14]

The extent of racial disparities in access to income from employment may be measured by what Bohmer calls the community earnings ratio. Comparing the access to earned income of blacks versus whites, the ratio takes account of both the likelihood of having a job and the level of income likely to be received if one has a job. Bohmer found that, over the early to mid post-World War II period, black women greatly improved their access to income. Black men made less strong but significant gains. For both, the trend was reversed in the late 1970s (see Figure 4.4).

Reconstructing the Racial Order

Progress toward racial economic equality sputtered in the late 1970s. Since 1979, however, three aspects of Federal Government policy have combined to intensify the attack on the economic status of people of color: macroeconomic policies, spending priorities, and civil rights policy.

Figure 4.4
Declining Access to Income

Community Earnings Ratios— Black Access to Earnings Relative to Whites, 1949-1983*							
	1949	1959	1969	1974	1977	1980	1983
Women	.43	.47	.77	.85	.92	.87	.88
Men	.48	.49	.58	.56	.53	.52	.52

Source: Peter Bohmer, "The Impact of Public Sector Employment on Racial Inequality: 1950-1983," Unpublished Doctoral Dissertation, University of Massachusetts, Amherst, 1985, pp. 55 and 58.

*The community earnings ratio is the percentage of blacks who have earnings multiplied by black median earnings, expressed as a ratio to the analogous figure for whites.

The "last hired, first fired" status of people of color in labor markets means that generally high levels of unemployment hurt people of color disproportionately. What this logic implies is that the cyclical swing of unemployment is more pronounced for certain segments of workers. Black and Latino workers are thrown out of work at higher-than-average rates during a recession, and return at faster-than-average rates as the demand for labor increases during expansion.

One Bureau of Labor Statistics study found that, while both black and white workers were thrown out of work during contractions in the postwar period, unemployment grew faster for black than for white workers during the contraction. Black workers were disproportionately hurt during periods of slow economic activity. Conversely, when workers returned to their jobs during expansions, unemployment rates for blacks, although higher in absolute terms, went down at faster rates.[15]

In short, while all workers are subjected to the discipline of unemployment in the capitalist economy, the unequal impact of the business cycle upon people of color makes them a "buffer" against the full effect of the cycle upon other segments of workers. The ability of the Reagan administration to gain political support for a macroeconomic policy of high unemployment may be connected to the fact that the costs of unemployment and under-employment are heavily concentrated among people of color.

The second prong of the de facto assault on the economic status of people of color is the reduction in government employment and the shift in spending priorities from social programs to military procurement (see Chapter 9).

Cuts in federal social programs have hit people of color especially hard. According to recent studies, the average black family lost three times as much in income and benefits as did the average white family in 1981. The average Latino family lost twice as much.[16]

Ten major programs have suffered the largest budget cuts (see Figure 4.5). Most of these programs directly or indirectly subsidize poverty rates for the working poor. Poverty rates for the people of color who work are substantially higher than for other sectors of the population. The largest cuts have been for programs which directly affect the functioning of the labor market and the training available for the working poor. While the administration's rhetoric proclaims that the alternative to the welfare system must be employment, the programs which support training and employment have been the most affected by the reorganization of the budget.

Besides employment and training-oriented programs, the affected programs include food subsidies to children and families, education, housing, and cash subsidies to families.[17] All these are programs in which participation is based on financial need. Although there is no

Figure 4.5
Budget Cuts' Impact on People of Color

Size of Budget Cuts in Programs With High Black and Latino Participation

Program	Dimensions of Cuts for FY1985 %	% of Participants Who Are: Black	Latino	Black and Latino
CETA	100.0	30.3	14.7	45.0
Employment Training	38.6	37.3	11.9	49.2
Work Incentive	35.1	33.6	17.2	50.8
Child Nutrition	28.0	17.4	9.9	27.3
Legal Services	28.0	24.4	13.5	37.9
Compensatory Education	19.5	31.5	13.5	45.0
Pell Grants, for Higher Education	15.6	34.0	—	—
Food Stamps	13.8	36.8	10.5	47.3
AFDC	14.3	45.7	13.5	59.2
Subsidized Housing	11.4	45.3	10.8	56.1

Source: J.L. Palmer and I.V. Sawhill, Ed., **The Reagan Record: An Assessment of America's Changing Domestic Priorities,** Urban Institute, August 1984, based on data from the Office of Management and Budget.

conclusive data, a preliminary assessment suggests that the chronically unemployed, those who only work a small portion of their adult life, constitute a minority of the recipients of these subsidies. The majority are people who work most of their adult life.

The Reagan administration reorganized not only government expenditures but has moved to reorganize the tax structure as well. The 1981 tax act enacted a tax-cutting package for the affluent taxpayer. The "supply-side" tax reform package ended a tradition of regular revisions which benefited low-income families. The revisions to tax laws included standard deductions, personal exemptions, and earned income tax credit. The end result of changes in federal tax policies have been a shift in the tax burden to the middle and lower income groups (see Chapter 9).

Reagan's budget and tax policies have generated a substantial redistribution of income; not just from poor to rich, but also from people of color to whites. Since blacks and Latinos are heavily overrepresented in low and moderate income groups (given their limited access to business ownership and financial assets), tax reform aimed at affluent taxpayers benefits them very little. The Congressional Budget Office projected that households with income under $20,000 a year would lose $19.7 billion between 1983 and 1985. Conversely, affluent taxpayers with income above $80,000 a year would gain $34.9 billion. Sixty percent of Latino families and 63% of black families are in the under $20,000 income category. On a per capita basis, this redistribution of income represents a loss of $1,100 on average for families below $10,000 a year and a gain of $24,000 for families with income over $80,000. Income losses per household in 1982 due to tax changes averaged $575 for Latino and $457 for blacks.[18]

The reorganization of the budget will also alter the structure of employment and the position of people of color in the labor market. Defense spending is projected to rise from 5.2% of GNP and 22.7% of the budget in 1980, to 7.5% of GNP and 36% of the total federal budget by 1990.[19] Although the overall effect of military spending on employment is controversial, there is less doubt about its employment effect upon people of color.[20]

Most of the increase in military spending under Reagan comes out of the investment account—weapons procurement, research and development, military construction—which is capital-intensive and concentrated in industries largely closed to people of color. The investment account will grow from 37.3% of each defense dollar in 1980 to 50% in 1986. The growth of the investment account is at the expense of expenditures in military personnel, operations and maintenance. Expenditures in military personnel will shrink from 28.6% in 1980 to 22.8% in 1986; operations and maintenance will be reduced from 32.2% to 25.6%.

The shift in U.S. government spending priorities from human services to military procurement has lowered job opportunities for people of color. Blacks and other people of color, as well as white women, are significantly under-represented in the major military procurement industries. Rather, they are disproportionately employed in human service occupations. Using 1980 employment data, a hypothetical shift of a million jobs from health services, educational services and social services to aerospace, communications, and electronics (prime military industries), would generate a net loss of 320,000 jobs for white women, and 66,000 jobs for black women. By contrast, white men would gain 386,000 jobs. The job losses of black men, who have more employment in the military-related industries, would be almost exactly offset by job gains.[22]

Equally important is the slowing down and leveling off in the growth of government employment. Because the government at all levels employs disproportionately greater numbers of people of color than the private sector, the recent shift in jobs from the public to the private sector of the economy has tended to reduce employment opportunities for people of color. Bohmer calculated the impact of this slowdown of public sector growth on total employment for black workers. He concludes:[23]

> If government employment had continued to grow at its
> 1962-1976 annual rate ... and employed blacks and whites at
> the 1984 composition of the government [employment],
> 247,000 more black men and half a million more black wo-
> men would have had jobs in 1984. ...[T]he continued growth
> in public sector employment would have eliminated about
> half of the growth in the unemployment gap for men and
> the entire growth of the gap for women.

The administration's rhetoric proposes that the private sector will
fill the vacuum left by the government in the economy. Ironically, the
Reagan administration has not only withdrawn support for workers
of color; it has also pulled the rug out from under the time-honored
conservative approach to the advancement of people of color:
"minority" capitalism. All small businesses in general and "minority
business enterprises" (MBE's) in particular, have been hurt by cuts in
non-military federal programs and the reorganization of the budget.

During the first three years of the Reagan administration, the
number of loans granted by the Small Business Administration was
reduced from 31,700 to 19,200; the number of MBE loans shrank from
6,000 to 2,700, representing a decrease from 19% of all loans in 1980 to
14% in 1983 (see Figure 4.6). The hole in the safety net for MBE's was

Figure 4.6
What Ever Happened to "Black Capitalism"?
Small Business Administration Loans to
Minority Business Enterprises

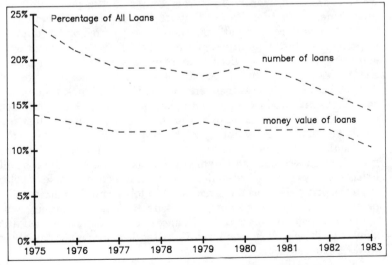

Source: **U.S. Bureau of the Census Statistical Abstract of the U.S.**, 1985, Table No. 870

opened at the worst of times. The 1981-82 recession was particularly hard on small businesses: the incorporation of all new businesses fell by 5 percentage points and the rate of business failures increased from 42.1% in 1980 to 61.3% and 89.0% in 1981 and 1982, respectively.

More important is the administration's general stance on discrimination in employment:

— affirmative action to redress historical inequities has been under persistent attack. Numerical hiring targets and quotas are increasingly opposed, even in prohibiting and redressing discriminatory practices by federal contractors. The administration's opposition to affirmative action goals is so strong it has tried to impose its views on local and state governments— making a mockery of the traditional conservative championing of local autonomy and states rights. The Justice Department has told more than 51 cities, counties, school districts, and state agencies to stop using numerical goals in the hiring of women, blacks and Latinos. As of October 1985, only two cities had agreed to do so. But the attack has affected the racial climate even where affirmative action goals are still in place. As one detective noted of the Indianapolis police department: "prejudice is a little more blatant";[24]

— the administration has altered the very definition of racial discrimination, seeking to disallow the use of simple statistical evidence of discriminatory patterns of hiring. Rather than evaluating claims of racial discrimination based on hiring outcomes, the Reagan administration has argued that *intent* to discriminate must be proven. In upholding the Nixon administration's use of such evidence, the U.S. Court of Appeals for the Ninth District in California wrote in 1985:[25]

Since the passage of the Civil Rights Act of 1964, the courts have frequently relied upon statistical evidence to prove a violation. ...In many cases the only available avenue of proof is the use of racial statistics to uncover clandestine and covert discrimination by the employer or union involved.

Conclusion: The Politics of Race

People of color have received an economic and social blow during the 1980s, the effects of which will last for decades to come. Perhaps unwittingly, the conservative logic of high levels of unemployment, a military buildup, social program cuts and dogmatic faith in the market is well on the way to reconsolidating the old social order where white people benefit relative to people of color. The civil rights movement induced a direction of change that undermined a centuries-old system of racial oppression. Racial policies, overt or subsumed in the intricacies of national economic policies, are an important element of the emerging realignment of social and economic forces in American society.

Can a new civil rights movement be rekindled to counter this assault? Much depends on coming to terms with the thorny question of who benefits from racial discrimination. Mobilizing a mass movement against racism in the U.S. will involve confronting the perceived interests of some whites in perpetuating the racial order.

Employers, for example, can turn racism into higher profits in two ways: directly, when they pay less-than-average wages to people of color; and indirectly, when they are able to keep a divided labor force in a weak bargaining position. In 1980, employers' direct gain from wage discrimination—the amount extra they would have had to pay if black workers earned the same as whites—reached $25 billion, a substantial fraction of corporate profits.[26]

But these were only the direct profits. A more accurate estimate would also include the additional profits from lower wages paid to white workers because of a divided labor force. This amount is equivalent to the income loss of white workers' due to racial discrimination. Indeed, there is a strong inverse relationship in local U.S. labor markets between the relative income standing of people of color and the real income of white workers: where the income gap between whites and people of color is particularly wide, the average income of white workers is lower than where the gap is narrower.[27] In short, white workers as a whole are made poorer, not richer, by racial discrimination.

Nonetheless, white workers also benefit from racism. If there is a certain amount of unemployment to be "shared" by workers and a given number of good jobs to go around, white workers benefit from their relatively lower unemployment, their better access to good jobs, and a higher income relative to workers who face discrimination.

The issue of white workers' gains or losses from racism in labor markets is controversial. Its resolution depends not so much on the technical intricacies of statistical procedure but upon what is taken to be given. To an individual white worker—unable alone to alter the distribution of income between capital and labor or the availability of well-paying safe jobs—racial preference for whites in hiring increases the chances of economic and personal well-being and security. This worker will likely see the economy as a zero-sum game in which any other worker's gains reduce his or her chances. And in a society rampant with racial prejudice, it is not surprising that many focus their wrath on people of color.

But for workers and communities as a whole, being divided from within is clearly not advantageous. The long history of U.S. labor movement struggles for higher wages, better working conditions, and greater say in the political and economic process reveals that inter-racial and inter-ethnic unity is typically the key to success—and its absence, the assurance of failure. Furthermore, whites have some-times gained from the spillover effects of the struggles of people of color. At the City University of New York, for example, black and Puerto Rican students recently demanded and won a policy of open admissions. Although many white students and community leaders opposed the policy, white working-class students who were previously excluded have benefited greatly.[28]

Demographic trends may favor an increase in the political power of people of color. Partly because of the increasingly large electorate of people of color, the economic reverses of the past decade have not been mirrored in the electoral sphere. It also seems likely that electoral success by black and Latino political figures will continue. According to estimates by political scientist Kenneth Dolbeare, people of color will comprise over a quarter of the population in such pivotal electoral states as Texas, New York, Florida, and Illinois before the end of the century. In California, they will form half.[29] In at least ten other states, people of color will comprise at least a quarter of the population. Political strategists will ignore the swing potential of this group of voters at their peril.

Whether or not a new civil rights movement will emerge depends on the political strength, unity, and dynamism of people of color in pursuing economic and social equality. It also depends on the willingness of whites—workers and others—to reject the self-defeating logic of racial exclusion in favor of the more general logic of racial unity. The potential impact of such a movement, as the Civil Rights Movement of the 1960s demonstrated, extends far beyond the racial order to nearly every social, economic, and political institution in America.

Footnotes

1. "People of color" refers to all ethno-racial groups. We do not use "minorities" because the numerical connotation suggests that discrepancies in social status, political power and/or wealth are primarily the result of population differences. In many regions and urban areas, a racial group or groups form the majority; yet they remain second-class citizens. Power and wealth, in short, are simply not proportional to numbers.

2. Michael Reich, "Postwar Racial Income Differences: Trends and Theories," Mimeo, University of California at Berkeley, 1985.

3. Sheldon Goldman, "Reaganizing the Judiciary: The First Term Appointments," *Judicature*, Volume 68, Numbers 9-10, April-May 1985, p. 319.

4. "Decline Found in Proportion of Blacks in Medical Schools," *The New York Times*, October 10, 1985. The study was published in the October, 1985 issue of *New England Journal of Medicine*.

5. William K. Stevens, "Black and Standard English Held Diverging More," *The New York Times*, March 15, 1985.

6. Edward B. Fiske, "Minority Enrollment in Colleges Is Declining," *The New York Times*, October 27, 1985.

7. *Economic Report of the President*, 1974, pp. 151-152.

8. Peter Bohmer, "The Impact of Public Sector Employment on Racial Inequality: 1950-1984," Unpublished Doctoral Dissertation, University of Massachusetts, Amherst, 1985, pp. 34-42.

9. U.S. Census Bureau, occupational data.

10. In urban areas outside the South, the median income of black males relative to white males fell considerably, from .73 in 1949 to .67 in 1979. By this measure, virtually all major Northern cities except Los Angeles and New York comprised a more racially discriminatory economic environment in 1979 than they did three decades earlier: in Chicago, Cleveland, Detroit, Philadelphia, Pittsburgh, San Francisco, and St. Louis, black males did worse relative to whites in 1979 than in 1949. Reich, *op. cit.*, Tables 4 and 6.

11. U.S. Census Bureau, occupational data.

12. U.S. Department of Labor, "Employment and Earnings Characteristics of Families, Second Quarter 1985," USDL, 85-337, August 21, 1985.

13. Bohmer, *op. cit.*, pp. 246-247. The adverse trend in the black unemployment rates over the period 1976-1984 is a departure from the earlier period in which a weak trend of improvement existed for men and no discernable trend existed for women. The post 1975 adverse trend for both men and women is highly significant statistically.

14. *Ibid.*

15. See Bureau of Labor Statistics, *Handbook of Labor Statistics*, 1980, Table 26.

16. Southwest Voter Registration Project, "Growing Problems in a Growing Community," Washington, D.C., 1984; and Center on Budget and Policy Priorities, "Falling Behind," Washington, D.C. 1984.

17. No separate data for women is offered in the sources of the table. A good source for the unequal impact of these cuts upon women is Coalition on Women and the Budget, "Inequality of Sacrifice," National Women's Law Center, Washington, D.C.,1984.

18. Center on Budget and Policy Priorities, *op. cit.*

19. See Defense Budget Project, "Fiscal Year 1986 Defense Budget, The Weapons Build Up Continues," Center on Budget and Policy Priorities, Washington, D.C., April, 1985.

20. The Congressional Budget Office estimates insignificant differences in the multiplier effect of military spending relative to other government programs. Critics, however, maintain that multiplier effects are lower and that military spending generates net job losses. See Robert W. DeGrasse, *Military Expansion, Economic Decline*, Council on Economic Priorities, New York, 1983; David McFadden and James Wake, *The Freeze Economy*, Mid-Peninsula Conversion Project, Mountain View, California and National Clearinghouse, Nuclear Weapons Freeze Campaign, St. Louis, Missouri, 1983; and William D. Hartung, "The Economic Consequences of a Nuclear Freeze," Council on Economic Priorities, New York, 1984.

21. Defense Budget Project, *ibid.*

22. Calculated from Bohmer, *op. cit.*, Table 23.

23. Bohmer, *op. cit.*, pp.260-262.

24. Joe Davidson, "Quotas in Hiring Are Anathema to President Despite Minority Gains," *Wall Street Journal*, October 24, 1985.

25. Robert Pear, "Rewriting Nation's Civil Rights Policy," *The New York Times*, October 7, 1985.

26. These estimates ignore the Latino population in order to simplify calculations. The assumption of differences in wages mostly as a result of wage discrimination crucially depends on equal levels of productivity for white and black workers. For the plausibility of the argument, see Omer Galle, Candace Wiswell and Jeffrey Burr, "Racial Mix and Industrial Productivity," *American Sociological Review*, vol. 50 (Feb. 1985), pp. 20-33. See also Victor Perlo with Gordon Welty, "The Political Economy of Racism and the Current Score," in Marvin Berlowitz and Ronald Edari, *Racism and the Denial of Human Rights*, Minneapolis, MEP Publications, 1984; and Lester Thurow, *Poverty and Discrimination*, The Brookings Institution, 1969.

27. The evidence is examined in Michael Reich, *Racial Inequality*, Princeton: Princeton University Press, 1981.

28. Richard Gambino, "Whatever Happened to CUNY?," *The Village Voice*, April 2, 1985.

29. Kenneth M. Dolbeare, *Democracy at Risk: The Politics of Economic Renewal*, Chatham House, New Jersey, 1984, Table 11.5.

5 Women and Children Last

Conservative economics has brought some bad news for women, as well as some not-so-bad news. The not-so-bad news is that the availability of paid employment (albeit in segregated occupations at low wages) and of government income support programs (however inadequate) has meant that women's access to income is no longer restricted to that which is redistributed to them through marriage. The bad news is that women with children but without male breadwinners are more likely to be poor.

Three quarters of the 6.2 million new jobs which opened up between 1979 and 1984 went to women. But women have not succeeded in closing the gender gap in living standards. Despite dramatic increases in the number of employed women, women's average income—obtained either from wages, the government, and/or husbands—relative to men's income did not improve over these years.[1] Almost a million more families headed by women fell below the official poverty line between 1979 and 1984 (see Chapter 3).[2]

The increased employment of women relative to men in the labor market was offset, on the one hand, by cuts in the public programs on which women's—and children's—living standards depend; and on the other hand, by the continuing increase in the number of women whose household income is not augmented by a male paycheck. Just short of half of all adult women now live in such households.[3]

Yet conservative economic policies are not the only thing working against women and their families. There is also a distinct conservative social "gender agenda" that aims to restore the male-headed, nuclear family—which they call *the* family—to its former prominence. The Reverend Jerry Falwell writes:

> The strength and stability of families determine the vitality and moral life of society. The most important function performed by the family is the rearing and character

59

formation of children, a function it was uniquely designed
to perform, and for which no remotely adequate substitute
has been found. The family is the best and most efficient
"department of health, education and welfare."[4]

Cutbacks in government health, education and welfare programs—
especially those which support unmarried women with children—are
welcomed as a crucial strategic victory in what fundamentalist Tim
LaHaye calls "The Battle for the Family."[5]

Does the agenda of patriarchal fundamentalism dovetail with
other programs of the new economic orthodoxy—an overvalued
dollar, high interest rates, and the attack on organized labor? The
answer, ironically, is no. These national economic policies decimated
the predominantly male manufacturing, mining, and construction
sectors, and pushed many women into a depressed labor market. This
is hardly what Reverend Falwell had in mind.

The conservative social and economic agenda has been a response
not only to the structural crisis of the capitalist economy, but to the
crisis of the traditional family as well. Much of the support for the
conservative agenda over the past decade has come not from the
businessman's concern with the long-term decline in profits or from
the bankers' project to restore the Almighty Dollar; rather, it springs
from an attempt to buttress a traditional concept of what it means to
be a man and a woman in our society. Ironically, by drawing more
women into the labor force, the economic policies of the right have
done as much to challenge as to support their preferred form of "the
family."

Thus the implicit industrial policy of conservative economics—to
shift labor out of well-paid manufacturing and into lower-wage
services—is on a collision course with the overt family policy of the
right—to accept no substitutes for the patriarchal family. Women and
children are caught in the middle.

Women Hold Up Half the Economy (at Less Than Half the Price)

Many women have entered the labor market over the past two decades
(see Figure 5.1). Why has their standard of living relative to men not
improved?

Important changes in women's economic status have occurred
over the past two decades, in both access to earned income and to
governmental transfers and in-kind services. But the relative earnings
of full-time female workers have shown little improvement. In 1970,
women earned 62.3% of what men did. By 1983, the figure inched up to
66.5%, then dipped in 1984 to 64.8% (see Figure 5.2).

Figure 5.1
Women Enter the Labor Market

Labor Force Participation Rates of Women by Marital Status and Race for Persons 16 Years and Over

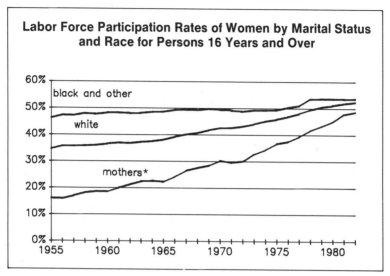

Source: U.S. Department of Labor **Handbook of Labor Statistics,** 1985 Table 5, pp. 18-19, 22.
*Mothers refers to married women with children under 6.

Figure 5.2
Women Run Hard to Stay in Place
Ratio of Female to Male Median Weekly Earning for Full-Time Wage and Salary Workers, 1974-1984

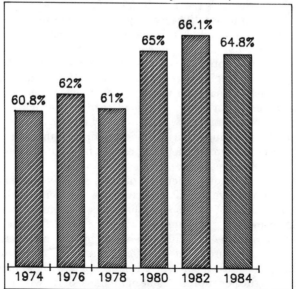

Source: For 1984 figures: **Employment and Earnings,** January 1985, p 210; for all other years, various **Statistical Abstracts of the United States.**

61

Many have pointed out the disappointingly slow pace of im-provement. Responding to 1984 projections of further gradual im-provements, Sandra Farha, President of the California National Organization of Women said:

> I hear them saying to women, "Hey, its getting better. You're increasing your earning power. Don't feel bad if you're only making 59 cents. You'll be making 74 cents soon."[6]

At the rate of improvement between 1970 and 1984, the 74 cent figure would be attained in the year 2031—by our granddaughters.

Conservatives point to the increased visibility of professional women as evidence of economic progress. While the percentage of women in law, medical and management professions increased between 1979 and 1984, most women remain in low-paid, "pink-collar" job ghettos. Changes in the federal classification of occupational categories in 1983 make long-term comparisons difficult.[7] But a look at some detailed occupational categories shows that close to 50% of all women are employed in 20 occupations out of over 200 possible occupations. The top 10 occupations, which account for one-third of all women employees, changed little between 1980 and 1984.

Between 1979 and 1983, the ratio of year-round full-time female to male workers' income improved for women, moving from 59% to 64%. But this "improved" ratio was based on a descending target—men's income. During this four-year period, the real income of men fell a crushing $1483. Women's real income increased by less than $24 over the entire four-year period.[8] The average women's earning power was stuck on a treadmill, barely keeping up with inflation.

Furthermore, a slight rise in women's recorded income and the entry of a few women into professional and managerial positions does not spell generally improving living standards for women. This is because "income" measures only earnings and government transfers, and not transfers from other household earners, particularly hus-bands. The amount of money women actually receive in their house-holds simply does not appear in income statistics. Changes in the real economic picture of women, therefore, cannot be accurately assessed in earned income figures alone.

To gain a more comprehensive picture, we have estimated a measure of the relative standard of living of women which takes account of all sources of livlihood: spouse and other family members, government transfers, and wage and other income. Of course, we do not know how income is actually shared by the members of a household. Our measure must therefore be an approximation. We measure the per capita income of all households with women and compare that to the per capita income of all households with men. We thus measure the average access to livelihood (measured in dollars) of women compared to men on the assumption that income is equally shared within households. We term our measure the *Per* capita *A*ccess to *R*esources or PAR (see Figure 5.3).[9]

Taking account of sharing within households, the per capita income of women in 1983 was 87% of the per capita income of men. We term the difference between men's and women's income 13 points under PAR. Since 1967, the first year for which we were able to calculate the index, the amount by which women were under PAR gradually increased through the late 1970s, and has remained constant since. Between 1967 and 1983, the gap between men's and women's income has doubled almost exactly, despite the fact that the ratio of female to male incomes of full-time workers was rising.

Much of the decline in the relative living standards of women stems from the rapid increase in the percentage of women living in households with no adult male. This change in family structure has been made possible in part by changing social attitudes and legal practices concerning divorce. It has also been facilitated by women's reduced economic dependence on men, caused by the expansion of jobs available to women and some sources of income support through AFDC, Food Stamps, and other government programs.

Reduced economic dependence on men is a major gain for many women, but the monetary costs of being without a man are still high. Well over a third of female-headed households live below the poverty line, and the fraction is rising (see Chapter 3). Indeed, per capita household income varies greatly with marital status. By comparison with married-couple households, the per capita income of divorced men is 57% greater; divorced women are 26% poorer; men with wife absent are 27% richer; and women with husband absent are 56% poorer.[10]

According to the logic of conservative economics, what the market does not provide, the family will. But the market has provided women with jobs in unprecedented numbers and partly as a result, the male-centered single-earner family of conservative lore is a fast-fading myth. Many of the budgetary decisions and policy and legislative initiatives of the current administration can be understood as an attempt to offset the increase in women's autonomy that the growing demand for labor has afforded.

Government Off Whose Backs?

Triggered by the dissolution of the male breadwinning family and the "ghettoization" of women into low-paying jobs, women's under-PAR income has been exacerbated by changes in the role and philosophy of

Figure 5.3
The Gender Gap in Income Widens*

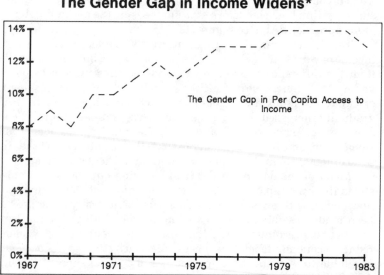

Measuring the PAR Index

The PAR index is an estimate of the average per capita income of women relative to men. To construct it, we made the hypothetical assumption that income is shared equally by household members.

We first calculated the total income of married women by multiplying the number of married couple households by their per capita income. We then calculated the income of unmarried women and other female headed households (these include married women with husband absent, divorced women, single women, and widows) by multiplying the number of such households by their per capita incomes. We added the two incomes together and then divided the sum by the total number of households with women in them to get the numerator of the ratio. Performing the same operation for men yields the denominator.

---

*One minus the PAR index measures the gap between gender equality (PAR equals one) and the actual situation.

government under the reign of the new right. Conservatives not only identify the government as the source of all evil in the economy; they also decry government "intervention" in the family.

Embracing a political philosophy that goes beyond the New Federalism, Reagan has publicly stated his admiration for family traditionalist George Gilder, author of *Wealth and Poverty*. In his book, Gilder argues it is the government—in the form of the welfare state—which is responsible for the collapse of the family, as well as the stagnation of the economy.

According to Gilder, income-support programs for poor and unemployed women undermine the breadwinning role of the father. As a result, men have lost the incentive to work and labor productivity has suffered. Furthermore, Gilder claims, the high taxes required to support the welfare state have caused family after-tax income to fall, driving women out of their homes and into the labor force. The male-headed nuclear family has been the casualty.

The policy prescriptions that emerge from these views are clear: cut personal income taxes and slash public income support for unmarried women and their children. The advantage of such a strategy, based on unleashing the "free" market, is that the same policies implicitly double as prescriptions for the economy and for the family.

The stated objectives of Reagan's conservative economic policies, however, have obscured their implications for women and for family structure. Under the rubric of getting government "off our backs," conservatives have advocated not only cuts in public support specifically for women but generally in domestic government spending.

But since militarism is one of the planks of the conservative economic approach, defense spending is exempt from conservative budget-cutting scissors. Instead, income-support and human development programs have been the primary target of conservative proposals to cut government spending. Congress and public opinion have curtailed the possibility of severe cuts in Social Security programs which support the elderly, leaving unemployed and poor families to bear the brunt of the budget cuts (see Chapter 9). While programs for low-income families constitute less than 10% of federal expenditures, they sustained 30% of all budget cuts between 1981 and 1985.[11]

Because women and children comprise a large and increasing proportion of the poor, the primary recipients of public income-support programs are women. Indeed, the number of poor persons in female-headed households rose by 100,000 a year between the mid-1960s and the mid-1970s. According to feminist analysts Barbara Ehrenreich and Frances Piven, two of three adults living below the poverty level in 1980 were women; more than half of poor families were headed by women.[12]

Because of the increasing "feminization of poverty," the cuts in income-support and other social programs which began in 1981 disproportionately affected women.[13] A study by the Coalition on Women and the Budget found that 94% of all families who receive AFDC (Aid to Families with Dependent Children) payments were maintained by women (as of March 1979); 63% of all SSI recipients (Supplemental Security Income) were women (as of December 1981). Moreover, Medicaid and Food Stamp recipients in 1983 were 60% and 85% female, respectively, while legal services clients were 67% female.[14] Women of color have been particularly hard-hit. In 1980, black female-headed families comprised 27.7% of all female-headed families but 43.4% of all families that are poor.[15]

The effects of the social spending cuts on women's living standards were worsened by the 1980-1982 recession, which generated the highest rates of unemployment since the 1930s. Prior to the conservative strategy of cutting the federal budget when the economy is contracting, income-support programs functioned precisely in reverse: to provide counter-cyclical assistance to people hurt by an economic downturn.

Cutting public support precisely at the moment when the market curtails economic opportunity, however, is the "stick" approach of conservative economics. The elimination of social welfare as a source of support "frees" large numbers of women workers for the expanding low-wage service economy.[16]

Besides the threat of poverty, there is an added twist when the stick approach is applied to women. Like men, they are subject to the "discipline of the market"; unlike men, they are also subject to the discipline of the family. Reduced options, either in the labor market or in social support programs, may force women into dependence on men. Once there, if they become victims of domestic violence, they will find battered women's shelters underfunded. Even before the Reagan budget cuts, battered women's shelters across the country were forced to turn away three times the number of people they served.[17]

Women and Children Last

A favorite target of conservative cuts in social spending programs is the AFDC program. Leading the attack is Charles Murray. In his book *Losing Ground: American Social Policy 1950-1980*, Murray argues that AFDC reduces the poor's incentive to work (see Figure 5.4). Perhaps more than any other social program, AFDC represents an alternative—however meager—to the male-headed nuclear family for women with children.

Figure 5.4
Finding Scapegoats: Charles Murray's Agenda

Battered proponents of government transfer programs report that their efforts had been "Charles Murrayed."[1] Murray's highly influential book, **Losing Ground: American Social Policy, 1950-1980,** is a picturesquely argued case for the conservative agenda of gutting social programs. Murray argues not that the poor are more shiftless than anyone else, but that a social policy elite changed the rules of their world by making it economically attractive in the short run to behave in ways that are destructive in the long run. Thus the government does the poor a great disservice by continuing these mistakes: the various expanded social welfare programs of the 1960s and 1970s.

One of Murray's most ferociously argued examples concerns the AFDC program, a favored target of other conservatives as well. According to Murray, it encouraged women to shun traditional family responsibility (that is, marriage), while they nonetheless allegedly persisted in having babies. And, in Murray's words: "The most flagrantly unrepentent seemed to be black, too."[2] According to Murray, AFDC did not reduce poverty. Rather it ensured that millions of poor children would never grow up with first-hand experience of the virtues of hard work. Murray compares total real federal cash expenditures on public assistance with the number of persons below the poverty line from 1950 to 1980, and concluded that increased assistance caused increased poverty.

This conclusion is very odd in view of the fact that poverty rates and government transfers—revealed in Murray's own figures—unmistakably move in opposite directions.[3] One could use these data to make a stronger prima facie case for the opposite assertion: that public assistance reduced poverty, and when transfers were cut, poverty began to rise.

Murray contends that rising transfers for the poor induced most reasonable people within the reach of eligibility to abandon work and embrace idleness. Since the major alternatives to wage work for most women are housework and childcare, Murray's assumption of carefree leisure is highly suspect. And existing research has found a small wage-work disincentive in AFDC. As demeaning as AFDC recipients know it to be, it does provide some alternative—or more often, supplement—to the most underpaid and degrading jobs.

AFDC probably also contributed to some of the rise in female-headed households until the 1970s. However, in the 1970s, real per capita AFDC benefits shrank under inflationary pressure. AFDC families as a percentage of all female-headed families also fell, while the extent of female household headship continued each year to set new records.

AFDC thus plays some modest role in giving women alternatives to bad jobs and to bad marriages. However, the labor market itself has been a bigger factor in the growth of female headed households, and hence in women's and children's poverty. The increased probability that white women will have paid jobs, and the increased opportunity for black women to hold jobs other than minimally paid domestic service, made women more economically independent of men throughout post-war U.S. history. The elimination of public assistance cannot stop this development.[4]

1. **Newsweek,** February 1, 1985.
2. **Ibid.,** p. 18.
3. **Ibid.,** p. 57.
4. See Victor R. Fuchs, "His and Hers: Gender Differences in Work and Income, 1959-1979," Working Paper No. 1501, National Bureau of Economic Research, 1984, and Elaine McCrate, "The Growth of Non-Marriage Among U.S. Women," Ph.D Dissertation University of Massachusetts, Amherst, 1985.

Conservative policies rest on the assumption that childbearing and childrearing are private, not social, responsibilities. But the costs of raising children—in labor and material resources—are disproportionately borne by women.[18]

Furthermore, it is unlikely that the long-term trend toward non-marriage will be reversed. An increasing number of children, therefore, will be part of female-headed households. Given that children take shares out of female income which is at poverty level or below, it is not surprising that the economic welfare of such households depends primarily on the age and number of children within them. Economist Nancy Folbre has termed this phenomenon "the pauperization of motherhood."[19]

Like public support to the elderly, public intergenerational transfers of income to children comprise part of government responsibility in most other industrialized countries. Indeed, according to a recent study, the United States does less to relieve the private costs of rearing children than any of the other industrialized countries.[20]

Government income support for raising children, which often takes the form of child welfare allowance, reflects the reality that child-rearing is not only work but work that is important to the long-term health of the economy. Indeed, child-rearing might be considered the most important of all long-term economic investments. Yet, it is labor which is unpaid.

Recent data on the amount of unpaid work performed in the home by women and men are difficult to obtain, but there is no evidence that men are participating substantially more. The available information suggests that the amount of time women spend doing unpaid work is falling, but that their total work week (waged and unwaged work) is rising. The bulk of necessary work at home is still left up to women. Victor Fuchs estimated that women performed 70% of "non-market" work in 1979.[21]

Women provide 30-40% of all wage work and 70% of all unwaged work; yet the ratio of average income of women with income relative to that of men with income in 1983 was 42%.[22] In other words, it is likely that women do over half of all the work that gets done in this country and continue to make less than half of what men do.

The New Double Standard

Our contention that conservative economics is about family policy as well as economic policy helps to explain aspects of it that otherwise appear to be contradictory. The 1985 *Economic Report of the President*, for example, emphasized a reduced role for the federal government in all aspects of the economy. In particular, it supported deregulation, competition and free choice. In other statements, Reagan administration officials have objected to government interference in the "free" labor market to overcome sexual and racial discrimination by mandating that all work of comparable value to the employer is paid equally. Indeed, Clarence Pendleton, head of the Civil Rights Commission, called comparable worth the "looniest idea since looney tunes."[23]

According to a report in *Business Week*, if women today earned even three quarters of what men did, the country's total wage bill would be an additional $100 billion.[24] That means that discrimination cost every employed woman $2,123.38 in 1984.[25] It is clear that what is meant by the "market solution" is the continuation of depressed wages for women because discrimination is part of the marketplace.

Furthermore, so committed are conservatives to the workings of the existing "free" market they have reduced government support for programs that help women compete in the market. The Women's Educational Equity Act, funded at $10 million in 1981, was cut to $5.8 million in 1984, and was slated to receive no funds at all in the proposed FY1986 budget.[26]

Similarly, Title IV of the Civil Rights Act of 1964, which provides school districts with technical assistance to comply with federal anti-discrimination laws, received $37 million in 1981, $24 million in 1984, and zero requested dollars in FY1986. Provisions of the Vocational Education Act (which mirrors the occupational distribution) have been proposed for elimination.[27]

According to a recent report in *The New York Times*, the Reagan administration has begun a review of regulations that, in the words of Vice President Bush, are perceived to be "burdensome, unnecessary or counterproductive." Among those guidelines under review are the sexual harassment guidelines of the Equal Opportunity Commission ("terms such as unwelcome sexual advances and verbal sexual conduct...rely greatly on individual perception") and those that prohibit a job selection process "that disproportionately excludes members of a race, sex or ethnic group." Title IX policies which require equal expenditures on male and female athletic programs are also slated for review.[28]

The President, who campaigned against the Equal Rights Amendment on the grounds that adequate legislation against sex discrimination already exists, has curtailed enforcement of those laws. Reagan's Justice Department has also changed the standard by which discrimination can be said to exist. According to an Urban Institute Report, court decisions in the years prior to 1981 have held that the effects of apparent discrimination, e.g. underrepresentation of women in a particular firm's pattern of promotion, was sufficient cause to order a remedy. The current Justice Department standard requires instead the more stringent proof of *intent* to discriminate.[29]

As a result, the Equal Employment Opportunity Commission (EEOC) failed to find violations in 40% of all new charges filed with it in 1984. The figure for 1981 was 23%.[30] Federal outlays for enforcement of equal opportunity statutes have also declined. Between FY1981 and FY1983 the EEOC saw its budget cut by 10% in real terms and its staff by 12%. The EEOC is authorized to initiate litigation against discriminators. Between 1981 and 1983 there was a 60% decline in lawsuits filed by the Commission.[31]

Ironically, an administration which campaigned on the platform of getting the government off the backs of the American people and out of the economy has also attempted to legislate the most private aspect of people's lives. The conservative attack on abortion, homosexuality, and family planning is directed at legislating people's—especially women's—sexual decisions. Restricting access to abortion is prominent among President Reagan's social policy goals.[32] Conservatives have gone so far as to support a so-called Human Life Amendment to the U.S. Constitution. And the New Right aims to overturn the *Roe vs. Wade* Supreme Court decision (1973) which ruled that a woman's decision to end a pregnancy was a fundamental right to privacy protected by the 14th Amendment.

Conclusion

The changing relationship of family, economy, and government in the U.S. today has not opened up new vistas of economic opportunity and personal choice to women: it has closed them down. Continuing labor market discrimination and cutbacks in income support programs leave many women with little choice but to endure unwanted marriages, exchanging their autonomy for their livelihood.

To improve women's—and children's—living standards and to make individual choice about family structure a reality, public policy must move in three directions: (1) it must increase women's employment opportunities and remuneration; (2) it must provide adequate public support for the work of child-rearing; and (3) it must provide adequate income support programs. As long as child-raising is devalued and unpaid, and as long as discrimination persists in labor markets, women will continue to share unequally in social income and their personal liberty will be constrained.

Establishing greater social responsibility for children and their caretakers through government is a high-priority step for reducing women's and children's poverty, involving a major reorientation of the relationship between state and family. By way of comparison, an enormous transformation of the relationship between government and the private economy was necessary to address the record levels of unemployment in the Great Depression. After the end of World War II, tremendous headway was made in reducing unemployment because the government made a commitment to moderate the effect of the business cycle. Likewise, poverty among the elderly was reduced because the government committed itself to transfers through the Social Security system. Something of the same order is now necessary to contend with the social challenge of female-headed families.

Women and men are increasingly choosing non-traditional family structures: many are single, many will pass through one or more marriages, many live in collectives, many live in lesbian and gay couples. Allowing a wide and broadening range of family choices must be a central tenet of any society which calls itself democratic. Neither the market nor the traditional family—the two pillars of conservative thought and social policy—will secure this liberty; indeed, we have suggested that they constitute obstacles to broadening the range of choices facing women and men.

Without active government intervention in markets to combat discrimination; without the recognition of child-raising as socially valued work worthy of social remuneration; and without the establishment of an adequate income floor, the freedom to choose will remain a mirage for most—and for many, an impoverished freedom.

Footnotes

1. See Figure 5.3 which presents our calculations of women's income relative to men's.

2. U.S. Census Bureau, Current Population Survey, P-60 Series, 1985.

3. Thirty-two percent in 1983, up from 30% in 1979 and 22% in 1967, U.S. Census Bureau, Current Population Survey, *Money Income of Families, Households and Persons in the United States*, P-60 Series, 1985.

4. Reverend Jerry Falwell, *The Fundamentalist Phenomenon: The Resurgence of Conservative Christianity*, Doubleday, New York, 1981, p. 206.

5. Tim LaHaye, *The Battle for the Family*, Fleming H. Revell Company.

6. *The New York Times*, October 31, 1984.

7. Nancy F. Rytina and Suzanne M. Bianchi document those changes in *Monthly Labor Review*, March, 1984, Vol. 107, No. 3, pp. 11-17.

8. *Economic Report of the President*, 1985, p. 264. The figures are in 1983 dollars.

9. The measure does not take account of taxes, or of in-kind transfers of any sort.

10. The data are from U.S. Census Bureau, Current Population Survey 1983. Elaine McCrate has measured the changing "cost of non-marriage" over the post-war period. While it has declined in the 1980s due to falling male incomes, it rose substantially in the 1960s and 1970s. Elaine McCrate, "The Growth of Non-Marriage Among U.S. Women," Ph.D. Dissertation, University of Massachusetts, Amherst, 1985.

11. Center on Budget and Policy Priorities, *End Results: The Impact of Federal Policies Since 1980 on Low Income Americans*, Washington, D.C., 1984.

12. Barbara Ehrenreich and Frances Piven, "The Feminization of Poverty: When the Family Wage System Breaks Down," *Dissent*, Spring 1984, p. 162.

13. Diana Pearce coined the term in "Women, Work and Welfare: The Feminization of Poverty," in Karen Wolk Feinstein, Ed., *Working Women and Their Families*, Sage Publications, London, 1979.

14. Coalition for Women and the Budget, *Inequality of Sacrifice*, National Women's Law Center, Washington, D.C., 1984. Food stamp recipients include women and children combined. Women also constitute more than 50% of Social Security recipients. This program, however, was not severely trimmed back.

15. Catherine L. Hammond, "Not Always 'Just a Husband Away From Poverty': Race, Class, and the Feminization of Poverty," Mimeo, University of Massachusetts, Amherst, 1982, p. 25.

16. Frances F. Piven, and Richard A. Cloward, *The New Class War: Reagan's Attack on the Welfare State and Its Consequences*, Pantheon, New York, 1982.

17. Coalition on Women and the Budget, *op. cit.*

18. Nancy Folbre, "The Pauperization of Motherhood: Patriarchy and Public Policy in the U.S.," *Review of Radical Political Economics*, Vol. 16, No. 4, 1985. While social conservatives like Gilder suggest that women shoulder the burden because welfare payments have undermined the traditional family, there is evidence that even within male-headed families, the time costs of bearing and rearing children fall disproportionately on women.

19. *Ibid.*

20. Alfred J. Kayn and Sheila B. Kamerman, "Income Maintenance, Wages, and Family Income," *Public Welfare*, Fall 1983.

21. Victor Fuchs, "His and Hers: Gender Differences in Work and Income, 1959-1979," Working Paper No. 1501, National Bureau of Economic Research, New York, 1984.

22. *Economic Report of the President*, 1985, Table B-27, p. 264.

23. *The New York Times*, November 17, 1984, p. A15.

24. *Business Week*, January 28, 1985, p. 81.

25. Calculated from a total female labor force of 47,095,000 in 1982. See *Statistical Abstract of the United States 1984*, p. 413.

26. Coalition on Women and the Budget, *op. cit.*

27. *Ibid.*

28. *The New York Times*, August 12, 1984.

29. John L. Palmer, and Isabel V. Sawhill, Ed. *The Reagan Record*, Urban Institute, Washington, D.C., 1984, p. 206.

30. *Coalition on Women and the Budget, op. cit.*, p. 51.

31. Palmer and Sawhill, *op. cit.*

32. *The New York Times*, July 21, 1985.

6 Crossroads for Labor

American labor relations are at a crossroads. Years from now, the 1980s may be seen as giving birth to a new system of labor/management relations—a change no less profound than that of the 1930s, which ushered in collective bargaining and the mass organizing of industrial unions.

In one direction lies the route of undermining existing union shops and reasserting management control. For business, this route offers the lure of raising profits by cutting wages and cutting corners on workplace health and safety. It also offers businesspeople the assurance that most economic decisionmaking will remain in their hands.

Most businesses and the Reagan administration have opted for this big stick strategy, and have already gone a long way towards fundamentally restructuring U.S. labor relations. While some businesses are experimenting with "quality control circles" and other cosmetic forms of worker participation, many have opted for an old-fashioned reassertion of management control. Nearly all have adopted an increasingly aggressive anti-union stance in the face of declining profits, increased competitive pressure on world markets, and deregulation. Since 1979, the federal government's policies of tight money and the over-valued dollar have promoted import penetration, sluggish economic growth, and high levels of unemployment, all of which have combined to erode the bargaining strength of unions. Cuts in social programs, deregulation, and changes in National Labor Relations Board (NLRB) policy have further weakened organized labor.

Unions are reeling under the impact of this assault. Between 1980 and 1984, the number of employed union members fell by 2.7 million, and the percentage of employees who are union members fell from 23%

to 19%.[1] With unemployment rates stuck at over 7%, workers as a whole are paying the price.

The other road that tomorrow's labor/management relations can take points toward the carrot rather than the stick. Based on the recognition that workers are not mere inputs who happen to take the form of human beings, the carrot approach offers high wages and worker participation in both production and investment decisions. Unions are welcomed as a way to negotiate wage and work disputes.

The pay-off for businesses that offer the carrot is higher productivity and reduced spending over workplace conflicts. For the national economy, the high unionization rates of the carrot approach make possible non-inflationary full employment through bargained price and incomes policies.

The logic of a democratic and egalitarian approach to labor relations is that labor markets and workplaces are not only economic but also political arenas. Even an assembly line depends on the successful resolution of potential conflicts among and between workers and management. Stick strategies tend to be wasteful simply because they promote conflict and heavy-handed methods of dealing with conflict—such as high levels of unemployment and a top-heavy system of management.

The "right" conditions for the stick strategy to work also include an inadequate system of income support, as well as a weak labor movement. Racial, sexual and other divisions among workers also make it easy for management to fire workers indiscriminately because there is no unified workforce ready to walk out if a person is fired unfairly.

Moreover, with a weak labor movement, a rational nationwide solution to the determination of the general levels of prices and incomes is impossible, for no solution which leaves labor out of the bargaining process can be accepted as fair and binding. And labor cannot be consulted if it is not organized.

In the recent stick strategy followed under Reagan, inflation fighting takes the slash-and-burn form of high interest rates, an over-valued dollar, high levels of unemployment, and a massive shortfall between the output of the economy and its productive capacity. These very policies cost the U.S. economy an estimated $2 trillion in lost output between 1981 and 1985 (see Chapter 8).

But if the stick is going to be retired and the carrot strategy implemented, both U.S. business and organized labor will have to change their ways.

Like business, the labor movement faces a fork in the road. Labor can merely hold on to all of the gains it has already secured for the minority of U.S. workers who are now union members. Or unions can choose an aggressive and all-embracing strategy aimed at becoming a voice for all working and unemployed people on the job and off, and committed to a democratic system of labor relations. The future of the entire U.S. economy may hang in the balance.

The Decline of the Postwar Labor Accord

Between the late 1930s and early 1950s, a particular set of labor/management relationships and institutions developed in the U.S. Representing a specific balance of power between employers and unions, this "labor accord" was best reflected in the relationship between core firms—large companies with significant market shares or establishments whose prices and profit rates were maintained by government regulation—and the unions which represented workers in such firms. These unions generally gained from employers' recognition of their rights to exist and to bargain collectively. The unions won legislation which mandated government enforcement of those rights and generally were able to achieve wage increases commensurate with increases in productivity.[2] Employers maintained control over the shop and office floor, the level of employment, the rate of investment, and plant location, unless explicitly stated otherwise in a contract.

But the majority of workers did not participate directly in this labor accord. During the mid-1950s when unionization was at its highest, only slightly more than a third of U.S. workers belonged to unions. Indeed, among the advanced industrial nations, only France and Japan had comparably low rates of unionization.[3]

Agricultural workers and public employees were not even included in the basic national legislation setting the legal framework for the accord, the National Labor Relations Act.[4] And most workers employed outside core firms in the "secondary labor market," were never able to organize successfully.

The secondary labor market workers, composed disproportionately of women and workers of color, generally faced great employer resistance to union organizing.[5] Economist Michael Reich found that unionization rates among production workers in core manufacturing firms were 30% to 40% higher than for workers in secondary manufacturing firms.[6] The Taft-Hartley Act of 1947, which amended the National Labor Relations Act, severely limited the tools available to organize workers. The Act restricted the use of secondary boycotts and permitted states to pass right-to-work laws.

By the late 1960s, declining profits began to strain even the exclusive labor accord. Business began trying to lower workers' wages and benefits. And employers stepped up their resistance to new union organizing and tried to sabotage existing union contracts[7] (see Figure 6.1).

The employer offensive of the past 20 years can be seen in the increased number of cases before the National Labor Relations Board

Figure 6.1
Employers Step Up the Attack on Unions
Percentage of Representation Elections Resulting in
Certification Which Were Conducted with Employer Consent

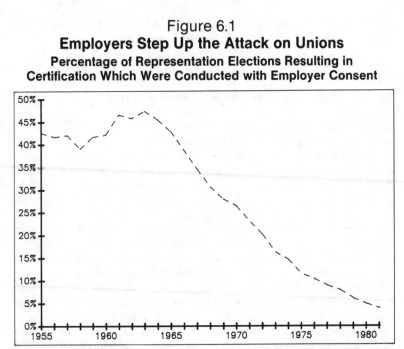

Source: 1950-1981: National Labor Relations Board, **Annual Report of the National Labor Relations Board**, Washington, D.C.: U.S. Government Printing Office, issues 15-46, 1950: Table 13, 1951: Table 9, 1953-1981: Table 11, reported in James B. Rebitzer, "Long Term Employment Relations in the United States," Ph.D. dissertation, University of Massachusetts, 1985, p. 162.

involving illegal activities of employers. According to labor economists Richard Freeman and James Medoff, the number of charges involving the firing of workers for union activity rose by 300% between 1960 and 1980. Meanwhile the number of workers awarded back pay or ordered reinstated rose by 500%. The number of NLRB elections, on the other hand, scarcely changed.[8] Freeman and Medoff also estimate that, in 1980, one in twenty pro-union workers got fired, and one person was illegally discharged for every NLRB-sanctioned election.[9]

The defeat of the proposed Labor Law Reform Act in 1978 continued to reflect labor's profound weakness. Without these reforms, the labor accord and the limits of union power declined even further. The unsuccessful 1978 Act aimed to correct abuses under previous labor law, including management's ability to delay union elections.[10]

Recent conservative economic policies and court rulings on unions also bear the imprint of the declining accord between business and unions. In his first year in office, Ronald Reagan ordered 8,590 members of the Professional Air Traffic Controllers Organization (PATCO) dismissed after they did not follow his order to return to work.[11] Reagan also ordered that PATCO members not be hired into government positions.

Donald L. Dotson, Reagan's Chairman of the National Labor Relations Board, has clearly expressed the hostility between conservative economics and collective action by workers. In 1984, Dotson argued that collective bargaining "frequently means labor monopoly, the destruction of individual freedom, and the destruction of the market place as the mechanism for determining the value of labor."[12]

Reagan administration nominees gained a majority on the NLRB in December, 1983. Within six months, a minimum of eight major pro-labor precedents were overturned.[13] The NLRB broadened the right of employers to interrogate union supporters about their union sympathies and narrowed the circumstances in which such questioning would be considered "coercive."[14] The Board also reversed a previous NLRB decision and ruled that an employer is not required to bargain over plant relocation, if the relocation did not hinge on issues of labor costs.[15]

In 1984, the Board also reduced the kinds of worker activities protected by the NLRB and reduced the circumstances in which unions can file a complaint with the NLRB. These decisions have obviously increased employers' ability to resist bargaining with unions, reduced the protection afforded workers attempting to form unions, and restricted the areas in which unions can expect government intervention on their behalf.

The decline in the power of unions can also be seen in the deterioration of union wages. From 1954 to 1973, first-year median wage *increases* averaged 2.6%, corrected for inflation. Between 1973 and 1979, wages declined slightly (0.2% average) each year. But between 1979 and 1984, real wages *fell* by an average of 1.6% a year according to a widely-used measure of union wage settlements.[16]

Since 1979, the list of unions forced to give back existing benefits includes two of the largest U.S. unions—the United Auto Workers and the Teamsters. Unionized workers have also lost major strikes, such as the air traffic controllers of PATCO and union workers at Continental Airlines.[17]

Union membership has also plummeted, particularly in manufacturing and other non-service industries. Between 1980 and 1984, union membership in goods-producing industries alone fell by 1.9 million people.[18]

Roots of Union Decline

The decline in union membership is the result of three developments: the anti-union strategies of business; increased unemployment; and the changing structure of the economy. The particular organizing strategies and policies of some unions have also pushed union membership downward. According to Freeman and Medoff, the amount of union resources and energies devoted to shopfloor organizing appears to have had a major influence on the outcomes of elections.[19]

A number of studies document the effects which the anti-union strategies of business have had on unions and on the outcome of NLRB elections. Freeman and Medoff conclude that "despite the considerable differences among the studies...virtually all tell the same story. Managerial opposition to unions, and illegal campaign tactics in particular, are a major, if not the major determinant of NLRB election results."[20] They estimate that one quarter to one-half of the decline in union electoral success can be attributed to rising management opposition.

Part of the decline in union membership is the result of long-term structural changes in the economy, such as the shift from goods production and manufacturing to service production; changes in the relative occupational mix from blue collar to white collar occupations; and changes in the composition of the labor force. These changes have resulted in the movement of workers out of higher unionized industries and occupations into those with lower unionization rates.

But the sharp decline of unionization *within* such bastions of the trade union movement as construction, mining, and durable goods manufacturing between 1980 and 1984 suggests that sectoral shifts cannot account for all or even most of the overall decline. While union membership in goods-producing sectors declined by 1.9 million between 1980 and 1984, these sectors had an *increase* of 1.1 million new jobs.[21]

Further caution concerning the "sectoral shift" explanation is suggested by the fact that many countries experiencing roughly similar structural shifts in the economy have not experienced a relative decline in union membership. The fraction of the non-agricultural employed labor force which is unionized rose between the early 1970s and early 1980s in Australia, Belgium, Canada, Denmark, France, Germany, the Netherlands, Sweden, and the United Kingdom. And most of these countries experienced far more severe declines in employment in manufacturing than the U.S.[22]

Other structural shifts may have been more important. Unions are more successful in achieving wage gains from monopoly or oligopoly firms—for the simple reason that these firms can pass on wage increases to consumers. Competitive firms do not have the market power to set prices and cannot easily pass on wage increases. The increasingly competitive nature of the economy since the mid-1960s—the combined result of increasing international competition and deregulation—has no doubt undermined the ability of unions to deliver the goods for their members.

Finally, high levels of unemployment during the first half of the 1980s and the weakening of the social safety net have forced workers to take seriously business threats to close up shop if the union pushes too hard. This is the unspoken logic of conservative economic policy at work.

Because of a longer search for new jobs and a lower percentage of unemployed workers who received unemployment insurance, workers displaced during the recession of the early 1980s lost a far larger share of their expected lifetime income than those who lost their jobs during the mid-1970s recession. With so many people unemployed, and with the costs of not having a job mounting, general economic conditions have made it relatively easy for business to attract non-union labor. As a result, unions have become more cautious in the use of strikes and have been less successful in winning strikes.

Unions and Economic Performance

Orthodox economists generally argue that unions reduce economic efficiency and promote inequality. Unions succeed in raising wages for their members, they point out, by restricting the supply of labor to unionized firms or industries. "Unnaturally" high wages create unemployment because firms hire less labor when it is more expensive. Furthermore, reduced employment opportunities in unionized firms may generate an increased supply of workers to secondary labor markets, forcing down wages for non-union workers and producing a polarized distribution of income among workers. Finally, orthodox economists claim that union work rules, which usurp management control on the shop and office floor, restrict the efficient allocation of labor within the firm, thus reducing productivity and increasing product cost and price.

But unionized firms and countries with strong labor movements appear, on balance, to exhibit better productivity performance than the "union-free" environments advocated by orthodox economists.

A broad view of the relationship between unionization rates and economic performance can be gleaned by examining the post-World War II period in the U.S. and Western Europe. While no strong conclusion can be derived from a simple historical correlation, the U.S. trend is clear: the period of high unionization and union strength in the immediate postwar decades was a period of strong productivity growth. The decline of union strength in the 1970s and 1980s has been accompanied by a productivity slowdown.[23]

Furthermore, a comparison of the U.S. and Western Europe in the postwar period does not support the conservative argument for an anti-union stance on economic grounds.

Belgium, Denmark, and Sweden are the most unionized of the advanced Western industrial nations, with unionization rates ranging from 60% to 96%. Furthermore, the strength of these European unions has grown over the postwar period. Concurrently, the productivity growth rates in manufacturing have been consistently higher in these nations than in the U.S. Today the U.S. unionization rate, declining since the mid-1950s, totals about one-third that of Belgium, Denmark and Sweden (see Figure 6.2).

Between 1950 and 1984, the average annual productivity growth rate in manufacturing for these countries was approximately 80% to 150% higher than in the U.S. In addition, both Germany and Japan, which have outperformed the U.S. in terms of productivity growth over the postwar period, have had higher rates of unionization in recent years. Labor/management conflict—as measured by the frequency and size of strikes—has also been considerably less in Belgium, Denmark and Sweden (see Figure 6.2).

The superior economic performance of the highly unionized countries extends considerably beyond the immediate terrain of the workplace itself. Between 1960 and 1982, investment (measured as the average of fixed capital investment as a percent of Gross Domestic Product—GNP) was approximately 12% to 16% higher in Belgium, Denmark, and Sweden than in the U.S. And in this same period, no country lost as large a share of world trade as did the U.S.

Compared to the U.S., all three countries averaged much lower unemployment rates and more rapid rates of growth of wages (corrected for inflation) with only slightly higher levels of inflation. The trade-off between inflation and unemployment—how much unemployment is needed to reduce inflation by 1%—was considerably more favorable in these countries over the postwar period.

One measure of the inflation-unemployment trade-off is the misery index—the sum of the unemployment rate and the rate of inflation. Between 1959 and 1983, the U.S. scored higher than Sweden on this index of stagflation in every year but two.[24] Data for Belgium and Denmark and for earlier years in Sweden are not sufficiently comparable to allow a reliable comparison.[25]

The relative success of the highly unionized countries cannot be attributed unambiguously to unionization; no doubt many factors contributed. But these comparisons suggest a number of possible national and industry-based ways that unions increase productivity.

At the national level, unions have consistently pressed for full employment and full utilization of economic resources. Where unions have remained strong, as in Austria and Sweden, government policy

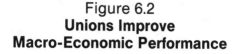

Figure 6.2
**Unions Improve
Macro-Economic Performance**

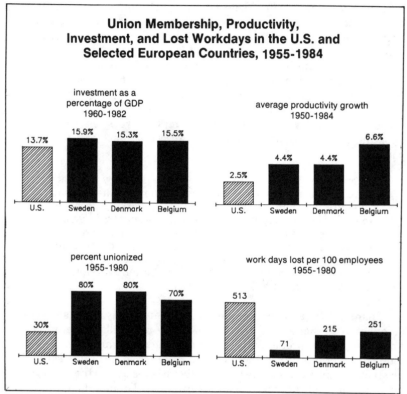

Source: U.S. Department of Labor, **Handbook of Labor Statistics 1983,** and Office of Productivity and Technology (unpublished data).

has been expansionary, leading to more rapid rates of economic growth and less waste of human resources and material inputs. Unions have also pressed for public expenditures on human resource development. Resulting programs in education and health, for example, have undoubtedly contributed to the economic well-being of the entire society. Finally, where strong unions encompass most of the population, they have been able to bargain with employers and with the government for a package of wage and price increases which are in line with productivity increases, thus contributing to a more favorable inflation-unemployment trade-off.

The beneficial economic effects of unions may also operate at the level of the individual industry or even firm. While some analysts link unionization to reduced productivity, recent studies suggest that the opposite is the case—that unions boost productivity. Labor economists Charles Brown and James Medoff found that output per labor hour in U.S. manufacturing industries was 10% to 25% higher in those states with higher rates of unionization.[26] Industrial economist Kim Clark conducted case studies of productivity (measured in tons per labor hour) at six cement plants before and after they were unionized. His study suggested that unionization led to productivity increases of 6-8%.[27] And labor economist Steven Allen found higher productivity for unionized establishments in construction.[28]

Unions, apparently, can transform the work environment, boosting productive efforts. As Harvard economist James Medoff concluded:[29]

> When a union comes into a competitive industry and gets increased compensation for the employees, as unions typically do, then everything has to be working to bring about higher productivity or the establishment will go out of business. You'll find efforts on the part of management because it wants to stay in business. You'll find efforts on the part of unions because they want to keep their new members. And you'll find efforts on the part of workers because they want to keep their jobs.

If unions are good for economic performance, why are businesses so opposed to them? The paradox is easily resolved. While unions apparently raise productivity, their collective bargaining strength tends to lower profits. Through unions, a larger share of the fruits of production tends to go to the workers themselves and to the public at large, through larger social spending programs. Unions also enhance worker input into the work process and expand public control over a nation's economy, reducing the domain of corporate decisionmaking. While profits are the bottom line for business, it is clear that enhancing profits and enhancing economic performance are not the same thing.

Nonetheless, since profitability guides investment, conservative economists argue that reducing profits is itself inefficient. But in some countries, high rates of unionization are apparently linked to high levels of investment. Sweden, for example, has had consistently lower profits and consistently higher investment in its manufacturing sector than the U.S.

A New Accord?

Is a strong U.S. labor movement a thing of the past? While some predict a continuing deterioration in union strength and membership into the next century, U.S. history offers examples of previous periods of severe union decline followed by vigorous growth.

In the 1920s, unions experienced bitter attack and severe defeat. Union membership declined by over 40% between 1920 and 1932, leading analysts and critics to predict continued decline (see Figure 6.3). George Barnett, President of the American Economic Association, offered this view to his fellow economists in 1932:[30]

> American trade unionism is slowly being limited in influence by changes which destroy the basis on which it is erected. It is probable that changes in the law have adversely affected unionism... I see no reason to believe that American trade unionism will...become in the next decade a more potent social influence...

By 1934, union membership began to explode. New organizing strategies were developed and workers who had been on the sidelines of the established labor movement—particularly blacks and unskilled workers—became part of the mainstream. By 1935, the Committee for Industrial Organization was formed, the National Labor Relations Act was passed, and industrial unionism had begun to expand rapidly. In the next five years, union membership more than doubled (see Figure 6.3).

Like the 1920s, the current period of structural change in both the economy and the labor movement may also be sowing the seeds for a "new unionism" of the 1980s and 1990s. Public sector unions, for example, grew vigorously in the 1960s and 1970s.

Public employees were left out of the postwar labor accord since collective bargaining legislation excluded public employees until the early 1960s. By 1980, however, almost half of the states had laws giving collective bargaining rights to some public workers, and thirteen states extended such rights to all workers. Similar advances have continued into the 1980s.

Federal workers gained limited bargaining rights through a series of Presidential orders and congressional revisions of the Civil Service Act in 1976. These bargaining rights, however, do not include the right to strike or to bargain over compensation.

By 1984, government employees constituted approximately one-third of all employed union members. And unlike the experience in the private goods- and service-producing industries, there has not been a significant decline in the number of union members among government workers since 1980. The unionization rate among government workers remained constant between 1980 and 1984 at 35.9%.[31]

Figure 6.3
The Decline in Labor Union Membership

*The post 1978 series is not exactly comparable with the earlier data. Data for 1981 are not available.
Source: 1930-1960: U.S. Department of Commerce, **Historical Statistics of the U.S.**, Washington DC, Government Printing Office, Series D-946-951, p. 178;
1961-1980: U.S. Bureau of Labor Statistics, **Directory of National Unions and Employee Association,** Washington, G.P.O., 1979, p. 59, and "Corrected Data on Labor Organization Membership, 1980," News Release, September 18, 1981;
1982: Courtney Gifford, **Directory of U.S. Labor Organization,** Washington DC, The Bureau of National Affairs, Inc., 1984, p 2.

A possible turnaround in the fortunes of unions is also suggested by the fact that the most rapidly growing sectors of the labor force—women and people of color—appear to want to join unions (see Figure 6.4). The number of women and people of color entering the workforce has increased over the postwar period and now makes up half the U.S. labor force. There has also been an increase in the group's union membership: women now make up approximately one-third of employed union members and black workers make up over 14% (see Figure 6.5).[32]

Traditionally, unionization rates have been lower among service workers and among women, who are disproportionately concentrated in service sector jobs. Today, however, nonrepresented women employed in the private sector and workers of color, who are also disproportionately concentrated in service jobs, are more likely than their white male counterparts to vote for a union to represent them.[33]

Some measure of the labor movement's potential future may be gained from the recent successful strike at Yale University by clerical

Figure 6.4
Women, People of Color and
Service Sector Workers Favor Unions

Untapped Union Strength and Projected Labor Force Growth		
	Percentage of non-represented private-sector workers who answered "for" to: "If an election were held with secret ballots, would you vote for or against having a union or employees' association represent you?"	Projected per cent change in the share of the labor force, 1982-1995
All nonrepresented sector wage and salary employees	33%	
Sex		
Male	27%	−6%
Female	41%	8%
Race		
White	29%	−2%
Nonwhite	69%	13%
Selected Industries		
Mining	16%	
Construction	22%	
Manufacturing	36%	
Wholesale and retail trade	34%	
Finance, insurance, real estate	31%	
Services	37%	

Source: R. Freeman and J. Medoff, **What Do Unions Do?**, Table 2-2, p. 29 (original data from **Quality of Employment**, 1977, Institute for Social Research, University of Michigan; and Howard Fullerton and John Tschetter, "The 1995 Labor Force: A Second Look," U.S. Bureau of Labor Statistics, **Employment Projections for 1995**, U.S. Government Printing Office, Washington, D.C., March 1984, p. 6).

and technical workers of Local 34, Federation of University Employees. A central issue was pay discrimination against women and workers of color. After a ten-week strike, the workers won a contract which included provisions aimed at ameliorating sexual and racial discrimination. Achieved with solidarity between Locals 34 and 35 (Local 35 represented the service and maintenance workers), the success at Yale indicates what workers can accomplish in the private service sector.[34]

A number of other unions are actively pressing employers for pay equity for their female members and members of color. Equal pay for

Figure 6.5
Union Membership

Employed Union and Employee Association Members by Race and Sex, Average for Year Ended September 1984		
	Percent Unionized	Percent of All Union Members
Race		
Black	26.2	14.3
White	18.2	83.1
		97.4
Sex		
Women	14.0	33.7
Men	23.3	66.3
		100.0

Source: Adapted and calculated from Larry Adams, "Changing Employment Patterns of Organized Workers," *Monthly Labor Review*, February, 1985. Table 2, p. 29.

work of equal value to the employer, known as comparable worth, is currently a major bargaining issue for at least six unions: American Federation of State, County and Municipal Employees (AFSCME), Communication Workers of America (CWA), International Union of Electrical Workers (IUE), Service Employees International Union (SEIU). United Electrical Workers (UE) and United Auto Workers (UAW).[35]

In spite of the anti-union policies and court rulings in recent years, new coalitions have emerged among unions and between unions and community groups. In response to employment declines of 17% at Westinghouse and 10% at General Electric since 1982, twelve unions formed a coalition representing 100,000 GE and Westinghouse workers. They wanted to be in a better bargaining position to increase job security for their members.[36]

A successful union-community coalition recently prodded a reluctant Campbell Soup Company to negotiate with the Farm Labor Organizing Committee (FLOC). Campbell finally agreed to negotiate after church groups joined the consumer boycott called by the FLOC. Campbell also agreed to cooperate with a commission set up to "establish ground rules" for union elections at independent farms from which Campbell buys vegetables. Because farm workers are not covered by labor law, the agreement amounts to a private labor relations board.[37]

This new kind of coalition among unions and community, religious and civil rights organizations was also a key factor in pro-union campaign victories against J. P. Stevens and Beverly Enterprises. The coalitions raised labor issues at stockholder meetings, and with corporate creditors, customers and government regulators.

If more unions continue to take the route of expansive organizing—extending their membership and leadership beyond their traditional bases of support—the labor movement could well experience an unprecedented upsurge. The success or failure of tomorrow's union battles will help determine if the U.S. economy continues to be run on the basis of the big stick or takes the route of higher wages and higher productivity.

Footnotes

1. Between 1977 and 1980, by contrast, union membership among employed wage and salary workers grew by 800,000. These data are from the Current Population Survey of the U.S. Census Bureau. Including unemployed union members would change the picture little: union and employee association membership (including the unemployed) fell by 2.6 million from 1980 to 1982. By contrast the recession of 1974-76 saw a loss of membership of only 147,000. Larry Adams, "Changing Employment Patterns of Organized Workers," *Monthly Labor Review*, February, 1985, p. 26; U.S. Department of Labor, Bureau of Labor Statistics, *Directory of National Unions and Employee Associations*, U.S. Government Printing Office, Washington, D.C., 1979, p. 59; and Courtney Gifford, *Directory of U.S. Labor Organizations, 1984-5 Edition*, The Bureau of National Affairs, Washington, D.C., 1984, p. 2.

2. Richard Edwards and Michael Podgursky, "The Unraveling Accord: American Labor in Crisis," in Richard Edwards, Paolo

Garonna, and F. Todling, eds., *Unions in Crisis and Beyond*, Dover: Auburn House, 1986.

3. U.S. Department of Labor, "Union Membership as a Percentage of Nonagricultural Wage and Salary Employees, 13 Countries, 1955-1983," Bureau of Labor Statistics, Office of Productivity and Technology, Division of Foreign Labor Statistics and Trade, October 1984.

4. Public employees beginning in the 1960s began to obtain collective bargaining rights and are continuing to win such rights.

5. David M. Gordon, Richard Edwards, and Michael Reich, *Segmented Work, Divided Workers: The Historical Transformation of Labor in the United States*, Cambridge University Press, 1982.

6. Michael Reich, "Segmented Labor: Time Series Hypothesis and Evidence," *Cambridge Journal of Economics* 8 (1984), p. 73.

7. See Figure 6.1.

8. Richard B. Freeman and James L. Medoff, *What Do Unions Do?*, Basic Books, New York, 1984, p. 232.

9. *Ibid.*, pp. 232-233.

10. Edwards and Podgursky, *op. cit.*, p. 45.

11. Adrian Paradis and Grace D. Paradis, *The Labor Almanac*, Littletown Libraries Unlimited, Inc., 1983, p. 34.

12. "NLRB Rulings That Are Inflaming Labor Relations," *Business Week*, June 11, 1984, p. 127.

13. *Ibid.*, p. 122.

14. Rossmore House, Los Angeles, California, and Hotel and Restaurant Employees (Local 11), AFL-CIO, Case Numbers 31-CA-12388 and -12422, April 25, 1984, 269 NLRB No. 198, reported in *Labor Relations Reference Manual*, Vol. 116, The Bureau of National Affairs, Inc., Washington, D.C., pp. 1025-1029.

15. Otis Elevator Company, a wholly owned subsidiary of United Technologies, Mawah, New Jersey and East Hartford, Connecticut and Automobile Workers (UAW) Local 989, Case No. 22-CA-8507, April 6, 1984, 269 NLRB No. 162, reported in *Labor Relations Reference Manual*, Vol. 115, pp. 1281-1290.

16. U.S. Department of Labor, *Handbook of Labor Statistics*, 1985, p. 330, "Major Collective Bargaining Settlements in Private Industry," News Release, 24 January, 1985, p. 7, and *Economic Report of the President*, 1985, p.296.

17. Edwards and Podgursky, *op. cit.*, p. 3.

18. Adams, *op. cit.*, pp. 25-81.

19. Freeman and Medoff, *op. cit.*, pp. 228-230.

20. Freeman and Medoff, *op. cit.*, p. 233.

21. Adams, *op. cit.*, pp. 25-31. The percentage of employees who are union members fell in *every* sector of the U.S. private economy between 1980 and 1984. Government employees were 36% union members in both years, higher than any sector in the private econ-

omy. The estimated drop in union membership in finance, insurance and real estate was so minor as to be statistically insignificant.

22. U.S. Department of Labor, "Union Membership as a % of NonAgricultural Wage and Salary Employees, 13 Countries, 1955-82," Bureau of Labor Statistics, Office of Productivity and Technology, October, 1983; and "International Comparisons of Manufacuring Productivity and Labor Cost Trends for 1984," Bureau of Labor Statistics, USDL News Release 85-230, June 10, 1985. See also Henry S. Farber, "The Extent of Unionization in the United States," *Challenges and Choices Facing American Labor*, Thomas A. Kochan, Ed. MIT Press, Cambridge, 1985, pp. 22. Farber concludes that industrial, regional, occupational and sexual shifts in the composition of the labor force can account for at most 40% of the decline in the extent of unionization over the past twenty-five years.

23. The average annual rate of growth of output per hour in the business sector was 2.9% between 1950 and 1965. The annual rate of growth of productivity averages only 1.7% between 1966 and 1984, a period of lower unionization. Calculated from *Economic Report of the President*, 1985.

24. In 1965 the misery index stood at 6.2 in both countries; only in 1966 did the U.S. outperform Sweden. Computed from U.S. Department of Labor, "Consumer Price Indexes, Fifteen Countries, 1950-1983," Bureau of Labor Statistics, Office of Productivity and Technology, June, 1984; and U.S. Department of Labor, Bureau of Labor Statistics, *Handbook of Labor Statistics*, U.S. Government Printing Office, Washington, D.C., June 1985, Table 126, p. 419.

25. The misery index is a very crude index of stagflation. The index weights inflation and unemployment equally. However, most people probably care more about a percentage point change in unemployment—well over a million jobs, or people out of work—than a percentage point change in the rate of inflation. And because inflation rates tend to vary from year to year, while unemployment rates are more stable, most of the change in the misery index is a reflection of inflation, not of unemployment.

26. Charles Brown and James Medoff, "Trade Unions in the Production Process," *Journal of Political Economy*, vol. 86, no. 3 (1978), pp. 355-378.

27. Kim B. Clark, "The Impact of Unionization on Productivity: A Case Study," *Industrial and Labor Relations Review*, vol. 33, no. 4 (July 1980), pp. 451-469.

28. Steven Allen, "Unionized Construction Workers Are More Productive," (North Carolina State University, 1981, mimeographed), and "Unionization and Productivity in Office Building and School Construction," (North Carolina State University, 1983, mimeographed), pp. 27-30, reported in Freeman and Medoff, *op. cit.*, pp. 165-169.

29. *Fortune*, December 1, 1980, p. 149.

30. George Barnett, Presidential Address at the Forty-Fifth Annual Meeting of the American Economic Association, Cincinnati, Ohio, 29 December 1932, *American Economic Review*, XXII, no. 1, March 1933, p. 6.

31. Adams, *op. cit.*, p. 26.

32. Adams, *op. cit.*, p. 29.

33. See Figure 6.3.

34. "Beep, Beep, Yale's Cheap: Looking at the Yale Strike," a *Radical America* Forum with Aldo Cupo, Molly Ladd-Taylor, Beverley Lett, David Montgomery, pp. 7-19; and Teresa Amott and Julie Matthaei, "Comparable Worth, Incomparable Pay: the Issue at Yale," in *Radical America*, vol. 18, no. 5 (Sept.-Oct., 1984), pp. 7-29.

35. Amott and Matthaei, *op. cit.*, pp. 22-23.

36. *Business Week*, July 8, 1985, p. 31.

37. *Ibid.*, p. 30.

7 Trouble in Farm Country

David Bowen knows that the farm sector is in trouble. His farm near Cedar Rapids, Iowa is under Chapter 11 of the Federal Bankruptcy Act. But Bowen claims that he has not yet given up: "I'm going to keep fighting till there's nothing left to fight for."

Meanwhile, absentee farmers in the Imperial and Central valleys of California enjoy high rates of profit while the workers on their farms live in the worst poverty in the state. Like David Bowen and other family farmers throughout the Corn Belt, agricultural workers in California are not sharing in the benefits of what Wall Street until recently called a recession-proof industry. Neither are rural communities in the South, nor the growing number of hungry people in the U.S.

How did farms and rural communities get into this mess? The Reagan administration argues that the fault lies with farmers, who got greedy during the good years in the 1970s and expanded production beyond what the market could bear. Many farmers blame the government or bankers, claiming they were encouraged to expand and become more mechanized to support the government's foreign policy objectives or the profits of bankers.

Government policies and the overexpansion they promoted in the 1970s explain part of what happened. But the crisis in American farming is rooted in structural changes in the U.S. economy which could not have been completely avoided by any short-term farm policy. Furthermore, the crisis cannot be solved by new policies unless they address its three basic causes: (1) the "technology treadmill," which prompts increased mechanization, as well as chemical and biological innovation; (2) the increasing control of large agribusiness corporations over food production and distribution; and (3) changes in the farm sectors' relations with the international economy.

Far from ameliorating the underlying causes of the farm crisis, Reagan's economic policies have exacerbated them. Shaped with virtually no attention to their consequences for agriculture, conservative economic policies—monetarist, militarist, and supply-side—have helped drown most farmers in red ink and push many off their farms. The farm policies adopted by the Reagan administration to deal with the crisis, consistent with the pattern since the end of the New Deal, are only band-aids: short-term, reactive, and porkbarreled into shape.

Trouble Down on the Farm

American agriculture faces a severe crisis (see Figure 7.1). Many family farms face a crippling combination of overproduction, depressed prices, rising debt, and falling land values. As a result, farmers in the Midwest and elsewhere have not only failed to make a profit; increasingly, they cannot even make payments on their debts. Farm debts totalled $225 billion nationwide in February 1985, more than the debt of Brazil, Mexico and Argentina combined.[1] The dollar value of delinquent farm loans quintupled from mid-1980 to mid-1984 and the rate at which farms are going out of business doubled from 1983 to 1985.[2] And the Farm Credit System, a government-instituted but privately-run agency that holds one-third of farm debt, asked for federal help in September 1985 for the first time in its history. Almost $10 billion of its $74 billion in loans were 90 days or more past due.[3]

Finding the way out of the crisis is not possible without a convincing explanation of how we got into it. David Stockman, former Director of the Office of Management and Budget, argued in February 1985 that farmers brought on their own problems by borrowing too much. Their growing debts, declared Stockman, were "willingly incurred by consenting adults."[4] For this comment he got into trouble with his mother, who is a farmer, but not with the President, since Stockman's proposed solution to the farm problem is a good dose of "free market" competition. To make farming more market-oriented, President Reagan vetoed emergency farm credit legislation in 1985 and Agriculture Secretary Block called for a 17% reduction in the federal farm budget from 1986-1988.[5]

Another administration response is that farm problems are not really so bad. Paul Volcker, Chairman of the Federal Reserve Board, argued in testimony to the Joint Economic Committee in February 1985 that the credit problem was only regional, not national.[6] Only particular commodities and areas of the country have been hit, he claimed, proving that only those farmers who are bad financial managers or inefficient producers are in trouble—and they deserve to be. According to Volcker, farm foreclosures signal a "shakeout" of inefficient producers, making the farm economy as a whole more healthy.

Like the administration, many corporate spokesmen also blame the victim. At a December 1984 conference on farm policy, Sherman T.

Figure 7.1
Contours of the Farm Crisis

1. In 11 Midwestern farm states, land values dropped by an average of 17% from 1981 to 1984. The decline was 12% in 1984, the largest one-year decline since the Depression.

2. On January 1, 1985, 6% of family-sized commercial farms were technically insolvent (debt/asset ratios greater than 100), another 7% of all farms had debt/asset ratios over 70 and an additional 20% had debt/asset ratios of 40 to 70. In total, 33% of family-sized commercial farms were in severe financial stress.

3. Agricultural bank failures are running at 10 times the annual rate for the past 30 years. In 1984, agricultural banks accounted for 32% of the total of 78 bank failures in the U.S., up from 13% of total failures in 1983.

4. Interest on farm liabilities in March 1985 was more than $21 billion, while total farm income averaged only $23 billion in 1983 and 1984.

5. More than 25% of all U.S. cropland, much of it highly productive, is eroding at rates exceeding the soil's regenerative capacity. This is an erosion rate greater than 5 tons per acre.

6. Retail food prices rose by 24% from 1980 to the end of 1984. Only 3% went to farmers; the rest went to processors and distributors.

7. The share of American farm products in the world markets has fallen from a peak of 62% in 1979-1980 to an estimated 48% in 1984-1985.

8. In 1980, the average export price per ton for Argentine wheat was $25 more than the U.S. export price. By March 1985, the Argentine price was about $30 **less** than the U.S. price.

9. Wharton Econometrics estimates that the cost of the high dollar to American farmers through loss of export markets was $4.42 billion between January 1983 and February 1985 for just corn, wheat and soybean producers.

10. The Department of Agriculture estimates that farm income in 1985 will be $10 billion less than the $33 billion estimated.

Sources: 1. "The Current Financial Condition of Farmers and Farm Lenders," USDA Economic Research Service, Agriculture Information Bulletin No. 490, p. 6; "Farmland Values Dropped 12% in '84," **The Boston Sunday Globe,** June 9, 1985, p. 15.
2. "A Summary report on the Financial Condition of Family-size Commercial Farms," USDA Economic Research Service, Agriculture Information Bulletin No. 492, pp. 3-5.
3. USDA Bulletin No. 492, **op. cit.** p. 7; Robert Pear, "Farm Banks' Troubles Are Worsening," **The New York Times,** March 6, 1985, p. B11.
4. William Robbins, "Despair Wrenches Farmers' Lives," **The New York Times,** February 10, 1985, p. 1.
5. "Analysis of Policies to Conserve Soil and Reduce Surplus Crop Production," USDA Economic Research Service, Agricultural Economic Report No. 534, p. 2.
6. USDA, Agricultural Handbook No. 637, p. 33.
7. Wendy Wall, "Sudden Worsening of Nation's $37 Billion Farm-Export Market," **Wall Street Journal,** March 25, 1985, p. 6.
8. **Ibid.**
9. William Robbins, "Surging Value of Dollar Spurs Chaos on Farms," February 1, 1985, p. 1.
10. Peter Kilborn, "Reagan Plan to Cut Farm Aid Felled by Agriculture Crisis," **The New York Times,** July 18, 1985, p. A17.

Rice, Vice-president of Continental Grain, pointed the finger at farmers who complain about falling prices: "You can't do it? He's (the Argentine farmer) doing it. He doesn't care. And you're going to have to compete with it."[7]

Other businessmen are concerned about the impact of government policies on sectors and firms which depend on agriculture. The Payment-In-Kind program (PIK) for example, paid farmers not to produce in 1983, reducing the demand for seed, fertilizer and farm equipment. As a result, International Harvester, the machinery giant, filed for bankruptcy. Nicholas L. Reding, Executive Vice-President of Monsanto Chemical Co., noted laconically that "Many of us in agribusiness remember the PIK program the way London remembers Jack the Ripper."[8] In his view, no government involvement at all would be better than government actions that hurt his firm or help competitors.

Populist farmers offer an alternative to simplistic conservative economic explanations which focus on "too much" government involvement or bad farm management. Instead, the populists blame the collapse of farms on particular policies of the Reagan administration, the control and pricing policies of big grain dealers and food processors, and/or greedy bankers. Texas Agriculture Secretary and populist spokesman Jim Hightower emphasized in 1985: "It comes down to one key question: Are we going to have a system of hard-working, efficient, independent, family farms in this country, or are we going to turn control of our food supply over to a handful of conglomerates and superfarm combines?"[9]

These explanations have some truth to them. The major goal of the Reagan administration was to control inflation, and the anti-inflation package introduced in the early 1980s had a significant impact upon farmers. Reagan relied mainly on monetary policy to keep prices down. Tight money forced up interest rates, triggering the deep, worldwide recession of 1981-1982, and farmers got a one-two punch. First, high interest rates added millions of dollars to farm debt. Second, the world recession reduced demand by poor countries for U.S. grain. In fact, some of these countries, like Argentina and Brazil, are now forced to sell their grain on the world market at very low prices because they are desperate to earn foreign exchange to pay off their huge international debts.

A side-effect of conservative economic policies is the strong dollar, which has devastated farmers by devastating farm exports. Between 1980 and 1984, the value of total farm exports fell by a quarter, from $51.9 billion to $37.6 billion (see Figure 7.2). Loss of export markets cost American farmers over $4 billion between January 1983 and February 1985 just for corn, wheat, and soybean production.[10]

Besides high interest rates and a strong dollar, farmers and rural banks have been hurt by financial deregulation which claimed "to provide a more market-oriented, competitive financial environment."

Figure 7.2
Transformation of the American Farm

Changes in 10 Characteristics of U.S. Farming, 1950-1984			
Farm characteristic	1950	1980	1984
Population in agriculture as percent of total population	15%	3%	2.5%*
Number of farms (millions)	5.4	2.4	2.4
Average size of farms (acres)	216	429	436
Percent of farm labor that is hired	23%	35%	39%
Value of machinery per worker (1984 dollars)	5303	32934	31263
Crop production per acre (1984 = 100)	52.7	88.4	100
Ratio of prices received to prices paid by farmers (1984 = 1.0)	1.45	1.06	1.0
Farm debt as a percent of assets	9.3	16.5	20.8
Farm exports (billions of 1983 dollars)	12.5	51.9	37.6*
Number of people fed by one farmer	15	76	75**

Sources: Rows 1-3, USDA, *Agricultural Statistics*
　　　　Rows 4-9: *Economic Report of the President,* 1985.
　　　　Row 10: USDA, Economic Indicators of the Farm Sector, Productivity and Efficiency Statistics, 1983.

*1983 data
**1982 data

According to a USDA report, a serious problem for farmers in the 1980s is that they are more dependent on borrowed money since the mid-1970s. Therefore, farmers are more affected by what goes on in the financial system. Today's mechanized farms are strongly affected by increased volatility in interest rates.[11]

Banks also played a part in farm troubles, offering farmers loans based on unrealistic expectations about future land values. When loans were made in the 1970s, the average value of land was increasing at a rate which would have doubled land values in a decade (see Figure 7.3). This inflated the value of farm collateral, allowing farmers to assume more debt without excessively high debt/asset ratios.

Figure 7.3
Land Values Exploded in the 1970s

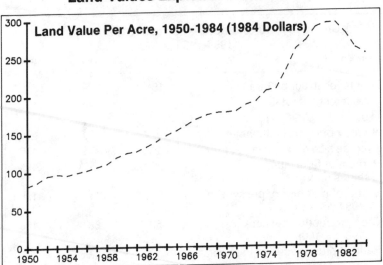

Sources: **Economic Report of the President**, 1985, p. 297, Column 1, USDA Economic Indicators of the Farm Sector, Income and Balance Sheet Statistics, p. 106, Column 3.

But between 1974 and 1978, a time of peak borrowing, net income per farm fell by 22% in real terms. By 1982, it had fallen another 50%, dramatically reducing farmer capacity to service their higher debts. When land prices started falling, the debt-to-asset picture started looking grim. While farmers themselves paid insufficient attention to price and income trends, both they and the banks argue that their practices were sound at the time, given expected international demand for U.S. food exports. Neither farmers nor banks could have been expected to anticipate the collapse in land prices which resulted from falling exports and rising interest rates.

Conservative economic policies brought the current crisis to a head. As *The Nation* editorialized in 1985, "Reagan's do-nothing farm policies will, in fact, do nothing to revitalize agriculture."[12] But farm problems started before the switch toward more market and less government support. The most recent policies—which have amounted to kicking farmers when they are down—are only the tip of a very large iceberg. Indeed, a chronic tendency toward overproduction has plagued U.S. farms since the 1870s. It is the interaction of farm policy with structural change throughout the U.S. economy, especially since 1950, that has generated the current breakdown in American agriculture.

Squeezing Popular Access to Land

The farm sector of the American economy looked quite different in 1984 than it did in 1950 (see Figure 7.2). A small farm which relied on family labor and relatively little capital in the 1950s has likely switched to large-scale, mechanized, and "chemicalized" production using more hired labor in the 1980s. Repeating a trend which followed the Civil War, farms are also more dependent on exports: in 1950, exports accounted for only 8.8% of farm sales; by 1980, 27.4% of farm sales came from exports.[13]

The Reagan farm policies certainly have pushed the family farm to the brink of extinction. But why were farms such a pushover for high interest rates and the high dollar? To find out, we have to go back a bit into the history of how earlier government policies and basic shifts in the whole U.S. economy have interacted to make farms look more and more like "factories in the fields."

Historically, government policy to control access to land and to water has been an important force in shaping the farm sector. Beginning in the middle 1800s, land and water resources were increasingly channeled away from small farmers and toward larger producers. Land policy took away land first from Native Americans and then indirectly from independent white farmers. While we are taught in grade school that homesteading laws made land available to common people, some of the best and most accessible land never came under the Homestead Act (such as the railroads' millions of acres). Furthermore, legal subterfuges made it easy for speculators, banks, and cattle barons to get around the stipulations of the Act.[14]

Tenancy—leasing or occupying land that belongs to someone else—was quite common. Blacks, for example, were effectively excluded from homesteading. For black farmers, the ideal of "40 acres and a mule" was betrayed by Andrew Johnson and replaced by the reality of sharecropping.[15] Furthermore, land and other resources supposedly available to independent white homesteaders went disproportionately to large landholders and to corporations.[16] At a very early point in American history, government intervention, advertently and inadvertently, pushed control of land, water and timber resources into fewer and fewer hands.

But these policies did not go unchallenged. Populist agrarian movements aimed at constraining the power of large landowners and keeping small farmers on their land exploded in the Midwest between the 1870s and the 1930s. As a result, government policies were enacted to equalize the distribution of resources. The National Reclamation Act of 1902 limited the amount of federally financed water available to any one farm to an amount sufficient to water only 160 acres. Land ownership patterns were also attacked. In 1936, the Committee on Farm Policy, appointed by President Roosevelt to investigate rural poverty, concluded that poverty was mainly caused by rural tenancy. To overcome absentee landlordism, speculation, and depletion of natural resources, the Committee called for the federal government to repurchase land and resell it to tenant farmers.

The laws aimed at redistributing resources, however, fell far short of their intentions. Large landholders, sometimes with the approval of local authorities, consistently ignored the water laws, despite law suits by small farmers that were upheld in federal courts.[17] A strong populist movement uniting farmers and industrial workers in the 1930s could not stop large landholders and businessmen from undermining legal remedies against concentrating land and timber resources.[18] With the teeth pulled from redistributive laws, the stage was set for a post-war agricultural system of large farms and skewed access to resources.

Laws to help tenants become farmers were abolished at the end of World War II. Instead, the *status quo*—the existing pattern of land ownership—was taken as a given by government policy-makers. Agricultural policy then focused on four major areas: developing water resources; supporting research and development of seeds, fertilizers and pesticides; supporting research and development of mechanization and technological innovation; and protecting farmers' incomes from swings in market prices.

Policies aimed at these objectives have directly or indirectly favored large farms over small and the concentration of farms into fewer and fewer hands.

The benefits of water resources in the post-war period have gone disproportionately to large farms. For example, two recent reports by the Natural Resources Defense Council and the California Rural Legal Assistance Foundation estimated that the Interior Department illegally provided nearly $1.5 billion in subsidies to irrigate farms in California's Central Valley, many of which are owned by large corporations.[19]

The distribution of the benefits of research and development of seeds and chemicals, as well as machinery, are harder to evaluate. However, while researchers argue that new technology is adaptable to all size farms, they also admit that large farms are in a significantly better position to use the new technology.[20]

The fourth area of government policy, protecting farmers' incomes through direct subsidies and credit, has also benefitted large farmers disproportionately. In 1978, farms with more than 500 acres—which comprised only 10% of all farms participating in commodity programs—received 46% of all commodity support payments. A 1981 government report on agriculture concluded from these data and other research that "...of the participants, the largest farmers receive most of whatever benefits the programs offer."[21]

Furthermore, the yield-increasing impact of the new, publicly-supported technologies has undermined the objective of stabilizing and supporting farm incomes. Federal farm policies have been so incoherent and contradictory that the government has supported acreage restrictions while at the same time prompting research on new high-yield crop varieties!

Credit policies, too, now tend to favor large producers. According to the U.S. Department of Agriculture, government-sponsored credit agencies (Farm Credit System) and insured loan programs (Farmers' Home Administration) gradually shifted their priorities during the 1950s and 1960s. Originally these programs were designed to maintain low-income, self-sufficient farms. Now the emphasis is on "bringing about commercially viable enterprises."[22] In 1978, in response to cash-flow and credit problems in the farm sector, the emphasis shifted again and legislation was enacted to provide emergency loans. Emergency credit has been a major emphasis of USDA programs during the past five crisis years. These loans have higher ceilings than other forms of government assistance ($400,000) and corporate farms are now eligible.[23]

Price supports are the farm policy that most people think about when they argue that farmers already get a lot of government help. But these policies simply recognize that farming is an unusually risky business. The basic problem is that most people don't buy much more food if prices fall. No one except very poor people will buy *twice* as much food if prices fall by 50%. This means that low prices give farmers very low incomes. Since prices change quickly in the markets for farm products, farmers' incomes are highly unstable, not because of what they do but because of the nature of people's demand for food.

Price supports simply protect farmers from the tremendous riskiness of farm income. But a problem with supports has always been that they may encourage farmers to grow more. With a floor on prices, farmers can get more income if they grow more, even if they can't sell it. Price supports, in short, go hand in hand with surpluses. To make the problem more complicated, when surpluses rise, market prices fall and the amount the government must pay to hold up the floor under support prices also goes up.

In the early 1950s, when both the productivity of farmers and price supports were rising, farm surpluses began to accumulate. In response, Public Law 480 was enacted in 1954 to allow the government to buy up surplus crops for export. This "Food for Peace" became a pillar of U.S. foreign policy and the primary way of dealing with surplus problems. By the mid-1960s, however, surpluses had accumulated to such an extent that PL 480 exports were not sufficient to eliminate surpluses. Following the lead of PL 480, the Berg Commission of 1966, convened by President Johnson, called for restructuring agricultural production around export crops. Reduction of support prices to meet world market prices meant that farmers would be encouraged to grow more corn, wheat, soybeans, and cotton for export.

The government's orientation toward export crops shows how U.S. agricultural policy was affected by changes outside the domestic economy. During the 1950s, the U.S. was the dominant economic and military power in the world. As the largest producer of agricultural products and the world's banker, the U.S. was in a very good position to take advantage of renewed economic growth abroad. These were boom years for exports of U.S. manufactured goods. Exports of agricultural products in turn helped reduce U.S. grain surpluses.

This was an important role for farm exports to play, because exports relieved pressure on the farm price floor held up by government price supports. But by the beginning of the 1970s, agriculture was playing a second important role: it was the key to keeping the U.S. balance of payments deficit under control.

The deficit was a problem because the U.S. was in trouble in the world economy. Productivity declines relative to Western European and Japanese industry had begun to dry up the world markets for U.S. manufactured goods. The dollar was no longer secure once demand for U.S. goods was no longer guaranteed. And the U.S. role as world banker finally ended in 1971 with a devaluation of the dollar and the end of the convertibility of the dollar into gold.

The loss of markets for the products of U.S. industry and the end of the dollar as the world currency marked a fundamental structural change in the U.S. economy. In 1973, a further shock happened when OPEC organized and raised oil prices.

In response to severe balance of payments deficits generated in part by the skyrocketing value of oil imports, the Nixon administration looked to agriculture to save the day. It was "Food for Crude," as farmers were encouraged to plant "fence row to fence row." Rather than address the root causes of the international trade deficit, successive administrations seized on agriculture (and other exports, such as arms and military equipment) as a quick fix. As a result, farmers were dragged into the chaos of the international trade and financial systems of the 1970s. Since then, any time the dollar rises or falls, farmers' fortunes swing in the opposite direction.

The Big Get Bigger

The push to export has had far-reaching effects on the structure of agriculture. One of the most important is the change in the mix of crops produced. Between 1969 and 1980, the share of the major export crops—corn, wheat, soybeans, and cotton—rose from 58% to 70% of total acres of cropland.[24] According to agricultural economist Philip Raup, this land use shift is "...creating a pattern of one-crop, export-based agricutural activity [in the grain belt]...that is very similar to the type of monocultural dependence formerly associated with colonialism."[25]

Just like export policy, tax policy has also changed the structure of agriculture. Most researchers agree that specific agricultural tax policies and general tax policies have encouraged absentee ownership of farms and land speculation. The most important of these policies are a cash method of accounting, capital gains provisions, deductions for interest payments and tax write-offs.

Under cash accounting, farms offer big tax advantages because expenses are deducted in the year they are paid and income is recognized in the year it is received. As a result, an investor with a tax problem can buy feed for cattle to be sold next year, thereby reducing this year's taxable income and in effect obtaining an interest-free loan from the federal government.[26] This has been one factor in taking cattle feeding off middle-sized family farms and into large feedlots, shares in which are bought by absentee owners of the cattle. This artificial advantage to large-scale competitors deprives middle-sized family farms of a potential source of income, making them more dependent on a few crops.

Capital gains taxes, tax write-offs, and deductions for interest payments encourage absentee ownership and speculation. This added demand for land helps bid up land prices and prevents promising entry-level farmers from starting up their operations. In addition, these tax provisions are expensive in lost tax revenues. The Congressional Budget Office has estimated that the combined cost of cash accounting and capital gains in farming produced a loss of $815 million in 1980 and $970 million in 1982 in tax revenues.[27]

Since 1976, farm land has also offered estate tax breaks designed to permit family farms to survive from one generation to the next. The overall impact of these tax provisions has been, in the words of agricultural economist Michael Boehlje, that "tax policy has exerted upward pressure on the price of farmland...encourage the expansion of individual farm firms...encouraged incorporation of farm and agribusiness firms...and stimulated the production of tax-sheltered crops."[28] Indeed, agricultural economist Harold Breimyer argued in 1985 that "the income tax code virtually confines new capital to that coming in under shelters."[29]

Government research reports agree.[30] These tax advantages are most attractive in times of inflation, when they provide an unusually powerful tax shelter. But this means that when general inflation leads to increases in land values and fuels speculation, tax policy further pushes up land prices, intensifying a vicious circle of rising land values and increased ownership of land for tax advantages and speculative gain, rather than for production. As an agricultural economist at Nebraska's Center for Rural Affairs has noted, "Under these conditions, simply owning land comes to be rewarded more highly than producing food on it—and unearned wealth becomes a bigger factor in farm expansion than is earned income from farming."[31]

All of these policies and the impact they have had in the farm sector have helped create a system of concentrated ownership and large farms. In 1978, the largest 5% of landowners owned a whopping 75% of the land.[32] The average farm acreage in 1980 was double that of 1950 (see Figure 7.2). The percentage of farms in the largest size category (measured by value of sales in constant dollars) quadrupled between 1960 and 1980, from less than 1% of all farms to 4.4%. One force behind this structural shift is increased mechanization, reflected in the fact that large farms (sales of $200,000 or more) use more than twice the amount of machinery per acre as middle-sized farms (those with sales of $40,000 to $200,000).

The character of the farm has changed as its size has increased. In 1949, less than 1% of all farms were classified as larger than single family farms. In 1980, 49% of farms were larger than a single family could run without substantial wage labor.[33]

A second important element of farm structure, the extent of corporate farming, is difficult to measure. Corporate farms accounted for roughly 2.5% of farms in 1982, 14% of land, and 24% of sales. But most of these corporate farms have only ten or fewer stockholders and are typically family-owned and operated.[34] Less than 1% of all farms are corporations whose income comes mostly from non-farm activities.

Farming, in short, is still a family business in most places. But the largest family farms are more like the family-owned oil companies on the soap operas "Dallas" and "Dynasty," rather than mom and pop stores. In California, for example, only 45 corporations owned nearly half of the state's crop land in 1980, but most of these owners were family companies, not corporations like Del Monte and United Brands. In fact, industrial corporations may find the prospect of becoming farmers themselves unattractive, because profit margins are small and prices very variable. Large industrial corporations can do better by pushing the risks of farming off on to smaller producers, whose products the corporations can then contract to buy.[35]

The fact that ownership of farms still rests with families, in other words, should not obscure the fact of concentration of land ownership. To keep these various kinds of farms straight, we use here the term family farm to mean only middle-sized farms (sales between $40,000 and $200,000) or those that can be run by a single family. Larger farms which are family-owned are not counted as family farms, but as corporate farms.

Agriculture Supply and Food Distribution

While government policies have encouraged large mechanized farms, industries important to the farm sector have also experienced major structural shifts. Concentration in the farm supply industry has increased substantially since the 1950s. U.S. Department of Commerce data show that for harvesting machinery, the top four firms had approximately 80% of total sales by the late 1970s, compared to 66% in 1954. In agricultural chemicals, the largest eight firms had 64% of sales in 1977, a rapid rise from 57% in 1972. The pesticide industry, too, became less competitive: the top four firms at the end of 1976 had almost 60% of the market, up from 33% in 1966.[36]

The costs of concentration in these farm supply sectors was estimated in a 1972 Federal Trade Commission study. The study calculated the profit margin due to monopoly based on the opportunity cost of capital: how much the firm could have earned on its capital if it had invested in another industry which was not highly concentrated. The Commission found monopoly overcharges of almost 6% in farm machinery and more than 4% in feed. These overcharges, which are like rents that farmers must pay to the firms in concentrated industries, amounted to 8% of net farm income in 1972. In effect, farmers in that year paid to uncompetitive suppliers an 8 cent tax on each dollar earned.[37]

Concentration among agricultural suppliers and the monopoly prices they generate are partially to blame for the skyrocketing input costs faced by farmers since the early 1970s. The price of fertilizer, for example, jumped by 17% between 1974 and 1979 and then rose by another 32% by 1984.[38]

Concentration in processing has been expensive, too, for both farmers and consumers. Today, over 90% of food is processed, and agricultural processing and distribution are characterized by large-scale corporations with fewer and fewer firms.[39] Concentration is apparent in both assets and sales. The largest 100 food corporations increased their share of total industry assets from 46% in 1950 to 75% in 1981, largely as a result of conglomerate mergers. In 1984, Beatrice Foods, a conglomerate with companies that make a range of products from baking products to soft drinks to organic chemicals, had sales of $12.6 billion after it bought Esmark, a meat processor. Beatrice is now the largest food manufacturer in the nation.[40]

The share of industry sales made by the top four food manufacturers rose by about 10 percentage points between 1958 and 1977, to about 50% of total industry sales. However, if we look only at those food manufacturers that produce differentiated products, for example brand name products, the share of industry sales going to the top four rose by 18 percentage points, to almost 70% of total industry sales in 1977. This has led one study to conclude that advertising, and in particular television advertising, "appears to be the major force behind the upward pressure on sales concentration."[41] Advertising expenditures are higher for food than for nearly all other goods, and the top 500 food manufacturers in 1980 spent about 13% of the value of sales on advertising.[42]

Competition among food outlets has followed the pattern for production and processing of food. Using Census data, a recent study of food retailing found that, in 1958, the top four supermarket chains captured more than half of all sales in about 40% of local markets. By 1977, the top four firms accounted for more than half of food sales in 67% of local markets. This has happened largely because of national concentration in retailing. The share of sales going to chains with more than 11 stores rose from about 42% in 1958 to almost 60% in 1982. The growth of chains was most rapid after 1975, apparently because of the relaxation of enforcement by the Federal Trade Commission of laws regulating "horizontal mergers" of chain stores.[43]

The last important change in the structure of agricultural production is the rise of vertical integration. This is the incorporation within one firm of many or all stages in the production of a product, from providing seed to growing crops or feeding animals to processing and marketing the product. A closely related arrangement is vertical coordination, in which agreements are made for farmers to sell their products to one processor.

These arrangements mean that even middle-sized family farms, those that seem to fit most closely the image of the rugged, independent farm family, may not be what they seem. When farmers enter into these arrangements, they lose the freedom to choose where and at what time to sell their product. They get some protection from sudden collapses in prices, but they lose their autonomy—what the USDA calls "loss of entrepreneurial independence"—and end up being in effect divisions of large food processing corporations. To accurately measure the degree of corporate control over farming, the integration arrangements between the family farm and the companies that buy their farm products must be taken into account.

Today, virtually all the chickens we buy at the supermarket fall under these two arrangements, as do products made of sugar from sugar beets and sugar cane. Overall, the percent of agricultural output vertically integrated or coordinated has risen from 19% in 1960 to a little over 30% in 1980.[44] According to a government report on the state of agriculture in 1981, vertical integration and contract arrangements are one more force pushing family-sized farms to grow or die. Contract arrangements also limit the role of the open market in agriculture.[45]

All of this concentration has shifted the distribution of the consumers' food dollar and made food prices more dependent on marketing costs than on prices paid to farmers. In 1950, farmers' share of the food dollar was 47%; by 1980 it was only 27%. Although farmers have never completely captured the gains of food price increases, their share is lower than ever now. Between 1980 and 1983, most of the increase in food prices came after the food left the farm, in what is called the farm-to-retail price spread, or the retail spread. Of the almost 8% increase in food prices in 1981, for example, less than 1% went to farmers while almost 6% went to wholesalers and retailers.[46]

Consumers as well as farmers have been losers from increasing concentration of market power in the food system. A recent study suggests that if food distributors were forced to cut prices to a level that brought them a "normal rate of profit," American households would enjoy an increase of 1.1% in purchasing power. Poor people would gain even more, since they tend to spend a larger fraction of their income on staples like food.[47] A report by the Federal Trade Commission found that if the food distribution industry were more competitive—that is, the top four firms accounted for only 40% or less of the industry's sales—retail prices would fall by a whopping 25% or more.

But monopoly is good for business—the business of the concentrated industries, that is. Rates of profit in major food companies show that concentration leads to relatively stable and high profit rates. In 1980, for example, Kellogg's after-tax return on equity was 26%; for General Foods it was 21%. These profit rates, garnered primarily from consumer overcharges, are as high as those of big oil companies.[48]

Are Big Farms More Efficient?

Important shifts have occurred in the structure of the farm and in the structure of those industries which dominate and shape farming. But why should economists be concerned about these changes? After all, output per acre grew by 70% over the years between 1950 and 1980. Moreover, in 1950 one farm worker could feed only 15 people; in 1983 the same worker can feed 79 people. And isn't size associated with efficiency: aren't bigger farms more cost-effective?

Unfortunately, the structural changes have made the farm sector much more vulnerable—*without* making it much more efficient.

The family farm has always been vulnerable to economic change because it is a unique kind of business. It is not a corporation that can take its assets and move when the profit rate falls too low. In fact, family farms have to produce even more when prices and profits fall. If the price of corn or wheat falls by 50%, for example, corn and wheat farmers make 50% less income that year if they produce at the same level. The only way to keep farm income steady would be to *double* production. But other farmers would be in the same situation; when they double production, the resulting increase in market supply means another drop in price. Family farms have always faced this dilemma of income chasing prices in a vicious circle. Market prices of farm products have long been notoriously unstable and as a result, farmers have never been able to plan very far into the future. Concentration in agricultural supply industries has made the circle even more vicious. Concentration requires farmers to take on expensive loans for machines and fertilizers whose prices are *not* sensitive to the market, but are determined by the market power of oligopolistic equipment and chemical companies.

In this way, farms today are especially vulnerable to price fluctuations.

What about efficiency? Are farms at least controlling their costs better, now that they are bigger and more mechanized?

Efficiency can be defined as a low cost of production to a producer, or in this case, the farmer. Efficiency measures private cost advantage in the sense that the advantage belongs to the private producer. If markets are competitive—that is, there are no monopolies or oligopolies—the benefit of low-cost production will be passed on to the community in the form of low prices. Are large farms more efficient because they capture the cost advantage of economies of scale?

Because farms differ so much by crop and by region, it is difficult to talk about national averages for the best size of farm. Government studies have found, however, that U.S. farms today are larger than the size needed to gain the potential cost advantages associated with size. A detailed USDA study which takes these differences into account found that wheat farms could capture 90% of potential cost advantages with a size ranging from 14% of average size in North Dakota to 46% of average size in Oklahoma. A "small" wheat farm in North Dakota, in other words, could be just as efficient as its twice-as-big neighbor. For corn, the figures were somewhat higher and very similar across states: the size necessary to get 90% of the benefits of large scale was only approximately 60% of the average size.[49] These and similar findings in other studies have led the USDA to conclude that the problems of middle-sized farms cannot be blamed on their lack of "efficiency."[50]

Private cost advantages of larger-than-single family farms, in short, are not very large and it seems that the costs of concentration outweigh any benefits. But middle-sized farms may be less profitable, even if they typically operate at comparable levels of cost with large firms. As the markets for farm inputs and crops become more concentrated, the large farmers have advantages that come from the sheer volume of their purchases and sales, not from superior production efficiency. For example, a large farmer in a small Midwestern town can get preferred credit terms and bulk discounts from local suppliers of machines, seed, and money. The suppliers of credit and inputs have lower transactions costs in dealing with fewer, bigger farmers. Similarly, USDA studies show that large farms tend to get better deals in vertically-integrated selling arrangements because of their whole truckload or traincar deliveries to processors. Being large has advantages, but they do not necessarily have anything to do with production efficiency. In an industry of low profit margins, like farming, these advantages can be the difference between survival and foreclosure.

The conclusion that size has lttle to do with efficiency is even stronger if we take into account social as well as private costs. Social costs include both the private costs borne by producers and the costs of polluted water, dirty air, and depletion of of soil and water resources, which raises their cost to future generations. The structural changes in agriculture have raised the social costs substantially. But because these costs are not measured in private "efficiency" calculations, looking only at private costs gives a false reading of how farms are doing today.

The Social Costs of the Technology Treadmill

The first problem for social costs with a mechanized and chemicalized agricultural system based on a few crops that are easy to export is high rates of soil erosion. Corn and soybeans are row crops that leave more land surface exposed to wind and water. Wheat is grown close together, but it too is erosive because it leaves land exposed for part of the year. It is just these crops that the government encouraged farmers to plant on newly-cleared and highly-erosive land during days of "food weapon" diplomacy in the 1970s.

As a result, on 9% of U.S. cropland the rate of erosion is 15 or more tons per acre—three times higher than the rate at which the soil can regenerate; on 17% of cropland, the rate is 10 tons per acre or more.[51] The situation is even worse if we consider the off-farm consequences of erosion for water quality, lakes and reservoirs, and plant and animal life. A recent USDA study has found that "costs of off-farm erosion may be substantially greater than the costs of productivity loss *on farms.*" Citing research by government and non-government sources, this study estimates on-farm losses to have been $1.3 billion in 1980 and off-farm losses at $3 billion annually.[52] The total costs of an export-led strategy for getting rid of agricultural surpluses should then include some $4.3 billion to account for soil problems.

Water resources, too, have been affected by the trend toward export crops and monoculture, because these changes necessitate increased use of pesticides, and fertilizers compared to more mixed cropping. Farmland is now the major source of off-point pollution, or pollution which does not come from a well-defined source like a smoke-stack. Fertilizers, pesticides and sediment from soil erosion are all "pervasive" sources of pollution.

Another problem is the decline in water tables. Irrigation now accounts for 47% of all fresh water taken from the ground or lakes, rivers and streams. In 1958, 37 million acres of land were irrigated; by 1977, 63 acres got their water from ground sources. In some areas, water tables are dropping 7 to 10 feet a year. A USDA study concludes that "decreasing availability and increasing cost of ground water" may cause the loss of $2.5 billion (in 1980 dollars) of crop production and 6.6 million acres.[53]

The excessive use of water has been promoted by technological innovations such as center pivot irrigation, as well as price structures. The relative prices of corn and beef, for example, have given farmers the incentive to grow corn rather than graze cattle on semi-arid land. The price of water itself is distorted, often through federal or state subsidy. One 1985 study of California's Central Valley, for example, found that farmers paid $6.15 per acre-foot of water, while the cost of supplying the federally subsidized water was $72.99 an acre-foot.[54]

In summary, the structural evolution of the farm and food industry since World War II has not minimized either private or social costs. And *all* farmers contribute to the social costs, not just the biggest. A hard look at the family farm, a sentimental favorite, shows that these farms also deplete the soil and pollute ground water supplies. This isn't surprising, because these farms right now are being squeezed so hard that conservation is a luxury they can't afford.

Another serious consequence of the "modern" farm is potential instability in costs. Farms are using a much larger percentage of purchased inputs. From 1950 to 1960, purchased inputs rose by about 15% and non-purchased fell by 20%.[55] This trend has continued, and as a result farms are also more vulnerable to changes in the input prices of fertilizers, pesticides and farm equipment. Since production of these inputs is now highly concentrated, it means that the success or failure of farms depends on the pricing strategies of oligopolistic firms, and farms increasingly are squeezed between non-competitive suppliers and non-competitive processors and distributors.

Furthermore, the increased capital-intensity of production in agriculture means that farmers rely increasingly on heavy borrowing to finance machinery purchases. Increasing debt makes farmers highly vulnerable to fluctuations in interest rates. The more that farms borrow, the more the value of their asset base—land—becomes critical to farm survival. Between 1950 and 1960, land values changed by only about 4% per year in real value, increasing slowly and steadily. Between 1975 and 1980, the real change was almost 7% per year, reflecting a speculative land boom. But then the bottom dropped out, and real land value fell by almost 4% per year between 1980 and 1983 (see Figure 7.3).

Democratizing Access to Land

All of these features of the farm system indicate that farms can be seriously threatened by forces completely beyond their control. Inflation, the Fed's monetary policy, the value of the dollar, the size of the federal deficit, growth of foreign competition in agricultural products, bad weather, and decisions by monopolistic suppliers and processors all affect the ability of a family farm to earn a decent income.

Conservative economic policies, however, have speeded up the farm crisis exacerbating a long-term trend toward concentration of control over the land into fewer and fewer hands. A "solution" to the farm crisis which offers more of the same is bound to fail, at least in the long run. Agricultural surpluses and soil and water depletion will likely continue to get worse if the farm sector is left to "free market" forces.

Furthermore, increasing concentration of land ownership forecloses an economic and cultural option to ordinary people. Solving the farm crisis requires a reorientation of policies and programs toward expanding, rather than contracting, popular access to land. Amidst all the statistics and claims and counterclaims, greater access to the land is the fundamental issue.

Footnotes

1. David Moberg, "Disappearing Dreams," *In These Times*, February 13-19, 1985, p. 3.

2. *Ibid.*

3. *Newsweek*, Sept. 16, 1985, p. 60.

4. *The New York Times*, February 6, 1985 p. 6.

5. *The New York Times*, July 18, 1985, p. 1; *Congressional Quarterly*, February 23, 1985, p. 335, March 2, 1985, p. 396 and June 11, 1985, p. 1207.

6. *The New York Times*, February 6, 1985, p. 6; and Gregg Easterbrook, "Making Sense of Agriculture," *Atlantic*, July 1985.

7. Elizabeth Wehr, "Administration Plan to Cut Aid Leaves Congress Divided, Farm Groups in Disagreement," *Congressional Quarterly*, January 26, 1985, p. 136.

8. *Ibid.*, p. 140.

9. Quoted in Devorah Lanner, "A Farm Bill By and For Farmers," *The Nation*, July 6/13, 1985, p. 19.

10. William Robbins, "Surging Value of Dollar Spurs Chaos on Farms," *The New York Times*, February 1, 1985, p. 1.

11. USDA, Agricultural Economics Report No. 530, 1985, p. 244.

12. *The Nation*, March 9, 1985, p. 260.

13. *Economic Report of the President*, 1985, pp. 338 and 342.

14. Charles C. Geisler, "A History of Land Reform in the United States: Old Wine, New Battles," in Charles C. Geisler and Frank J. Popper, Ed. *Land Reform American Style*, Rowman and Allenheld, Totowa, New Jersey, 1984, pp. 11-14.

15. Harold A.McDougall, "Land Reform and the Struggle for Black Liberation: From Reconstruction to Remote Claims," in Geisler and Popper, Ed., *op. cit.*, pp. 173-174.

16. Geisler, *op. cit.*, pp. 16-18.

17. Philipp E. LeVeen and George E. Goldman, "Reclamation Policy and the Water Subsidy: An Analysis of the Distributional Consequences of an Emerging Policy Choice," *American Journal of Agricultural Economics*, Vol. 60, December, 1978.

18. Geisler, *op. cit.*; Frederick H. Buttle, "Agricultural Land Reform in America," in Geisler and Popper, Ed., *op. cit.*

19. Cass Peterson, "Hidden Subsidies Alleged in California Irrigation," *Washington Post*, August 22, 1985, p. A8.

20. Norbert A. Dorow, "The Farm Structure of the Future: Trends and Issues," *The Farm System in Transition*, University of Michigan Cooperative Extension Service, No. 45, 1985; and Lyle Schertz, *Another Revolution in U.S. Farming?*, USDA, Washington, D.C., 1979.

21. USDA, *A Time To Choose*, 1981, p. 103.

22. USDA, Agriculture Information Bulletin No. 483, 1984.

23. *Ibid.*; and *Small Farm Advocate*, Winter 84-85.

24. USDA, Field Crops: Estimates By States, 1909-1974 and Crop Production: 1980 Annual Summary, cited in James Wessel (with Mort Hantman), *Trading the Future*, Institute for Food and Development Policy, San Francisco, California, 1983, p. 55.

25. Phillip M. Raup, "Some Questions of Value and Scale in American Agriculture," *American Journal of Agricultural Economics*, Vol. 61 (May), 1979, p. 303, cited in Wessel, *op. cit.*

26. *Small Farm Advocate*, Winter 1984-1985, p. 9; Schertz, *op. cit.*, p. 179; USDA, Agricultural Economic Report No. 530, p. 247-251; USDA, *A Time to Choose*, 1981, pp. 92-94.

27. Michael D. Boehlje, 1985, *An Assessment of Alternatiave Policy Responses to Financial Stress in Agriculture*, USDA, p. 3.

28. *Ibid.*, p. 6.

29. Harold F. Breimyer, "Agriculture's Problem Is Rooted in Washington," *Challenge*, May-June, 1985, p. 53.

30. USDA, *A Time to Choose*, 1981, p. 76 and USDA, Agricultural Economics Report No. 530, p. 247.

31. Wessel, *op. cit.*, p. 52.

32. USDA, *Landownership in the U.S., 1978*, Agriculture Information Bulletin No. 435, cited in Geisler, *op. cit.*, p. 8.

33. Terminology for describing farms is confusing because different terms are used to describe the same farms. For these classifications, single family or middle-sized family farms are those with sales between $40,000 and $200,000 in real terms (1980 dollars) and larger-than-single family farms as those with sales in real terms over $200,000. USDA Statistical Reporting Service, 1984.

34. USDA, Agricultural Economics Report No. 441, p. 23.

35. Roger Burbach and Patricia Flynn, *Agribusiness in the Americas*, Monthly Review Press, New York, 1980.

36. Wessel, *op. cit.*, p. 116.

37. *Ibid.*, p. 118. Input prices are found in *Economic Report of the President*, 1985, p. 341. Data for 1984 is preliminary.

38. John M. Connor and Bruce W. Marion, "Food Manufacturing in the Farm and Food System," in *The Farm and Food System in Transition*, University of Michigan Cooperative Extension Service, No. 43, 1985.

39. William F. Mueller, "Large Conglomerate Corporations in the Food System," *The Food and Farm System in Transition, op. cit.*

40. Connor and Marion, *op. cit.*, p. 4.

41. Connor and Marion, *op. cit.*, p. 3; Mueller, *op. cit.*, p. 4.

42. Bruce W. Marion, "Food Retailing and Wholesaling: Trends in Competition," in *The Farm and Food System in Transition, op. cit.*, p. 45.

43. Alden Manchester, "The Farm and Food System: Major Characteristics and Trends," 1983, No. 1, p. 7; and B. F. Stanton, "What Forces Shape the Farm and Food System?" in *The Farm and Food System in Transition, op. cit.*

44. USDA, *A Time To Choose*, 1981, p. 62.

45. USDA, Agricultural Handbook No. 258, 1983, p. 161; USDA Agricultural Handbook No. 637, 1984, p. 33.

46. Connor and Marion, *op. cit.*, p. 297.

47. Wessel, *op. cit.*, p. 120.

48. USDA, *Economic Indicators of the Farm Sector*, "Productivity and Efficiency Statistics," 1983, p. 56.

49. USDA, *A Time To Choose*, 1981, pp. 58-59.

50. USDA, Agricultural Economics Report No. 438, 1979, p. 112.

51. USDA, Agricultural Economics Report No. 534, 1985, pp. 1-4; USDA, *A Time To Choose*, 1981, pp. 81-82.

52. USDA, Agricultural Information Bulletin No. 486, pp. 10-12.

53. These are "acres on which groundwater mining is expected to become impractical." USDA, Agricultural Information Bulletin No. 486, 1985, pp. 16-17; and USDA, "Water and Related Resources In the United States," 1980, pp. 191 and 207.

54. Cass Peterson, "Hidden Subsidies Alleged in California Irrigation," *Washington Post*, August 22, 1985, p. A8.

55. USDA, Agricultural Handbook No. 258, 1963, p. 38.

Part III
Mortgaging the Future

Preface

Conservative economic policies have not improved the lives of most Americans. The fundamental problems of the U.S. economy, however, are structural and pre-date the Volcker-Reagan strategy. The havoc brought on by the new economic orthodoxy might be justified in the long run if it was needed to get the U.S. economy back on its feet again. But escalating poverty, growing inequality and social divisions, attacks on the economic and social gains made by women and people of color, a farm crisis, and an assault on the living standards of trade union members have only weakened the economy further.

The new orthodoxy has not reversed sluggish growth in productivity, growing domestic and international economic instability, or the long-term trend towards greater income inequality at home. Despite its rhetoric of unleashing the entrepreneurial spirit, it has not even generated productive investment. Conservative economic policies have also increased the average level of unemployment and further eroded U.S. international competitiveness.

The one success of conservative economics is that it sledge hammered down the rate of inflation. But the cost was crushing and the U.S. public has just begun to pay it. It will pay more in the years ahead, as the growing indebtedness of the U.S. economy and the U.S. government reaches its limit and the bills come due. Repaying our debt to our foreign creditors will require squeezing living standards to allow the U.S. to export more than it imports. For a decade to come the government deficit will—perhaps deliberately—hamstring the ability of the public sector to deal with the mounting human costs of a bankrupt economy.

The result will likely be a divided and stalemated United States, held together not by shared commitments and hopes but by an imposed order of anxiety, austerity, and pessimism.

8 Double Debt Crisis

The new economic orthodoxy promised a miracle and delivered a debacle:

— the supply-siders promised lower taxes without government deficits and without cuts in needed government services. They delivered tax cuts and wound up with record-setting government deficits despite taking the axe to domestic social programs;

— the monetarists promised a surgical strike against inflation with few casualties and a swift victory—a kind of economic equivalent of the Grenada invasion. They ended up presiding over the recession they had created—the most severe in the post-war era. The operation looked much like the Philadelphia police department's slash and burn approach to the dissident group MOVE.

The costs of the debacle are only now becoming apparent. The impression that Reaganomics is working may be attributable to the President's own popularity and persuasion powers. But it also results from the fact that both the U.S. government and the economy as a whole have gone deeply into debt, masking the severity of the failure, delaying the day of reckoning, and allowing the President—assisted by the myopia of sympathetic economic commentators—to proclaim victory.

When a family or a business tries a new course of action and ends up after some years, deeply and unexpectedly in hock to the future, we tend to conclude that they made a mistake. We think it is reasonable to apply this elementary reasoning to the track record of the new orthodoxy.

The heyday of orthodox economic policy under the tutelege of Paul Volcker and Ronald Reagan has taken place under adverse circumstances not entirely of its own making. Since the mid 1960s signs of weakness in basic economic structure and performance have

been accumulating. The after-tax rate of return on corporate capital—
the capitalist's eye view of the economic health of the economy—
peaked two decades ago, and has languished since (see Figure 8.1).
Growth rates of output have also been failing over the long term, not
only in the U.S. but in other industrial and developing countries as
well (see Figure 8.2). While the U.S. and world economy have
continued to endure the ups and downs of cyclical recession and
recovery, the long downward secular trend has been the primary
backdrop for domestic economic policies.

When Ronald Reagan kicked off his first presidential election
campaign in 1979, the U.S. economy was in serious trouble. Inflation
was running at 13% a year. The unemployment rate was 5.8%. And the
so-called Misery Index—the sum of the unemployment rate and the
inflation rate—was the highest it had been in the entire post-war
period.

Beset by low productivity growth, spiralling oil prices and
declining international competitiveness, Jimmy Carter had given up
on his strategy for dealing with the problems of the American
economy. With the help of G. William Miller, then Chairman of the

Figure 8.1
The Two-Decade Long Profit Slide

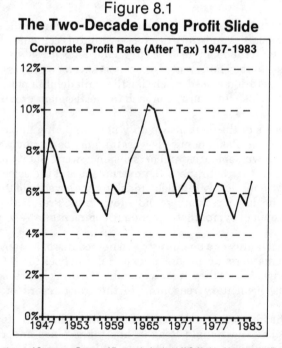

Source: Department of Commerce Bureau of Economic Analysis, **U.S. National Income** and **Product Accounts,**
reported in Samuel Bowles, David Gordon, and Thomas Weisskopf, "Power and Profits: The Social Structure of
Accumulation and the Profitability of the U.S. Economy" **Review of Radical Political Economics,** forthcoming,
1986.

Figure 8.2
The Shrinking Pie
Average Growth of Per Capita Domestic Product (%), 1960-1985

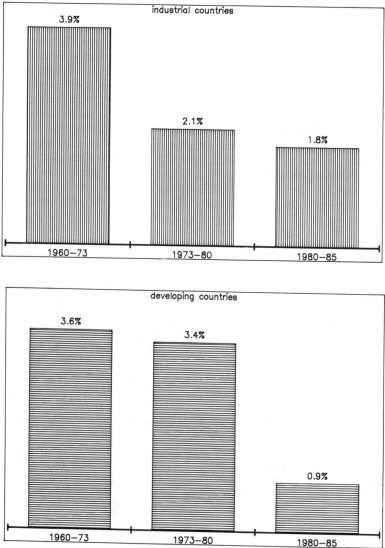

Source: World Bank **World Development Report,** Washington DC, 1985, p 138.

Federal Reserve, Carter's approach was to run a loose monetary policy and a tight budget policy. The easy credit policies of the Fed resulted in generally lower interest rates in the U.S., and this encouraged people with money to desert the dollar in favor of currencies that carried higher interest rates. This caused the dollar to fall *vis-a-vis* U.S. competitors.

The lowered value of the dollar made U.S. exports cheaper and imports to the U.S. more expensive. This, in turn, allowed American manufacturers to increase their sales abroad and maintain their profits, even while raising their prices at home to cover their increased oil costs.

The problem with Carter's policy of low interest rates, economic expansion and dollar depreciation was that it generated inflation. As a result, it shifted the burdens of America's long-run economic problems onto U.S. banks and financial institutions. Bankers found that the interest they had to pay on deposits climbed faster than those they took in as charges on loans. Bond dealers found it difficult to sell long-term bonds in an inflationary environment because of the great uncertainty about their long-run value.

As the dollar's value sank with inflation, large banks and corporations holding dollars in 1978 and 1979 began to panic. By the summer of 1979, a major sell-off of the dollar occured and a full-fledged currency crisis broke out. Miller resigned and Carter appointed Paul Volcker as chairman of the Fed. Carter hoped that Volcker, a banker's banker, could restore the world's confidence in the dollar and American banks. Almost immediately, Volcker's Federal Reserve System raised interest rates to break the inflationary spiral and dollar depreciation. In the process, the Fed sparked a sharp recession just prior to the 1980 election.

Volcker's appointment, in short, meant the abandonment of the Carter strategy, and soon thereafter, of Jimmy Carter. In combination—but not always in cooperation—Volcker and Reagan fashioned a new economic strategy which promised to find a non-inflationary solution to the U.S. economy's problems.

It did not work. They beat inflation. But they did not reverse the long-run structural decline of the U.S. economy. Instead, conservative economics generated a double debt crisis of government budget and foreign trade deficits. To pay for these deficits, the U.S. government is now billions of dollars in debt. This money will have to be repaid eventually, with interest.

The Logic of Conservative Economics

The objective of conservative economics was to restore profitability, international competitiveness, and sustained economic growth without inflation. This was no easy task. To try and accomplish it, the Federal Reserve and the Reagan administration combined well-worn recipes into a novel concoction.

Monetarism, the first ingredient, came from the Federal Reserve System's classic cook book. In its most recent guise, monetarism is an academic and rather technical doctrine which advocates close control over the money supply. Milton Friedman is the best known economist associated with this view. But historically, monetarism has been an intellectual disguise for the kind of policy which central banks often seem to like most: tight money and high interest rates.

Government central banks often perceive their primary responsibility as protecting financial institutions from the profit-damaging effects of inflation. And the Federal Reserve demonstrated its preference for tight money with zeal.

The real rate of interest[1]—which measures interest after adjusting for the rate of inflation—was nine times higher during 1980-85 than it had been for the entire period of 1949-1969 (see Figure 8.3). And after being *negative* between 1974 and 1979 on average, it jumped to over 4.4% on average between 1980 and 1984.

The logic of high interest rates is simple. High interest rates reduce inflation by generating a recession, which shrinks markets; and by increasing the foreign exchange value of the dollar, which lowers the price of imported goods, increasing domestic competition and putting downward pressure on the price of domestically-produced goods.

Figure 8.3
Real Interest Rates Soar

Average Nominal and Real Interest Rates, Period Averages, 1949-1985

	Interest Rate	Inflation Rate	"Real" Interest Rate
1949-69	2.9	2.4	.5
1970-73	5.5	5.1	.4
1974-79	6.9	7.5	− .6
1980-85	10.3	5.9	4.4

Source: (1) 3-Month Treasury Bill, **Economic Report of the President (ERP)**, 1985, B-66, p. 310; 1985, average of first three quarters; Council of Economic Advisers, **Economic Indicators (EI)**, October 1985, p. 30. (2) Per cent rate of change of GNP Deflator, calculated from **ERP**, 1985, B-3, p. 236; 1985, average of first three quarters, **EI**, October, 1985, p. 2. (3) Column (1) minus column (2). There are many different measures of "real" interest rates. The measure used here is a commonly used measure of so-called "ex-post" real interest rates. Other measures would give the same general pattern of results for this period.

High interest rates will recess the economy by making it harder and more costly for businesses, home buyers, and others to borrow. Businesses and individuals cut back on spending for new plants and equipment and new consumer goods. This in turn reduces the demand for labor and thus increases unemployment. With unemployment high, labor's bargaining power erodes and workers lose the ability to fight for higher wages and better working conditions for fear of losing their jobs. According to the monetarists, lower rates of wage growth lead to lower rates of inflation. If workers' power is sufficiently reduced, their ability to organize and raise wages may be curtailed for many years to come.

Because high levels of unemployment tend to make people grateful to have *any* job, it also creates a climate of opinion unfavorable to any policies which business can claim are likely to force them to close their doors. Thus movements for consumer protection, labor unions, workers' safety and health, and environmental protection are also put on the defensive.

High interest rates also increase the value of the dollar by attracting investors around the world to buy up dollars to invest in high-yielding U.S. assets. This will lower the prices of many imported goods and domestic goods that compete with imports—thereby reducing the overall rate of inflation.

If fighting inflation were the only goal of economic policy, monetarism would be just what the doctor ordered. But economies cannot live on low inflation alone. A well working economy must make productive use of its resources—both human and material. Fighting inflation by putting people out of work and idling machines—even if successful—may leave the economy an inflation-free disaster area rather than a stable source of a plentiful livelihood for its members.

But capitalist economies run on profits and the U.S. economy is no exception. So the key to understanding why monetarism backfired is to analyze its effect on profits.

By increasing the cost and decreasing the availability of credit and recessing the economy, the Federal Reserve's high interest rate policy threatened rather than bolstered profits. Businesses welcomed their increased bargaining power with labor; but with high unemployment it became harder to sell products.

As a result, monetarism shifted the problems of the U.S. economy from banks and other financial institutions onto families trying to make ends meet and onto manufacturing corporations.

If high unemployment forced workers to take significant wage cuts, then firms could increase their profit margins, even without having to raise prices. However, profits depend not only on the amount of profits made on each good sold, but they also depend on how many goods the firm can sell. By recessing the economy, high interest rates reduced the amount firms could sell.

Enter Ronald Reagan and his administration's supply-side solution, the second ingredient of conservative economics. "Supply-side economics" rejected the somber trade-offs of monetarism; it was a plan for reducing inflation and increasing corporate profits at the same time.

If the idea behind the Federal Reserve's monetarist policies was to lower inflation by restricting the *demand* for goods, the idea behind "supply-side" economics was to reduce inflation by increasing the *supply* of goods. The key to increasing supply was to increase corporate incentives to produce by increasing business profitibility.

It made a lot of sense to focus on boosting supply rather than holding back demand. But the supply-side remedies turned out to be simply the latest revision of a perennial theme of economic orthodoxy: the government as culprit.

As Reagan saw it, bad government policies were at the root of declining U.S. production and profits:

> The most important cause of our economic problems has been the government itself... In particular, excessive government spending and overly accommodative monetary policies have combined to give us a climate of continuing inflation. That inflation itself has helped to sap our prospects for growth... High marginal-tax rates on business and individuals discourage work, innovation and the investment necessary to improve productivity and long-run growth.[2]

Moreover, the Reagan administration argued that by helping support citizens who did not have jobs, the spending policies of the "welfare state" had undermined workers' willingness to work hard on production lines or accept jobs with low wages. As a result, Reagan argued, productivity on the shop floor had suffered and firms were forced to pay "excessive" wages to get workers to work. Lower productivity and higher wages, in turn had increased costs. If these costs are not passed on as higher prices, they lower corporate profits. If they are passed on, they lead to more inflation. In either case, according to the administration, the "welfare state" was the culprit.

Given this diagnosis, Reagan's administration embarked on a carrot and stick "supply-side" policy of tax, spending and regulatory changes to reduce the "welfare state," encourage work, innovation, saving and the investment necessary to improve productivity and long-run growth.

On the tax side, the Reagan administration cut taxes for working and wealthy individuals. The idea was that the wealthy would save their tax cuts which, in turn, would make more funds available for investment. The ideology of tax cuts for workers was necessary to justify the tax cuts for the wealthy. The Reagan administration hoped that people would invest these increased tax savings into U.S. corporations.

The administration also cut taxes for corporations to increase their after-tax profits. In return, they thought corporations would increase their investment.

The third ingredient of conservative economics was a massive increase in military spending. Military spending increases profits for military contractors quite directly. More importantly, military spending provides the military muscle necessary to protect U.S. economic "interests" abroad.

Thus conservative economics combined tight money, "supply-side economics," and massive increases in military expenditures in a strategy aimed at reducing inflation for financial institutions, increasing after-tax income for the wealthy, and boosting profits for business. In return, the wealthy would save more, and business would invest more. Economic growth would follow, "trickling down" its benefits to everybody.

It Didn't Work

The competitive edge of U.S. business did not revive; it collapsed. The economy did not boom; it lapsed into a record setting recession.

By raising real interest rates, monetarism succeeded in driving up the value of the dollar, putting workers and unions on the defensive. But the promised harvest of plenty failed to materialize.

Every important economic indicator except inflation reveals continuing economic deterioration under conservative economics (see Figure 8.4). To forestall pointless debate and to avoid complex statistical manipulation, our data do not focus on any given year, nor do we emphasize the depth and length of the 1980-82 recession while ignoring the strength of the ensuing recovery or *vice versa*. Rather, we focus on average performance of the economy over a whole business cycle, which is the fairest means of evaluating our 6-year (1979-1985) experience with economic orthodoxy in action. Choosing the business cycle eliminates distortions that would result from comparing, for example, a recession year with a boom year.

We define a completed cycle as the entire period from one business cycle peak to another. We define the peak of a business cycle as the year when the unemployment rate hits a cyclical low. According to this measure 1979 was a peak and most likely 1985 will be as well.[3] We have thus identified the years 1979 to 1985 as a completed business cycle, one which coincides with the reign of the new economic orthodoxy.[4]

Figure 8.4
Sagging Economic Performance

Economic Indicators,* Business Cycle Averages, 1949-1985

	(1) Unemployment Rate	(2) Real GNP Growth	(3) Change in Real Wages	(4) Net-Exports/ GNP (%)	(5) Productivity Growth	(6) Inflation Rate
1949-53	4.1	5.0	4.0	.9	3.7	2.2
1954-56	4.7	2.5	3.5	.8	2.2	.5
1957-59	5.5	2.5	2.7	.8	3.0	2.4
1960-69	4.8	4.2	2.8	.7	2.9	2.3
1970-73	5.3	3.7	2.1	− .1	2.6	4.9
1974-79	6.8	2.8	.3	− .8	.8	8.6
1980-85 **	8.1	2.1	− .005	− 1.9	1.3	6.7
Memorandum:						
1949-69	4.7	3.9	3.2	.8	3.0	2.0

Sources: (1) All civilian workers, *ERP*, 1985, B-33, p. 271; 1985 *EI*, October 1985, p. 12. (2) Real GNP growth, average annual percentage rate. *ERP*, 1985, B-1, p. 232; 1984 and 1985, *EI*, October, 1985, p. 1; all converted to real 1984 dollars. (3) Rate of growth of real compensation, average. Business Sector, *ERP*, 1985 B-40, p. 278; 1985, *EI*, October, 1985, p. 16. (4) Net Merchandise Trade Balance as a percentage of GNP, *ERP*, 1985, B-98, p. 344 and *ERP*, 1985, B-1, p. 232; 1984 and 1985 data from (EI), October, 1985, p. 1 and p. 36. Trade data for third quarter of 1985 are from the Commerce Department and are not fully consistent with earlier data. (5) Rate of growth of output per hour, all persons, Business sector. *ERP*, B-40, p. 278; 1984 and 1985 from *EI*, October 1985, p. 16. (6) Year to year change in consumer price index, all items. *ERP*, 1985, B-56, p. 296; 1985 from *EI*, October, 1985, p. 23.

*Economic Indicators (EI), Council of Economic Advisors, compiled for the Joint Economic Committee of the U.S. Congress.

**1985 data refer to average of first three quarters.

Besides generating record rates of unemployment, between 1980 and 1985 conservative economics produced the lowest average rate of growth of real GNP of any cycle in the post-war period. Conservative economics did not restore U.S. international competitiveness. Instead the merchandise trade deficit, as a share of GNP, *doubled* from .8% between 1974 and 1979 to 1.9% between 1980 and 1985.

A look at business cycle peaks rather than averages offers another view of the relative performance of conservative economics. In 1985, unemployment was higher than it had been at any cycle peak since the Great Depression. Inflation fighting was the clear winner, falling to the lowest rate for a peak year since 1959 (see Figure 8.5). And in 1984, the economy grew at an overall rate of 6.8%.

Do not these achievements—low inflation and a strong expansion from the depths of the 1980-1982 recession—indicate the success of conservative economics? To answer this question we may ask: how much did it cost to fight inflation the Volcker-Reagan way? And what did it cost to achieve one year (1984) of rapid economic growth?

Figure 8.5
Reagan's Lackluster Business Cycle

Economic Indicators, Business Cycle Peaks, 1969-1985			
	(1) Unemployment	(2) Inflation Rate	(3) Net-Exports/GNP (%)
1969	3.5	5.4	.06
1973	4.9	6.2	.07
1979	5.8	11.3	− 1.1
1985	7.1	2.6	− 3.4

Sources: See Table 8.4.

Question: How much does it cost to reduce inflation by a point?
Answer: 200 Billion Dollars

The problem with fighting inflation with recessions is that recessions are costly. Workers are thrown out of work, factories are idled, and businesses lose profits. Supply-side economics promised to reduce the cost by increasing the supply of goods. If the combination of monetarism with supply-side economics represents a new, improved method of inflation fighting, then it would have reduced the amount of unemployment required to reduce inflation.

For example, if before it took one percentage point increase in the unemployment rate to reduce inflation by one percentage point, then under the regime of conservative economics, a one percentage point increase in unemployment should reduce the inflation rate by *more* than one percentage point. In other words, if conservative economics is a better economic policy, it should improve the "trade-off" between inflation and unemployment.

But careful studies of the relationship between inflation and unemployment have found that conservative economics has not altered this trade-off. Taking into account the effects of raw material prices on inflation, it takes as much unemployment to reduce inflation now as it did before 1980. What made conservative economics different was that the Federal Reserve was willing to generate more unemployment and keep it higher longer than previous monetary policy makers had been willing to do. And the cheap imports, made possible by the overvalued dollar, helped keep the lid on prices.[5]

It has been a costly strategy. How many more goods and services could the U.S. economy have produced if, between 1980 and 1984, the government had put people back to work rather than throwing them out of jobs? In other words, how high would GNP have been if unemployment had been lower?

Lower unemployment increases the output of goods and services (GNP) in two ways: first, more people are working, producing goods and services. And many workers who had previously given up looking for jobs re-enter the labor force and get jobs. This further increases the number of people working and producing goods. Second, when more people are working, productive capacity is more fully utilized, and productivity is higher because there is less waste of plant and equipment.

To estimate the effects of these two factors we first calculated how many people would have been working had the unemployment rate been lower, taking account of the fact that the lower unemployment would draw "discouraged workers" back into the labor force. We consider these discouraged workers to be truly unemployed, even though they are not officially counted that way for they are no longer actively seeking work. We estimate the true size of the labor force and the true level of unemployment by choosing an unemployment benchmark of 3% and ask how many people would seek work and how many find it if this hypothetical high employment target were maintained over a period of years.[6] According to this estimate, there were 8.5 million officially unemployed workers. But unemployed discouraged workers not included in the official count added another 3.1 million to the ranks of the unemployed, giving a total of 11.6 million jobless on the average throughout 1984. The true unemployment rate was 10% in 1984, compared with the official estimate of 7.5% (see Figure 8.6).

Those who would have been working in our hypothetical high employment scenario would have produced more. We have estimated the output shortfall due to high unemployment using four different benchmark "high employment" rates of unemployment. By comparing how much would have been produced with how much was actually produced, we can calculate not only the true extent of unemployment but also the costs of using unemployment to fight inflation.[7]

At the hypothetical high unemployment level of 6%, the economy between 1980 and 1984 would have produced over 800 billion dollars more than it did.[8] If the economy had operated at full employment—around 3%—the lost output was a whopping two trillion dollars.

What if those responsible for macroeconomic policy had tried gradually to bring the unemployment rate down, rather than trying to raise it? If unemployment had been 5% in 1980, 4% in 1981 and 1982, and 3% in 1983 and 1984 instead of the average of 8.4% over the period, real GNP would have grown at an annual rate of 4.1% between 1980 and 1984 (see Figure 8.7). By post-war standards, this is not an

Figure 8.6
Hidden Unemployment

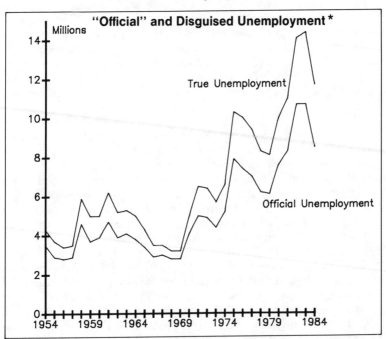

"Official" and Disguised Unemployment *

True Unemployment

Official Unemployment

*The number of discouraged workers and the "true" unemployment rate are calculated on the basis of an estimate of what the total labor force would have been had a 3% unemployment rate been maintained.
Source: See text and appendix.

unusually high rate. In fact, is is about equal to the 4.2% growth rate between 1960 and 1969 (see Figure 8.4).

The bottom line is that the cost of fighting inflation compared with a gradual move towards a 3% unemployment rate was 1 trillion seven hundred billion dollars, an average of over 10% of GNP, between 1980 and 1984. That is more than $28,000 for every family and over $10,000 for every person in the country.

If conservative economics brought down inflation by about 9 percentage points—from 13.5% in 1979 to 4.3% in 1984—then it cost almost 200 billion dollars for each point. That comes to almost $3,000 per family and almost $1,000 for each person for each point. As economists are fond of saying, you can buy just about anything for a price—even poverty.

Figure 8.7
The High Cost of Conservative Economics

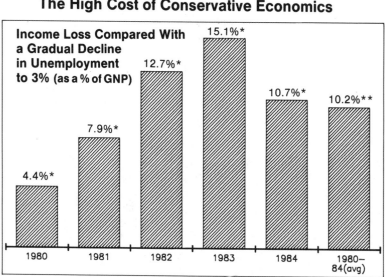

Income Loss Compared With a Gradual Decline in Unemployment to 3% (as a % of GNP)

4.4%*   7.9%*   12.7%*   15.1%*   10.7%*   10.2%**

1980   1981   1982   1983   1984   1980–84(avg)

*Assumed unemployment rates are: 1980 equals 5%, 1981, 1982 equals 4%, 1983, 1984 equals 3%
**Average for period.
Source: See appendix.

What Went Wrong

Conservative economists assumed that if the government handed out the carrots and wielded the sticks, corporations would deliver the investment and jobs needed for rapid and sustained economic growth. The government delivered, but the corporations did not.

The government delivered on its promise of major reductions in tax rates for corporations.[9] But rather than boost investment, corporations cut back. Between 1980 and 1984, net investment as a share of Net National Product was at its lowest level, on average, in the postwar period. The much-heralded 1984 "investment explosion" brought net investment to a level somewhat *below* that of 1981—the year of the tax cut—and below 1979 as well (see Figure 8.8).

With their tax rates slashed and with the power of workers declining, corporate investment should have soared. What happened?

Investment depends on the level of expected profit and on the cost of credit.[10] If the cost of credit is too high, relative to the expected profit rate, firms will not invest. For example, if a loan to buy equipment costs 10%, corporations won't buy the equipment if they believe they will only make a 10% profit. If they did borrow, all their profits would go to the bank, not to the firm.

Figure 8.8
Investment: Up from the Cellar
Net Non-Residential Fixed Investment as a Share
of Net National Product

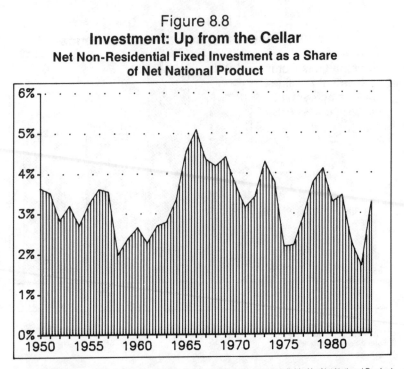

Sources: Net Investment Share: Net Private Non-Residential Fixed Investment divided by Net National Product, **Economic Report of the President,** Tables 1985, B-15 and B-19, and **Survey of Current Business,** June 1985.

From 1980 to 1984, the cost of borrowing was at a postwar high and profit rates at a postwar low (see Figure 8.9),[11] with the higher cost of funds due largely to the high real interest rates generated by the Fed's tight money policies.[12]

The lower rates of profit were certainly *not* due to workers' wage demands, since real wages actually declined over this period. Rather, falling wages, high unemployment and the high value of the dollar contracted markets for U.S. goods at home and abroad, prompting a fall in profitability and thus investment.

Rather than an investment boom, conservative economics gave us a financial speculation spree of wild proportions. With lower taxes leaving corporations with plenty of cash on hand, and with the incentive to engage in productive investment blunted by high interest rates, corporate leaders turned to paper investments. Mergers accounted for $122 billion in 1984, more than the value of net private domestic non-residential investment and 20% of the value of gross investment for that year. A Federal Reserve Board article reported that its Senior Loan Officer Survey "suggests that almost 20% of the dollar volume of new lending in the first quarter of 1984 was to finance mergers and acquisitions."[13]

Figure 8.9
High Interest Rates
Dampen the Incentive to Invest

**The Profit Rate and the Cost of Funds for
Non-Financial Corporate Businesses,
1954-1984**

	(1) Profit Rate	(2) Cost of Funds	(Difference Between (1) and (2)) (3) Real Return on Funds Borrowed for Purposes of Investment
1954-56	9.0	6.9	2.1
1957-59	7.6	6.3	1.3
1960-69	9.4	5.6	3.8
1970-73	7.5	5.5	2.0
1974-79	7.0	6.5	.5
1980-84	6.4	8.0	− 1.6

Sources: (1) Before-tax rate of return for non-financial corporate business; capital stock includes structures, equipment, land and non-interest bearing net financial assets. Barry Bosworth, "Taxes and the Investment Recovery," **Brookings Papers on Economic Activity**, 1, 1985, p. 26. (2) Cost of Funds calculated as a function of interest rates , debt/equity ratios, and taxes. Bosworth, ibid.

The irony of the new orthodoxy is that it succeeded in strengthening the hand of business on all fronts—labor, consumers, government—but it failed to induce business to invest. They can lead the horse to water, but they can't make it drink.

The Dollar

Part of the disappointing investment record is due to the overvalued dollar, itself the deliberate result of new orthodox policies. A major goal of the Federal Reserve's policy was to protect the value of the dollar. And indeed, the dollar's value was spectacularly protected. Between 1979 and the fourth quarter of 1984, the dollar's value increased by 67% against its major trading partners.[14]

Designed to reduce the power of labor and restore the profitability and competitiveness of U.S. industry, the high dollar has instead devastated U.S. manufacturers and knocked U.S. goods out of world markets.

International competitiveness depends on the costs of goods produced in one country relative to the cost of those goods produced elsewhere. Relative costs, in turn, depend on three things: relative growth of wages; relative growth of productivity; and changes in exchange rates, that is, currency values relative to competitors.[15]

If wages grow more rapidly, productivity grows more slowly and the value of the currency goes up relative to competitors, the country's products will be less competitive. However, a reduction in the value of the currency can compensate for faster-than-average wage growth or slower-than-average productivity growth.

Similarly, even if wages grow less rapidly and productivity grows as fast as one's competitors, a large *increase* in the value of the currency can wipe out the competitve advantage gained by that slower wage growth.

In 1983, the real wages of U.S. workers grew at a rate of 3.5% less than the wages of U.S. trading partners, while productivity growth was 9% lower. Since wage growth was so low, manufacturing should have become more competitive. But when the soaring value of the dollar is taken into account, U.S. trading partners gained a massive advantage. Measured in dollars, U.S. costs *increased* by 3.2% faster than our competitors in 1983 and 9.2% faster in 1984.[16]

The reason, as these data make clear, was not that U.S. wages ran ahead of our competitors, but that our productivity lagged and—much more importantly—the dollar soared.

Conclusion: Mortgaging the Future

The economy's rebound from the 1980-82 doldrums in 1984 helped to re-elect Ronald Reagan and breathe new life into conservative economics.

Economic growth, which averaged 6.8% in real terms in 1984, has since slowed dramatically to 3.3% in the 3rd quarter of 1985. But the stellar 1984 upswing, particularly in the context of the continuing long-term deterioration in economic performance, appears to be a puzzle. The answer, however, is simple: the policies of conservative economics looked good in 1984 because the U.S. economy was living on borrowed time.

Rather than laying the foundation for sustained economic growth, conservative economics has generated one of the largest government budget deficits in peacetime history and a massive trade deficit. Generating a double debt crisis, conservative economics is mortgaging our future.

The common view of the budget deficit is that it is an unmitigated evil because it raises interest rates, reducing investment and driving up the value of the dollar. However, the evidence suggests that the deficit has had little effect on interest rates.[17]

Indeed, recent large budget deficits, by increasing demand for goods and services, are probably responsible for much of the economic recovery from 1982 to 1985.

The trade deficit is also a cloud with a silver lining. Though widely regarded as the bane of our economic existence, the trade deficit has allowed the U.S. economy to live beyond its means, thus cushioning the fall in living standards and obscuring the failures of conservative economics. Between 1980 and 1984, the United States imported $275 billion more than it exported.[18] This meant the U.S. was able to spend $275 billion more than it made. Indeed, the trade deficit was nearly 3% of U.S. GNP in 1984 (see Figure 8.10). In 1985, the U.S. economy will live beyond its means by another $150 billion.

Being able to spend more than one produces has short-run advantages. For those who do not work in import-competing and export-competing industries, trade deficits can mean more for less. If the value of imports had equalled the value of exports between 1980 and 1984, U.S. national income—and therefore spending—would have been reduced by the value of the trade deficit. For example, the United States would have had to get by with $275 billion less in new plants and equipment, or housing, or health care.[19] Or the government would have had to spend $275 billion less on arms.

Figure 8.10
U.S. Trade Position Deteriorates

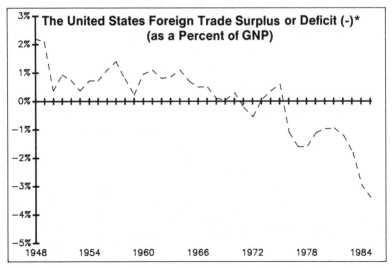

*The figures refer to the current account.
Sources: **Economic Report of the President,** 1985, pp 232, 344, **Survery of Current Business,** June, 1985 and **Federal Reserve Bulletin.** The 1985 figure refers to the second quarter.

But this opportunity to live beyond our means has been bought on borrowed time. Even the most obvious success of conservative economics, a dramatic reduction in inflation, has been partly acquired on borrowed time.

According to a number of estimates, around a third of the reduction in inflation has been due to the effects of the appreciating dollar. When the dollar falls—as it will eventually, either slowly or in a panic—prices of imported goods will rise and inflation will be reignited. When we repay our foreign debts the price dampening process will work in reverse: we will pay later for the relative price stability bought now.

And repaying our external debts means the U.S. will have to produce more than we consume and invest domestically. Writing in June 1985, National Bureau of Economic Research economist Jeffrey Sachs concludes:[20]

> ...exchange depreciation has reduced U.S. inflation by as much as three percentage points as of 1985. Given the strong likelihood of a depreciation of the dollar, those inflation gains will likely be lost, or more than lost in the future.

Even paying the interest and profits on U.S. debt to other countries is already putting a mounting strain on the economy.

Jimmy Carter may have won the prize for the Misery Index—the sum of inflation and unemployment; but Ronald Reagan has locked up the prize for the Penury Index, the percentage of gross national product that the country pays in profit and interest to foreigners every year. The Penury Index tripled between 1970-1973 and 1980-1984 (see Figure 8.11).

Moreover, the U.S. has run such large deficits abroad that, in 1985, the United States became a net debtor country. *We have borrowed more from foreigners than they have from us* for the first time since the First World War.[21]

But borrowing isn't necessarily detrimental to economic well-being. Whether borrowed money enriches or impoverishes depends on how it is spent. In fact, borrowing is a good idea if the borrowed resources are invested in productive activities that yield higher returns than the interest which must be paid on the loan. In that case, the loan can be repaid with interest and money is still left to spare. If the money is squandered, on the other hand, all that remains is a debt which will absorb future resources.

Have conservative economic policies led to sufficient productive investment to make the debts worthwhile? Or have these policies mortgaged our future?

Figure 8.11
Penury Index

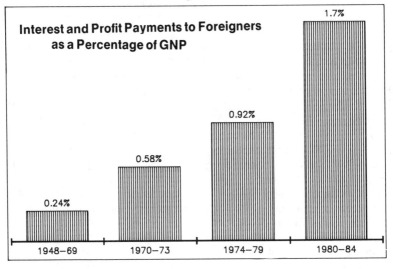

Interest and Profit Payments to Foreigners as a Percentage of GNP

1948–69	1970–73	1974–79	1980–84
0.24%	0.58%	0.92%	1.7%

Source: See text.

To answer, we must estimate the amount of productive investment in our economy. This must include more than investment in plant and equipment by firms. It must also include money that corporations, households, and federal, state and local governments invest in research and development, in material and cultural infrastructure, and in preserving the natural environment.

We have calculated such a measure: we call it TIME—the Total Investment Measure. TIME attempts to measure the total social productive investment in the U.S. economy.[22] It estimates the resources allocated for the future.

TIME includes non-defense government spending on investment goods; total spending on non-defense research and development by businesses, government and universities; total spending on education; state and local government capital spending, which is primarily infrastructure spending; and private non-residential net fixed investment.

If the share of TIME in national income is going up at the same rate as debt, then the economy is apparently investing its borrowings wisely, that is, in productive activities which can help pay off the borrowing.

If the share of TIME is not rising at the same rate as the debt, however, then it is likely the loans are being wasted and future generations will have to bear the price.

And indeed, TIME or social investment is falling while U.S. borrowing from foreigners is rising. This means that unless social investment can become dramatically more productive dollar-for-dollar, conservative economics has indeed mortgaged our future.

While research and development expenditures are increasing as a percent of GNP, federal and, more importantly, state and local spending on non-defense capital infrastructure is declining. Expenditure on education as a share of GNP is declining as well, as is net fixed investment (see Figure 8.12).

The Total Investment Measure (TIME) also includes expenditures on environmental protection. As one might expect, these expenditures, as a percentage of GNP, have decreased under the reign of conservative economics. Annual data compiled by McGraw-Hill show a steady decline in corporate expenditures for air and water pollution as a percent of GNP since 1979 (with a slight increase in 1984). The averages for this period also indicate that business expenditures for environmental protection during the reign of conservative economics were the lowest since the late 1960s.

Rather than using the opportunity of the budget deficit and the trade deficit to invest borrowed funds productively for the future, conservative economics has pursued policies which waste this borrowed money. We—and our children and their children—will have to pay the price.

Figure 8.12
Conservative Economics
Mortgages the Future

Average Percentage of GNP, Period Averages 1966-1984					
	Research and Development	State and Local Investment	Net Fixed Investment	Fed. Capital Investment	Educ.	TOTAL
1966-73	1.5	2.3	3.7	.3	7.3	15.1
1974-79	1.5	2.0	2.9	.3	7.4	14.1
1980-84	1.7	1.8	2.5	.3	6.9	13.2

Source: Fred Beamer, Department of Education, **Projections of Educational Statistics, 1990-1991**. 1970-1981; 1966-1969 and 1982-1984; U.S. Census Bureau, **Government Finances,** annuals and **Census of Governments,** 1977 and 1984; **Historical Tables of the Budget of the U.S., 1986,** Table 9.; **Statistical Abstract of the U.S.** Table No. 988, p. 574.

Footnotes

1. Real interest rates are a better measure of the cost of credit than market interest rates because inflation distorts the meaning of interest rates as it does the meaning of other values. For example, a business would find an interest rate of 10% on borrowed funds more burdensome if the price of its products were going up at 1% a year than if they were rising at 20% a year. In the latter case, a business could borrow $100 from a bank to pay its workers and suppliers, produce goods worth $100, hold on to them for a year, and at the end of the year sell them for $120. It would pay the bank $110 ($100 plus $10 of interest) and make $10 free and clear. If inflation were only 1%, the business would *lose* $9 on the deal since it could only sell its goods for $101 at the end of the year.

2. The White House, *America's New Beginning: A Program for Economic Recovery*, 1981, p. 4.

3. The civilian unemployment rate hit an apparent trough of 7% in August, 1985, and then *increased* to 7.1% in September. (See *The New York Times*, October 5, 1985, p. 41.) This gives a quarterly unemployment rate for 85III of 7.1 compared with 7.3 for 85I and 85II. Thus, by our definition of business cycles (for comparative purposes) 1985III is likely to be the peak of the current cycle. Factory utilization rates also peaked in the third quarter—they peaked in August at 80.5%, falling to 80.2% in September. (See *Wall Street Journal*, October 18, 1985, p. 18.) The forecasted sluggish growth for the rest of 1985 suggests that the unemployment rate is not likely to fall again, at least for a while.

4. The other business cycle peak years are 1948, 1953, 1956, 1959, 1969, and 1973. These dates differ from the business cycle peak years chosen by the National Bureau of Economic Research (NBER) which convenes the group that picks the "official dates" for business cycles. The NBER definition of a recession is two consecutive quarterly declines in real GNP. We use the period's low point in the *unemployment rate* to date our cycle peaks. By this dating, 1948-1969 dates the post-war "boom years," 1973-1979 dates the "stalemate" or "inflationary-fight back" years, and 1980-1985 represents the "reign of conservative economics."

5. Robert J. Gordon, "Understanding Inflation in the 1980s," *Brookings Papers on Economic Activity*, 1985, pp. 263-299. The Reagan administration's willingness to keep interest rates and unemployment high led to reductions in raw material and import prices which contributed a third of the reduction in inflation between the fourth quarter of 1981 and the fourth quarter of 1984.

6. The detailed calculations and similar estimates using benchmarks of 4%, 5% and 6% appear in the Appendix.

7. See the Appendix for details of how these calculations were made.

8. This is the figure which some economists think represents *full employment* today. Others believe that the full employment rate of unemployment is over 7%!

9. For details, see Chapter 9.

10. There is strong evidence that profit rates are important determinants of investment which, in turn, are crucial for productivity growth and overall economic growth.

11. If, as an alternative, cost of funds is estimated using the "real long-term interest rate"—the yield on Moody's AAA bonds minus the rate of change in the gross domestic product deflator—a similar pattern of disincentive to invest emerges.

12. The cost of credit also depends on other factors such as taxes. It is extremely difficult to measure cost of funds and real interest rates in an economically meaningful way. Our estimates (Figure 8.7) should be seen as very rough approximations. See Barry P. Bosworth, "Taxes and the Investment Recovery," *Brookings Papers on Economic Activity*, Number 1, 1985, pp. 1-47 for discussion.

13. Richard Medley, "High Interest Rates: It's Not Just the Deficit," Economic Policy Institute, Washington, D.C., Briefing Paper, June 1985, p. 9.

14. *Economic Report of the President*, 1985 B-104, p. 351. This number is the nominal appreciation. The real appreciation, which takes into account relative inflation rates, was almost identical: 64%.

15. A fourth factor which may be important is the quality of products relative to those of competitors.

16. United States Department of Labor, *News*, "International Comparisons of Manufacturing Productivity and Labor Cost Trends: Preliminary Measures for 1984," June 10, 1985, Table B, p. 5.

17. The Congressional Budget Office Reports that most empirical studies give mixed results: out of 24 studies of the relationship between deficits and interest rates, only 6 showed a definite positive relationship and even these are statistically unreliable. See CBO, *The Economic Outlook*, 1984, pp. 99-101, and CBO, *The Economic and Budget Outlook: Fiscal Years 1986-1990*, Feb. 1985, p. 83.

18. All of these figures are in 1984 dollars.

19. This ignores the possible expansionary effect on the domestic economy from a lower trade deficit.

20. Jeffrey D. Sachs, "The Dollar and the Policy Mix," National Bureau of Economic Research Working Paper 1636, June 1985.

21. *Survey of Current Business*, June 1985. The Penury Index measures interest and profit payments to foreigners. The U.S. also receives interest and profit payments from foreigners. Indeed, for the entire postwar period, payments to the U.S. have been larger than payments to foreigners. Thus some might think that the Penury Index

is misleading. Yet the same point could be made by looking at the rate of growth of *net* interest and profit payments as a percentage of GNP. Divided into the same periods as in the graph, 1948-69, 1970-73, 1974-79 and 1980-84, these rates of growth are (all in %): 3.3, 10.4, 7.5 and -16.0. Conservative economics still gets the prize for *reducing* the share of *net* interest payments as a percent of GNP for the first sustained period in the postwar period.

22. Data is not available for all productive investments, especially by households.

9 Strategic Deficit

They haven't cut these programs back to prepare for war; they've
declared *war—on us.*
> —A resident of the North End section
> of Springfield, Massachusetts, 1984.

We know full well that Congress will spend every penny—and
more—that is yielded in taxes. A cut in taxes means a cut in spend-
ing. There is no other way to get a cut in spending.
> —Milton Friedman, *Newsweek,* July 28, 1981.

Conservative economics represents a fundamental change in the
role of federal government spending and taxation in the economy.
Harking back to the Coolidge era which preceeded Roosevelt's New
Deal, the conservative strategy calls for shrinking the economic role
of government by slashing taxes, spending, and deficits. "This
administration is committed to a balanced budget," claimed Ronald
Reagan in 1981, "and we will fight to the last blow to achieve it by
1984."

The Reagan strategy of decreasing both taxes and spending half-
worked: revenues as a percentage of GNP declined as a result of tax
cuts and were even lower than projected between FY1981 and 1985.
But according to the President's own figures, the ratio of government
spending to Gross National Product (GNP) has *actually increased*
since 1981. Indeed, federal spending was almost a third larger in 1985
than what the Reagan team had projected (see Figure 9.1). With commitments expanding and resources shrinking, the promise of a balanced budget faded into the twilight which follows prime-time news.

What Reagan has accomplished instead since 1981 is a major
redirection of federal spending priorities and revenue sources. Expenditures on military procurements have exploded, while spending on
social programs has been cut.

Figure 9.1
Reagan's False Promise of a Balanced Budget
Projected and Actual Government Spending as a % of GNP

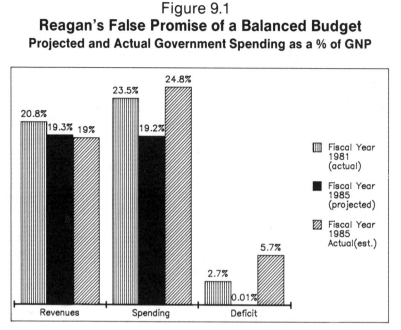

Source: Office of Management and Budget, **Historical Tables, Budget of the U.S. Government, Fiscal Year 1986,** Washington, G.P.O.

The winners in this reallocation have been large corporations, military contractors, and the rich. The losers have been workers, the poor, people of color, social service recipients, and children. A Congressional Budget Office study found that spending and tax changes between 1983 and 1985 reduced the annual incomes of families below $10,000 by a total of $23 billion. Those who make more than $80,000 enjoyed a total increase of $35 billion.[1]

Indeed, Reagan's much-vaunted 1985 proposal for "tax reform" would give progressively larger tax breaks to the wealthy. While taxpayers with incomes below $75,000 would gain about 1% of after-tax income, the gain would be 1.9% for income-earners between $75,000 and $100,000; between $100,000 and $200,000 it is 2.4%; and those few with incomes over $200,000 would get a tax break of a whopping 6%.[2]

As a result of the tax cuts, increased military spending, and increased interest payments, the federal debt almost doubled during Reagan's first term. By 1984, it totalled just under $2 trillion. The interest on the debt is now a major claim on the tax payers' dollar. It is paid almost entirely to the well-to-do who hold the bonds and it totalled $130 billion in FY1985.[3] This sum exceeds, by a considerable margin, the amount spent by the federal government on Medicaid,

AFDC, food stamps, school lunch programs, lower income housing assistance, low rent public housing, student loans, and all other programs for persons with limited income.[4] The interest on the federal debt is about double the amount spent on health, education training, and employment.

Generating a double debt crisis, conservative economics has not only mortgaged the future of the nation and funneled billions of tax dollars to the pockets of the rich; it has shifted the burden of debt largely to the shoulders of those least able to pay.

That Old-Time Religion

The centerpiece of conservative economics is, as Reagan explained in his 1981 inaugural address, less government: "Government is not the solution to our problem. Government is the problem." [5] The idea is that excessive government spending on income-support programs reduces the incentive to work hard by taking the teeth out of the threat of unemployment. Reduced incentives, according to the conservative view, explain the decline in the growth of labor productivity throughout the 1970s. Furthermore, conservative economics attributes the crisis in corporate profitability and investment spending to excessive taxation of corporate profits. Unsurprisingly, the government is also to blame for the erosion of U.S. international competitiveness. Excessive red tape and the decline in U.S. global power—the result of reduced military spending during the Ford and Carter years—lies at the root of lagging U.S. international performance.

Reagan revealed his economic vision shortly after taking office in 1981:

> The goal of this Administration is to nurture the strength and vitality of the American people by reducing the burdensome, intrusive role of the Federal Government; by lowering tax rates and cutting spending; and by providing incentives for individuals to work, to save, and to invest. It is our basic belief that only by reducing the growth of government can we increase the growth of the economy.[6]

Besides substantial decreases in the growth of federal spending, the size of the deficit, and personal and business taxes, the conservative plan called for business relief from Federal regulatory "burdens," a stable monetary policy to reinforce the other policies, and increased military spending, supposedly to enhance the deterrence capability of U.S. nuclear and conventional forces. Through reduced individual and corporate income taxes, the incentives for hard work and investment would invigorate economic growth.

Behind the benevolent rationale of orthodox economics, however, was a hidden agenda, one which emphasized the stick more than the carrot. Reduced social spending and higher unemployment would put labor on the defensive and drive wages down. Increased military spending would help to restore U.S. military and political dominance, improving the country's international economic and financial power. These policies, in turn, would improve U.S. business profitability. Higher profits would generate increased investment and improved productivity growth, leading to higher real incomes all around. With the government's economic role shrunk down to "proper" size, economic prosperity would eventually "trickle down" to everyone. Indeed, tax *cuts* would even generate an *increase* in government revenues by stimulating economic expansion.

The Government's Role in the Economy

Is a large role for the government a drag on the economy? Not if the experiences of most other advanced, industrialized countries are a guide. Indeed, the U.S. devotes a smaller percentage of its total output to the public sector than almost any other advanced Western country. And the U.S. economic record of productivity growth is dismal by comparison to most of these countries. In 1982, the ratio of total government expenditures to Gross Domestic Product averaged 47% for 23 OECD countries. For the U.S. the figure was 37.6%. From 1960 to 1982, government revenues relative to GDP also grew more slowly in the U.S. than the average OECD country.[7]

Government spending and regulation can boost the economy in four ways. First, government provides the material and cultural infrastructure—roads, postal service, courts, schools—upon which economic production and reproduction depends and which the market would not provide efficiently or at all. Second, since the Great Depression in the 1930s, the federal government has taken responsibility for the overall health of the U.S. economy. Through monetary, tax, and spending policies, the government has attempted to even out the ups and downs of market-generated business cycles, keep prices relatively stable, and avoid prolonged depressions.

Another role of government since the 1930s has been to reduce the inequality of market-determined income and wealth distribution. These social spending programs not only enhanced economic security by offering some protection from the uncertainties of the market; they also boosted aggregate demand, and helped maintain profitability, investment, and employment. Government programs also directly stimulated employment: by 1983, federal, state, and local employees constituted 14.4% of the civilian labor force, up from 10.1% in 1949.[8]

These government fuctions stem from an indirect form of macro-economic market failure—the inability of private enterprise to provide the conditions for a dynamic, healthy economy. The government's final responsibility has been to counter the abuses created directly by the market. Government's role has expanded since World War II to include programs and legislation that monitor environmental pollution, prohibit racial and sexual discrimination, create and enforce occupational health and safety standards, and inhibit the formation of monopolies.

The extent and specifics of the government's role in the economy, in short, have changed with economic conditions—and with changes in political power, which are manifested through the power to get out the vote. The aim of conservative economics is not so much to reduce the size of government; rather, it is to reverse the momentum toward an expanded egalitarian and regulatory public role in the economy—much to the approval of private business and the wealthy.

Decisions about what activities the government will pursue, what its spending priorities will be, and how they will be financed are determined via the political process. What happens in the public sector, in short, reflects the social distribution of political and economic power. Though they lack numerical voting strength, large corporations and the wealthy are able to use their inordinate economic power to influence governments to adopt policies and programs that are favorable to their interests (e.g. corporate tax cuts and military interventions).

On the other hand, the U.S. has a long tradition of citizen participation in government. Because of popular mobilization, the right to vote has been extended to more and more of the population. Through public opinion and political action, government can be pressured to regulate the private sector. Popular efforts have succeeded in curbing the power of the private sector in areas such as anti-trust, occupational health and environmental legislation and enforcement.

But attempts to challenge the power of private business are limited by the threat of "capital strike." If government actions threaten business interests or reduce profits, businesses can respond by curtailing investment capital, throwing the economy into a recession or depression. Through their control over jobs, corporations are often able to garner the votes of workers and their families for pro-business programs and policies. The economic role of the public sector, which reflects the dynamics of political struggle between different social groups, would likely look very different if jobs were not held hostage by the corporations.

Conservative Economics in Action

1. Tax Cuts for the Rich

The pledge to cut taxes is always popular with voters in a presidential campaign. In 1980, however, poor and middle income families felt a particular pinch. Because of inflation, all income-earners moved into higher tax brackets during the 1970s as their money incomes increased from year to year, a phenomenon called "bracket creep." For many, inflation was a one-two punch: money incomes failed to keep pace with price increases so real incomes fell even before paying taxes; and to add insult to injury, taxes took a larger bite from each dollar of income because money incomes had risen. Poor and middle income families were hurt the most because deductions were fewer and tax brackets narrower.

Furthermore, social security taxes increased in the 1970s: in real terms (adjusted for inflation), social security taxes on wages and salaries doubled during the decade.[9] While taxes increased, the growth of real wages slowed, stagnating during the 1970s and turning negative between 1980 and 1984. It is no wonder that Reagan's pledge to cut the "burden" of taxes and conquer inflation was warmly received.

Reagan's tax cut was modelled after the Kemp-Roth tax bill which had been introduced in Congress and pushed by conservative forces in the late 1970s. It called for cuts "across the board" in personal income tax rates of 10% a year over a three-year period. The gameplan, the Economic Recovery Tax Act of 1981 (ERTA), ended up cutting tax rates by 5% in 1981 and by 10% in each of 1982 and 1983. The top tax rate on individual investment income was also cut from 70% to 50%.

The Office of Management and Budget originally estimated that ERTA would reduce individual income taxes by $600 billion between 1983 and 1988—almost $9,000 per family. Represented as cutting everyone's taxes, the 1981 tax cut was in fact a program of "Robin Hood in reverse."

While individual income taxes as a share of federal revenues fell by 2.5% between 1980 and 1985, the overall tax burden increased for poor and middle income families because of inflation and the scheduled increases in social security taxes. Given these effects, only families earning more than $30,000 in 1981 enjoyed a net decrease in taxes between 1982 and 1984. For the 34% of families with incomes below $10,000, federal taxes *increased*, on average, by about 22% (see Figure 9.2).

In fact, the bottom 80% of taxpayers were net losers, while about 19% of taxpayers in the $30,000 to $100,000 group were "modest winners." On the other hand, the 0.2% of families with incomes above $200,000 were the big winners: on average, their taxes fell by almost $60,000, a 15% reduction. Indeed a Congressional Joint Committee on

Figure 9.2
Tax Cuts for the Rich

Average Tax Cuts Compared to Tax Increases
from Inflation and Social Security Taxes, 1982-1984

Income (thousands $)	Percent of all taxpayers	Effect of Reagan tax cut on taxes paid (¢)	Effect of Inflation and Soc. Sec. tax increases on taxes paid ($)	Net effect on taxes paid ($)	Percent change in taxes paid
Under 10	34.2	− 145	437	+ 292	+ 22
10-15	14.7	− 692	1,058	+ 366	+ 7
15-20	12.1	− 1,200	1,407	+ 207	+ 2
20-30	18.9	− 2,014	2,075	+ 61	+ 0.2
30-50	15.2	− 3,797	3,548	− 249	− 1
50-100	4.0	− 8,402	6,901	− 1,501	− 3
100-200	0.7	− 19,702	10,785	− 8,917	− 8
Over 200	0.2	− 73,635	13,647	− 59,988	− 15

Source: Calculated from data provided by the Joint Congressional Committee on Taxation and reported in Robert McIntyre and Dean C. Tipps, *Inequality and Decline,* Center on Budget and Policy Priorities, pp. 23-25.

Taxation study found that the richest 5.6% of all taxpayers would receive 35% of the total tax savings from the Reagan tax cut.[10]

The tax changes not only concentrated the tax cuts among high income taxpayers, but actually hurt the poor. According to a report by the Washington-based Center on Budget and Policy Priorities, the federal tax burdens of poor families doubled from 1978 to 1985.[11] Because there were no changes in the standard deduction, personal exemption, earned-income tax credit or tax brackets, inflation pushed many very low-income people into tax brackets that required them to pay taxes for the first time.

The earned-income tax credit of 1975 and 1978 was designed to create a "tax threshold" below which poor families basically paid no federal income taxes. From 1975 to 1980, this threshold was about $1,000 *above* the poverty level.[12] As a result, most very poor people did not have to pay any federal income taxes. Between 1981 and 1984, the income tax thresholds—despite the tax cut—averaged $1,250 *below* the poverty level, thus sending the tax collector to the doors of the homes of the poor and very poor. Between 1981 and 1986, the income tax threshold will average about $1,600 below poverty incomes. Because of their new federal income tax liabilities, as well as increased social security taxes, federal tax burdens for these poor families nearly doubled between 1978 and 1985 (see Figure 9.3).

Figure 9.3
Tax Burden on the Poor

**Income and Payroll Taxes as a Percentage
of Income for Families at the Poverty Level,
1978 and 1985**

Year	Family Size		
	One	Four	Six
1978	6.5	4.0	6.1
1985	11.3	10.5	11.1

Source: Joint Committee on Taxation, "Federal Tax Treatment of Families Below the Poverty Line," April 12, 1984, p. 9, reported in Center on Budget and Policy Priorities, "Taxing the Poor," April 1984, p. 5.

Besides cutting individual income taxes of the wealthy, the Reagan tax plan called for reducing business taxes. While the rationale was that cutting corporate income taxes would stimulate investment, the plan followed a long-term trend which has dramatically shifted the composition of federal receipts. Throughout the post-war period, the share of corporate income tax has consistently diminished. From 26.5% in 1950, corporate taxes as a share of federal receipts fell to 12.5% in 1980 and then to 9.0% in 1985 (see Figure 9.4). The effective corporate tax rate also declined from 45.2% in 1960 to 20% in 1984.[13] Did this shift of the tax burden and thus income from the poor to the rich increase savings, work, and incentives? Or did it simply line the pockets, the bank accounts and the portfolios of the rich?

From 1979 to 1985, personal savings as a share of disposable personal income decreased from 5.9% to 4.1%. In addition, the tax cuts did not put more people to work: the percentage of the population working remained constant from 1979 to 1985, countering a long-term trend upward (see Figure 9.5). The tax cuts, in short, have not led to an outpouring of either savings or total work effort.

The Reagan tax cut also called for reduced business taxes, primarily through investment tax credits and an "accelerated cost recovery system" (ACRS). The ACRS was based on a plan developed by business and conservative interests in the late 1970s to reduce corporate tax liabilities in an inflationary environment. Because inflation increased their capital costs, firms argued that they needed to depreciate their capital assets more rapidly. Accelerated depreciation would reduce their tax liabilities, enabling them to retain a greater portion of their profits to finance new investments.

The Economic Recovery Tax Act of 1981, including both the ACRS and an extension of investment tax credits, originally would

Figure 9.4
The Great Corporate Escape from Taxes

Composition of Federal Receipts
1950 to 1985, Percentage

Type of Revenue	1950	1960	1970	1980	1985
Corporate income taxes	26.5	23.2	17.0	12.5	9.0
Excise Taxes	19.1	12.6	8.1	4.7	5.0
All other receipts	3.4	4.2	4.9	5.1	4.8
Individual income taxes	39.9	44.0	46.9	47.2	44.7
Social insurance taxes and contributions	11.0	15.9	23.0	30.5	36.4
Personal Taxes (lines 4 plus 5)	50.9	59.9	69.9	77.7	81.1

Source: Office of Management and Budget, *Historical Tables*, Table 2.2.

Figure 9.5
Scorecard on the Supply-Side Tax Cut

Tax Cuts Did Not Boost Saving or Employment

	Change in Savings Ratio (peak-to-peak)	Change in Employment/ Population Ratio (peak-to-peak)
1959-1969	+ 0.2	+ 2.0
1969-1973	+ 2.2	− 0.2
1973-1979	− 2.7	+ 2.1
1979-1985	− 1.8	0.0

Source: *Economic Report of the President*, 1985, Tables B-23 and B-32. U.S. Department of Commerce, "Third Quarter 1985: Gross National Product, Corporate Profits," BEA, 85-56 November 20, 1985. The 1985 figure for the change in the savings ratio is for the first 3 quarters. The figure for the employment to population ratio is for December 1984.

have reduced corporate income taxes by over $500 billion by the end of the 1980s. About 80% of the reductions would have gone to the top 2,000 corporations, less than 0.1% of all U.S. businesses.[14] When the extent of the corporate tax cut was realized and when the federal deficit began to appear out of control, Congress passed the 1982 Tax Equity and Fiscal Responsibility Act, which reduced the corporate tax cuts by about $250 billion.

The corporate tax cuts failed to stimulate investment. Indeed, net investment as a share of Net National Product fell from 1979 to 1984. But they did give some of the largest corporations in the U.S. an enormous tax bonanza that could be used for increasing executive salaries, dividends, cash reserves, foreign investments, or mergers.

In August, 1985, the Washington-based Citizens for Tax Justice released their second in-depth study of the effects of the reduced corporate income taxes for major U.S. corporations over the 1981-1984 period. The study examined the profits and federal corporate income tax liabilities of 275 profitable corporations. Over the four-year period, the 275 corporations paid a total tax rate of 15.0% on domestic profits of $400 billion (compared to the 46% nominal rate by law). Fifty companies paid *no* taxes *over the entire four-year period*, and 129 companies paid no taxes in at least one of the years (see Figure 9.6). Seven received net tax rebates in excess of $100 million each.

In a previous study, Citizens for Tax Justice discovered a general pattern of reduced corporate taxes, reduced investment spending, and increased dividends. Between 1981 and 1983, 15 non-financial companies that paid no taxes in each of the three years *reduced* their investment spending by almost 30% and increased their dividends by almost 10%. Fifty-eight that paid no taxes over the entire three-year period reduced their investment spending by 16% and increased their dividends by almost 18%. One hundred-eighteen that paid no taxes in at least one of the years reduced their investment spending by 16% and increased their dividends by 21%.[15]

One of the largest tax escapers was Ronald Reagan's old employer, General Electric: it earned $9.5 billion in profits over the 1981-1984 period, paid no taxes, and got $98 million in tax rebates. During 1981-1983, it reduced its investment spending by 15% and increased its dividends by 19%. The nation's top 12 military contractors from 1981-1984[16] earned $27.7 billion in profits and paid taxes of $1.7 billion for an effective tax rate of 6.3%, about the same as a family earning $16,500.[17]

2. Spending Sprees

The second prong of the conservative attack against "big government" was to cut federal spending and achieve a balanced budget. Given that certain appropriations extend for more than one year and that some spending programs require yearly increases by law, the

Figure 9.6
Feeding at the Public Trough

Some Companies Which Paid No Taxes and Received Rebates from the Internal Revenue Service, 1981-1984

Company	Profit (millions $)	Tax Rebate (millions $)	Tax Rate (%)
Boeing Co.	2,099.0	285.0	− 13.6
Dow Chemical Co.	972.0	180.0	− 18.5
ITT	815.0	177.7	− 21.8
Tenneco	3,401.0	166.0	− 4.9
Pepsico	1,798.7	135.8	− 7.6
Santa Fe Southern Pacific Corp.	2,309.0	133.4	− 5.8
General Dynamics	1,579.5	103.8	− 6.6
General Electric	9,577.0	98.0	− 1.0
Transamerica Corp.	748.6	93.6	− 12.5
Texaco	1,819.0	68.0	− 3.7
Ashland Oil	336.1	62.0	− 18.5
Hutton (E.F.) Group	372.5	59.6	− 16.0
Weyerhaeuser Co.	929.2	59.1	− 6.4
Georgia-Pacific Corp.	783.0	59.0	− 7.5
IC Industries	534.7	55.4	− 10.4

Source: Citizens for Tax Justice, "Corporate Taxpayers and Corporate Freeloaders," Washington, D.C., 1985.

executive branch does not hold total discretionary power over the budget.[18] Nonetheless, the Reagan cuts reduced federal domestic spending about $56 billion below what it would have been in fiscal year 1985, almost $130 million per Congressional District. While this represents a 10% reduction, it is about half of what had been proposed during Reagan's first term in office.[19]

Far from shrinking federal spending, conservative logic has sparked a massive spending spree. Between 1981 and 1985, military spending increased by about $100 billion. Coupled with the massive income tax cuts, the federal deficit has soared: almost as much was added to the national debt during Reagan's first term as had accumulated in the entire history of the country.

While military expenditure soared, proposed spending cuts during Reagan's first term focused on programs which redistribute income toward the poor, provide economic security, and promote human development. According to the Urban Institute, the suggested cutbacks can be summarized as follows.[20] The harshest cuts (those over 50%) were intended for grants to state and local governments for education, health, employment, and social services (the smallest segment of social spending). Cuts of almost one-third were recommended in benefit programs for low income people (AFDC, food stamps, child nutrition, housing assistance, and Medicaid). Cuts of about 10% were called for in the largest social spending area, social insurance programs (Social Security, Medicare, unemployment compensation). All in all, the proposed social spending cuts meant that social spending was about 17% less than what it otherwise would have been in FY1985.

At first, Congress went along with many of the proposed cutbacks. In the later years, however, lawmakers responding to public outrage began to resist executive pressure to cut social spending. By 1985, social spending was about 9% less than what it would have been without the Reagan-inspired cuts.

Given the trends in place prior to 1980, non-military outlays would have been about 15.5% of GNP in FY1985; military outlays would have been about 5.8%. Reagan wanted the non-military share shrunk to 11.0% and the military share upped to 6.9%. Congress moderated the military buildup somewhat, however, and the military's share (based on the FY1984 budget) was 6.7% in FY1985. The non-military portion, on the other hand, was much higher than Reagan wanted, although at 14.1% it still reflected a substantial cut. Under the Kennedy-Johnson, Nixon-Ford and Carter years, federal social spending programs increased at an annual average rate of about 7% in real terms. Under Reagan, this rate was reduced to about 1.5%.

By contrast, national defense budget outlays (for the Pentagon, for the nuclear weapons portion of the Department of Energy's budget, and for other defense-related programs of the federal government) have increased in real terms at an annual rate of about 7% between 1980 and 1985 (see Figure 9.7). This real growth in military spending has been concentrated in military investment outlays: weapons procurement, research and development, and military construction. From FY1980 to FY1985, weapons procurement will increase by 100%, R&D by 80%, and military construction by over 90%.[21] During this same period, operations and maintenance budgets will go up by only 37% and personnel budgets by 13%. Spending on strategic weapons has tripled, to the point where these nuclear armaments constitute a majority of the weapons procurement spending in the FY1986 budget.

Since much of the weapons procurement is planned for future years, an increasing proportion of the military budget is identified as being "uncontrollable" by the Office of Management and Budget—38% by FY1986. The Department of Defense already has almost $300 billion of Congressionally approved funds that have not been spent yet. These unexpended funds totalled about $92 billion in 1980.

Figure 9.7
Guns (and Interest Payments)
—Not Butter

Changes in the Shares of GNP of Various Categories of Federal Spending and Revenues, FY 1981-FY 1985	
Spending Category:	Change in GNP share
National Defense	+ 1.1
Veterans benefits	− 0.1
Income security	− 0.2
Social Security and Medicare	+ 0.4
Social spending	− 0.8
Net interest	+ 1.0
All other	− 0.2
TOTAL	+ 1.3
Revenue category:	
Corporation Taxes	− 0.4
Excise taxes	− 0.4
All other receipts	0.0
Individual income taxes	− 1.4
Social insurance taxes and contributions	+ 0.6
TOTAL	− 1.7

Source: Office of Management and Budget, *Historical Tables*, Fiscal Year 1986, *Tables 1.2, 2.1, 2.2, 3.2.*

These facts point to continued high levels of military spending into the late 1980s. The Reagan administration projects that military spending will increase in real terms by about 6.5% per year to a total of $428 billion in FY1990. Given cost overruns in military weapons procurement, the relative underfunding of personnel and operations and maintenance budgets compared to the continued massive weapons buildup, and the rapid R & D effort, the prospect for pressures by the Reagan administration to raise military spending even further appears certain.

Since Reagan's election in 1980, administration officials including Reagan himself, former Secretary of State Alexander Haig and Secretary of Defense Caspar Weinberger rationalized this massive military buildup as necessary to catch up with Soviet military spending and power. These claims have proven to be as exaggerated as Kennedy's non-existent "missile gap" and other scares which tend to surface during presidential election campaigns. The CIA has admitted that its own figures for the level and rate of growth of Soviet military spending during the 1970s and early 1980s were overestimated.[22]

Rather than defend the U.S. from the "Soviet threat," the massive buildup in both conventional and nuclear forces aims to restore clear-cut U.S. military superiority in the world, allowing the U.S. to reclaim its political and economic dominance. This policy goal was also seen as complimentary to the master economic gameplan to restore growth and to re-experience the prosperity of the immediate post-World War II period, which rested in part on U.S. global dominance.

While the Reagan military buildup does not seem to have restored unquestioned U.S. economic dominance, it has contributed to an increased use of military force in U.S. foreign policy and accelerated the nuclear arms race. Its economic effects have been notable as well. Military contractors and the communities where they are located have experienced an infusion of funds for military business. Employment in the defense products industry increased by 12.6% from 1980 to May, 1985.[23] Industrial production in the defense and space equipment industry increased by 38% from 1980 to 1984; overall industrial production increased by only 11.2% during the same period.[24]

The military expansion, in short, has amounted to an industrial policy for the leading defense industries— aircraft, radio and communications equipment, guided missiles, ordnance, shipbuilding and repairs, and air transportation. Research and development funds are also flowing to these same industries for work on future weapons systems. Consequently, the massive Reagan military buildup will have a profound effect not only on the conduct of foreign policy but also on the long-run economic priorities of the U.S. economy, what it devotes its resources to and how it will develop in the near future. Indeed, the increased economic stakes in military production are likely to foster commitment to an aggressive foreign policy.

The consequences of the specific social spending cuts and the increased military contracting by the Reagan administration are not very well disguised. It amounts to an overt attack on women, children, people of color, the poor, and working people. Besides being unfair, it redistributes political power in the U.S. toward corporations and the rich and away from poor, working, and middle class families.

Low income programs, comprising about 10% of the budget, accounted for almost one-third of all of the budget cuts from FY1982 to FY1985. The list included: food stamps, AFDC, Medicaid, low income housing, public service employment, job training, low income energy assistance, legal services, compensatory education for disadvantaged children, health programs, school lunch and breakfast programs, summer food programs for poor children, student financial aid, unemployment insurance, and social security disability.

According to a study by the Congressional Budget Office, about half of the budget cuts for 1981 through 1983 affected families below the $10,000 income level; 70% affected those with incomes below $20,000. Households over $80,000 suffered only 1% of those same cuts.[25]

As late as March of 1985, Reagan wanted to take still more from the pockets of middle income and poor families. "Spending is zooming for one reason," claimed the president. "The domestic budget is still bloated with waste and unnecessary programs." His fiscal year 1986 budget proposed an increase in military spending of over $30 billion and a cut in domestic programs of an almost equivalent amount.

Federal spending is swelling not only because of military expenditures. The recession, high interest rates, and the deficits themselves add to the budget by requiring ever larger interest payments on the growing federal debt. Indeed, net interest payments absorbed $130 billion in FY1985, nearly double what they were in FY1981.

Interest is a transfer payment. Taxes are collected from the entire taxpaying population and then paid as interest to the people and institutions that hold government debt. In the FY1986 budget, interest payments were projected to be almost $50 billion more than spending for low income programs.

Not surprisingly, most of the interest income in the U.S. goes to the wealthy, who can afford to purchase government securities. According to one recent study, it is likely that the richest 10% of U.S. households hold about 70% of the government debt held by households.[26]

3. The Strategic Deficit?

There were always those who told us that taxes couldn't be cut until spending was reduced. Well, you know, we can lecture our children about extravagance until we run out of voice and breath. Or we can cure their extravagance by simply reducing their allowance.

—President Ronald Reagan,
February, 1981[27]

Notwithstanding the fact that the federal deficit had already swollen to $73.8 billion in the year before he took office, Reagan and his conservative team projected stunning success for their program: a balanced budget by 1984; a surplus of almost $7 billion by FY1985.

But the unleashed economy took a three-year nap. Instead of booming growth, the economy locked into its worst recession since the 1930s. Cuts in taxes far exceeded spending cuts. While Congress defended popular programs like Social Security, Reagan himself spurred a huge military spending binge. By FY1982, the deficit had grown to $127.9 billion; for FY1985, it was projected to be a mammoth $222.2 billion (see Figure 9.8).

Tax cuts and increases in spending on defense and on interest explain the widening gap between government receipts and expenditures: between FY1981 and FY1985, total government spending as a share of GNP increased by 1.3%; revenues decreased by 1.7%, leaving

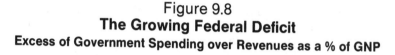

Figure 9.8
The Growing Federal Deficit
Excess of Government Spending over Revenues as a % of GNP

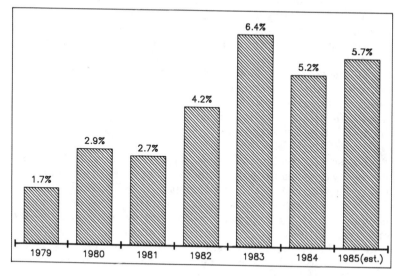

Source: Office of Management and Budget, **Historical Tables,** Tables 1.1 and 1.2

an increased deficit which amounts to 3% of GNP (see Figure 9.7). The winners—the categories of spending which increased—were defense, net interest, and social security and Medicare. But social insurance taxes were greater than expenditures. The social security system, in short, helped to *reduce* the deficit. The culprits were clearly military spending and net interest.

How could the economists who designed and promoted the Reagan strategy have erred so prodigiously? Increasingly, economic and political analysts charge that the deficit was created deliberately in order to generate political momentum to dismantle the "welfare state." Senator Ernest Hollings echoed the Democratic sentiment when he argued in January 1984, that Reagan "intentionally created a deficit so large that we Democrats will never have enough money to build the sort of government programs we want."[28] And Senator Daniel Patrick Moynihan claimed that David Stockman, President Reagan's former Director of the Office of Management and Budget, had told him that "the plan was to have a strategic deficit that would give you an argument for cutting back the programs that weren't desired. It got out of hand."[29]

Perhaps, but there is an underlying logic to the patterns of cuts, one which illustrates the characteristic analysis of economic orthodoxy. One way to measure the "success" of anti-worker conservative policies is the "cost of job loss" (CJL) measure. Constructed by Juliet Schor and Samuel Bowles of the Center for Popular Economics, CJL measures how much workers lose when they are fired from a job.[30] The more they have to lose, the less likely they are to withstand unreasonable employer demands.

The cost of job loss depends on two factors. The first is how long workers expect to be unemployed if they are fired. This depends on the duration of unemployment and is greatly increased by the slack demand for goods and services and the flood of imports promoted by the high interest rate and overvalued dollar policies of the Federal Reserve.

The second component of the cost of job loss is most strongly affected by the social spending policies of the government: it indicates how much workers lose by being unemployed each week. Their losses are higher the higher their wages are, and the lower—in unemployment insurance, food stamps, or other safety net payments—the amount of money they receive from the government when unemployed. Thus, the lower the government support for the unemployed, the higher the cost of job loss. And the higher the cost of job loss, the less the ability of workers to press their demands.

Of the two means of increasing the cost of job loss—increasing the duration of unemployment and reducing social spending—the latter is much better for business profits. Increasing unemployment by generating a recession can harm business by making it difficult for them to sell their goods. But cutting social spending has no such negative impact on corporate profits.

The high interest rate policies of the Federal Reserve and the social spending cuts of supply-side economics increased the cost of job loss by 50% between the late 1960s and the 1980s. In 1983, the cost of job loss was at a 20-year high.[31]

Though the strategic deficit has worked to put the screws to working people, it poses a dilemma. Helping to push up interest rates under a regime of tight money policies, the conservative deficit reinforces itself in a circular trap: tax cuts are transferred from the public purse into the hands of the wealthy; a deficit ensues and to cover it, the government borrows money from the wealthy; interest payments increase as a result of increased borrowing, further pushing up the deficit and transferring income to higher income-earners, and so on.

The deficit also raises the specter of a political stalemate. Even with economic growth, the only way to reduce the deficit is through some combination of tax increases and/or spending cuts. The Reagan administration refuses to consider raising taxes or significantly reducing military spending. Sensing strong public support for most domestic spending and a growing resentment at the sacred cow status of military expenditures, Congress is hesitant to go along with further cuts in social spending.

In mid-1985, Congress did pass resolutions cutting spending between FY1986-1988 by more than $200 billion (about one-third of which was in military spending). Even so, the Congressional Budget Office projects that the deficit will still be almost $150 billion in FY1988. For FY1989, even if Congress were able to continue the pace of spending cutbacks and reduced expected outlays by $132 billion, the deficit would total about $132 billion, or 2.5% of GNP.[32]

Couched in the language of domestic economic necessity and external threats, the battle over the deficit is a struggle over the fundamental priorities of the nation. Its resolution is likely to be difficult and slow and will stem less from economic analysis than political mobilization.

Footnotes

1. Congressional Budget Office, "The Combined Effects of Major Changes in Federal Taxes and Spending Programs Since 1981," April 1984, p. 9.

2. David E. Rosenbaum, "Tax Proposal Found Skewed," *The New York Times*, September 20, 1985, p. D2.

3. *Economic Report of the President*, 1985, Table B-71, p. 317.

4. Programs "for persons with limited income" are defined in Library of Congress, Congressional Research Service, "Cash and Non-Cash Benefits for Persons With Limited Income," Report No. 84-99.

5. Quoted in Hedrick Smith, "Reagan's Effort to Change Course of Government," *The New York Times*, October 23, 1984, p. 426.

6. The White House, *America's New Beginning: A Program for Economic Recovery*, February 18, 1981.

7. Peter Saunders and Friedrich Klau, *The Role of the Public Sector*, OECD Economic Studies, No. 4, Spring 1985, Table 1, p. 29.

8. U.S. Census Bureau, *Statistical Abstract*, 1985, Table No. 473.

9. Robert McIntyre and Dean Tipps, *Inequality and Decline*, Center on Budget and Policy Priorities, Washington, D.C., 1983, p. 11.

10. Reported in Center on Budget and Policy Priorities, *End Results*, Washington, D.C., September 1984, p. 12.

11. Center on Budget and Policy Priorities, "Taxing the Poor," Washington, D.C., 1984.

12. The poverty level is calculated to be three times the expenditure necessary to purchase food equal to a level of "minimum nutrition." It is adjusted for inflation on a yearly basis. An extra $1000 was added to take into account the payment of social security taxes.

13. Calculated from Office of Management and Budget, *Historical Tables*, FY1986, and *Economic Report of the President*, 1985.

14. McIntyre and Tipps, *op. cit.*, p. 33.

15. Citizens for Tax Justice, "The Failure of Corporate Tax Incentives," Washington, D.C., 1985.

16. They were: Rockwell, McDonnell Douglas, General Dynamics, General Electric, Lockheed, Boeing, Martin Marietta, United Technologies, Raytheon, Westinghouse, Grumman, and Litton.

17. See Joseph A. Pechman, *Who Paid the Taxes? 1966-1985*, The Brookings Institution, Washington,D.C., 1985, pp. 49 and 56.

18. Many appropriations mandate built-in annual increases.

19. John L. Palmer and Isabel V. Sawhill, Ed., *The Reagan Record*, The Urban Institute, Washington, D.C., 1984, p. 13.

20. *Ibid.*

21. Defense Budget Project, Center on Budget and Policy Priorities, *The FY1986 Defense Budget: The Weapons Buildup Continues*, Washington, D.C., April 1985, p. 47.

22. Center for Defense Information, *The Defense Monitor*, Washington, D.C., 1985, Vol. 14, No. 4, p. 6. The Joint Chiefs of Staff continue to testify in Congress that U.S. military forces are superior to those of the Soviets.

23. *Business Conditions Digest*, July 1985, pp. 91, 101.

24. *Economic Report of the President*, 1985, Table B-43, p. 281.

25. Congressional Budget Office studies quoted in Center on Budget and Policy Priorities, *End Results, op. cit.*, p. 12.

26. Thomas Michl, "Contractionary and Reactionary: Government Debt In a Simple Macroeconomic Model," Colgate University, August 29, 1985, p. 2.

27. Quoted in Daniel Patrick Moynihan, "Reagan's Inflate-the-Deficit Game," *The New York Times*, July 21, 1985.

28. Quoted in Tom Wicker, "A Deliberate Deficit," *The New York Times*. July 19, 1985.

29. *Ibid.*

30. Juliet Schor and Samuel Bowles, "The Cost of Job Loss and the Incidence of Strikes," Harvard Institute for Economic Research Discussion Paper, August 1984.

31. *Ibid.*

32. Congressional Budget Office, *The Economic and Budget Outlook: An Update*, August 1985, p. 66.

10 Market Failure

*The primary beneficiary of any true reform of the financial system
will the public...Bastille Day is near for these archaic laws and
regulations.*
— A.W. Clausen, then President of BankAmerica Corp.,
in *Bankers Monthly Magazine*, June 15, 1979, p. 23.

*The process of bank deregulation so far...has increased the
risks of bank failure, undermined the stability of the banking system, and increased the concentration of banking resources. Continuing deregulation in this vein will only exacerbate this trend.
The public receives nothing in return.*
— Honorable Byron L. Dorgan, *How the Financial System Can
Best Be Shaped to Meet the Needs of the American People*, Hearings on financial deregulation before the U.S. Congress, House
Committee on Banking, Finance and Urban Affairs, 98th Congress, 2nd Session, on H.R. 5734, Washington, D.C., 1984, Serial
No. 98-83, p. 69.

On May 16, 1984, a dramatic meeting took place at the Wall Street
offices of Morgan Guaranty Trust Company. Continental Illinois of
Chicago, the eighth largest bank in the U.S., teetered on the brink of
collapse. Bankers and government regulators feared its demise would
threaten the whole financial system of the U.S. and even the western
world.

Led by Federal Reserve Board Chairman Paul Volcker, the heads
of most major U.S. banks and top government bank regulators worked
out a rescue plan for Continental. The successful plan included a $7.5
billion aid package for the bank; a guarantee that the Federal Reserve
System would meet any of Continental's "extraordinary liquidity
requirements"; and a surprising waiver by the Federal Deposit
Insurance Corporation of the usual $100,000 limit on deposit in-
surance.[1]

Continental had behaved the way banks were supposed to in the new, increasingly deregulated environment. It had aggressively pursued large deposits throughout North America, Europe, and Asia to provide the funds for its equally aggressive loan program. Between 1975 and 1980, the bank's assets grew by 15% a year and its operating profits doubled. As the bank's profits soared, so did its reputation.

Then the severe 1982 recession and a growing oil glut sent profits plummeting. As word of its deterioration leaked out, Continental was hit by a "silent run": without ever having to form a line at the bank door, large depositors around the world withdrew their funds electronically. Only a dramatic government rescue prevented the bank's collapse. [2]

The panic at Continental sharpened debate over bank deregulation, a process which had begun in the late 1970s. Bankers and economists had promised that rolling back government regulation of banks would bring enormous benefits to the public. Indeed, the strategy of conservative economics called for dismantling the entire edifice of government social and economic regulation, which allegedly thwarted the beneficial effects of the "free" market.

The debacle at Continental raised some doubts.

The Role of Regulation

The market has never been allowed to operate uniformly throughout the private economy. Several important sectors of the U.S. economy have traditionally been regulated by the government, such as finance, transportation, communication, power, and agriculture. Examples include the railroads, traditionally regulated by the Interstate Commerce Commission; the airlines, regulated by the Civil Aeronautics Board and the Federal Aviation Agency; and the banks, regulated by the Federal Reserve System or Fed, the Federal Deposit Insurance Corporation (FDIC), and the Comptroller of the Currency. In some cases, government regulation of particular industries dates back to the nineteenth century.

A second type of government regulation is aimed not at one industry but at the economy as a whole. Examples include environmental, occupational safety and health, and consumer product safety regulation.

Industrial regulation is based on the belief that, without it, the profit-seeking actions of individual firms in certain industries will generate ill effects for the society. These include monopoly (for power, telephone, railroad, pipeline, and banking industries); destructive competition (airlines); information problems (securities markets, banking); safety problems (transportation industries); or some other socially undesirable outcome. In some cases, such as banking and transportation, an industry has large third party effects and public regulation is demanded to assure its growth, prosperity, and stability. In other cases, regulation is prompted by concern to conserve a natural resource (crude petroleum) or to assure a high quality, diverse product (broadcasting).

Industrial regulation is not unique to the United States. In most industrialized capitalist countries, the industries listed above are either regulated or state-owned and operated. Indeed, public ownership plays a much smaller role in the U.S. Rather, the government attempts to influence economic outcomes primarily by regulating the behavior of private businesses in such areas as price setting, buyer-seller relations, product characteristics, management practices, and new entry.

During the past decade, however, a new term has entered the language of economic policy: deregulation. Initiated under Carter and intensified under Reagan, significant steps have been taken to reduce or eliminate public regulation.

On August 12, 1981, Vice-President Bush announced a list of Federal regulations to be reviewed by the Presidential Task Force on Regulatory Relief. The Task Force was to determine if the regulations were among the "burdensome, unnecessary or counter-productive Federal regulations" that the White House planned to eliminate as a means of stimulating the economy.[3] Among them were:

— Equal Employment Opportunity Commission policies that prohibit hiring workers in ways which, in the EEOC's words, "disproportionately exclude members of a race, sex, or ethnic group";

— the "pesticides registration program" which required manufacturers to test and register products prior to sale;

— "sexual harrassment guidelines" of the Equal Employment Opportunity Commission;

— rules that limit the amount of lead in gasoline and which, in Bush's words, "place onerous capital requirements on small refiners"

— Rehabilitation Act provisions requiring that educational facilities which receive federal funds make their programs and buildings accessible to the disabled;

— Title IX policy interpretations which forbid discrimination against women's sports in educational institutions.

The list suggests the long reach of the deregulator's logic—stretching far beyond the boundaries of what are customarily considered to be economic concerns. Many of these regulations were only adopted in the 1970s.

The deregulation process began with the airlines in 1977, which are now largely free to determine fares and domestic routes as they wish. Trucking and long distance (though not local) telephone service is now largely unregulated. The Reagan-appointed members of the Federal Communications Commission are waging a battle to eliminate regulations governing radio and television broadcasts and have succeeded so far in ending limits to advertising time per broadcast hour.

While the lure of increased profits and the economic slowdown of the late 1970s provided some impetus to the deregulation movement, the aim in some cases was to undermine strong unions. The stability provided by regulation has fostered strong unions and high wages. The price wars sparked by the sudden entry of low-wage, non-union companies into a newly deregulated industry have enabled the established firms to win concessions on wages and benefits. For example, between 1980, when the Motor Carrier Act deregulating trucking was passed, and 1984, real average hourly earnings for workers in the trucking industry fell by 9.3%. For all workers in the private sector, the decline was 1.5%.[4]

The struggle over deregulation has probably been fiercest, however, in the financial sector, where the profit stakes are enormous. Proponents claim deregulation of banking will give a huge boost to the efficiency, growth, and prosperity of the entire economy. Opponents are likely to recall the crushing effect of the U.S. banking collapse in 1933.

Is deregulation, particularly bank deregulation, a boon or a disaster for the economy? The answer is important not only in its own right but because it would shed light on the social consequences of conservative economics, which has adopted deregulation as an article of faith.

Deregulation and New Orthodoxy

Conservative economics holds that unregulated markets always produce the best possible economic outcomes.[5] The bottom line for the new economic orthodoxy is that whatever makes money for business makes sense for the country as a whole.

According to the new orthodox logic, the pursuit of profits in unregulated "free" markets is "best" on four counts: (1) it is efficient, that is, it will produce products that consumers want at the lowest possible cost; (2) it yields an optimal rate of growth and technical progress by assuring an optimal amount of saving, investment, research and innovation; (3) it ensures full employment of all productive inputs, including labor; and (4) it produces the most equitable possible distribution of income, with each receiving in proportion to his or her productive contribution.

The underlying belief of these new orthodox economists, in short, is that as long as markets are "free" or unregulated, the self-interested actions of private individuals generally produce optimal social outcomes.

How might profit-seeking action serve the common good? How can it be true that "what's good for General Motors is good for the country?" The new orthodoxy holds that competition *compels* GM to serve all of us through seeking to serve itself. Competition is the "invisible hand" that guides selfish behavior in "free" markets toward socially productive ends.

But critics point out that the new orthodoxy rests on three assumptions which do not hold in the real world of U.S. capitalism. The first is each industry is freely competitive. Free competition means that no firm produces a significant share of any industry's output and that it is easy for new firms to enter any industry. In reality, the textbook ideal of a free market composed of thousands of competing buyers and sellers is more easily found on university blackboards than in real life. None of the major sectors of the U.S. economy conforms to its unrealistic assumptions. Many industries are dominated by a few giants that hold significant power over consumers and workers. Furthermore, new entry is rare in many industries.

The second assumption is that there are no "spillover effects" of production or consumption. In other words, no third parties are affected, for good or ill, by acts of production or consumption. But the real world is rife with such external effects: on the positive side, one person's polio vaccination reduces other people's likelihood of contracting polio; on the negative side, factories pollute the air and water used by many people. Indeed, it is often the case that the full social benefits of an act are not rewarded by the market, and equally that the full social costs of one's decisions are not paid for. If such external effects are frequent accompaniments to economic activity, then unregulated markets will not be socially efficient, producing too much pollution and too little vaccination.

Closely connected with external effects is the problem of "public goods." If one person eats an apple, it is no longer available for another person to eat. But some goods and services can be consumed by one person without using up the good or service. One person's "consumption" of a television broadcast, for example, still leaves it available for others, as the sprouting of dish antennas attests.

Most forms of information, such as new technologies, computer programs, video cassettes, weather reports, and medical cures, are public goods. National defense, uncrowded highways, and beautiful views also fit into this category. Because it is hard to charge money for something which can be made available freely to all, unregulated industries produce too little, or none at all, of such goods. When they do produce them, they will charge too high a price for them.

The new orthodoxy makes a third unlikely assumption, that everyone has complete and accurate information concerning all available products and all available jobs. When you buy a GM car or accept a job at Union Carbide, you are supposed to know exactly what you are getting, as well as knowing all the alternatives. Critics point out that corporations generally have the greatest amount of information about both products and jobs, while consumers and workers have far more limited information.

So far, we have dealt with the first two claims of the new orthodox theory: that unregulated markets assure the best possible levels of efficiency and growth. There is also a problem with the third claim, that unregulated markets assure full employment of labor. This claim is not supported by the historical record in the U.S. Rather than being the norm, full employment has not been achieved in any peacetime year during the past half-century. Only during World War II, the Korean War, and the Vietnam War years, when the free market was superceded in many respects, was full employment reached.

The fourth and last claim of the new orthodoxy is that the market is fair. Critics argue that even the freest of free markets will naturally produce growing inequality among individuals, as those initially wealthy, well-connected and successful, build on their head start while the rest have little on which to build. Furthermore, people's productive contributions have only a loose connection to economic rewards. Skilled mechanics or nurses can achieve at best a modest level of comfort through plying their trade, while expert stockbrokers and promoters of various types can gain great wealth. Wealth, once gained, can be passed on to heirs who lack even the skills of the originator of the fortune. And the major source of great incomes is large property holdings rather than any type of labor or effort.

Until about ten years ago, most economists agreed that the real-life failures of unregulated markets required some degree of government intervention. In particular, there was wide agreement that public regulation of such industries as railroads, telephone service, and banking was needed. How have the new orthodox economists been able to effect a major shift in the view of economic regulation?

This change of perspective was accomplished by shifting the terms of the debate. The question at issue gradually shifted from "do unregulated markets work well?" to "do regulated markets work well?" The new orthodoxy held that even where unregulated markets failed to achieve their promised results, the cure of regulation was worse than the disease of market failure.

Three main charges were leveled at economic regulation. The first was that it generated inefficiencies in the regulated industries. For example, it was claimed that absence of competition and barriers to new entry under regulation led to excessive costs and retarded new technologies. Guaranteed rates of return on investment in plant and equipment were blamed for excessive costs and overly capital-intensive technologies.

Second, deregulationists argued that the regulatory process itself entailed high costs. Much time and money was spent by regulatory agencies deciding such questions as the proper price to charge for a service or whether a railroad should be allowed to give up a particular route. By the time a decision was rendered, the underlying conditions might have changed so as to make the decision no longer appropriate. Furthermore, it was pointed out that regulated companies spent funds lobbying to attain their ends that might better have been spent on improving the product.

Third, the deregulationists borrowed a critique from radical and populist analysts of the regulatory process. This was the view that a regulatory agency is typically "captured" by the industry it is supposed to oversee. Instead of pursuing the public interest, the agency acts to protect the monopoly position of the companies in the industry.

There is a good deal of truth in the new orthodox criticisms of past regulatory practices. However, most of these problems have been known for years. The new element was the claim that the problems of regulation made it worse than the alternative of no regulation. And here a new and bold argument was introduced: it was asserted that the failures of unregulated markets could be corrected more efficiently and effectively by...the market mechanism itself!

Is monopoly a problem in some industries? Only temporarily, claim the deregulationists, for no private monopoly can last. Technological change, new entry or the threat of new entry, and competition from substitute products will soon erode any monopoly position.

Are external effects a problem? Anyone harmed by a negative externality, such as air or water pollution, can file a lawsuit for damages—and the expectation of such lawsuits will deter the act in the first place.

Do consumers or workers lack good information about, say, the health effects of a product or the hazards of working in a particular job? If so, the deregulationists are confident that someone will realize a profit can be made for supplying such information, and thus the market will insure that the right quantity and quality of information will be supplied. This eliminates the need for safety regulations, since consumers and workers will be able to judge for themselves whether to buy a product or take a job. And if any consumer is harmed by a product, the proper remedy is a lawsuit. The fear of consumer lawsuits will deter the sale of unsafe products.

For every problem that might justify government regulation, the deregulationists came up with an argument that the free market can solve the problem better and cheaper. Critics of this view find the new orthodox claims implausible.

The claim that monopoly power can only be a transitory problem flies in the face of the historical evidence. The Aluminum Company of America maintained a virtually complete monopoly over basic aluminum for several decades before World War II, until government antitrust action broke up its monopoly. For two decades after World War II, the big three auto makers effectively controlled the U.S. auto market, which allowed GM to make its 20% rate of profit year after year. And as a century of railroad regulation is ending, the specter of rail monopoly is appearing again. "We're going back to 1887—letting the railroads charge what the traffic will bear," charged Carl Bagge, president of the National Coal Association.[6]

The belief that lawsuits, and the fear of prospective lawsuits, can adequately solve the problem of negative external effects received a serious blow when the Johns Manville Corporation filed for bankruptcy under Chapter 11 in 1982. Thousands of people who believed they had contracted the deadly illness asbestosis due to exposure to asbestos—a classical example of an external effect—sued the producer, Johns Manville, for damages.[7] But the bankruptcy ploy leaves the disposition of such lawsuits to a bankruptcy judge, whose main concern is the survival of the company, not the problems of asbestosis victims. One might also note that Union Carbide Corporation was not deterred from its evidently sloppy handling of a deadly chemical in Bhopal, India, by fear of lawsuits by local residents. And lawsuits are, of course, a very cumbersome, slow, and costly process—one which makes public regulation appear cheap and efficient by comparison!

The fact that lawsuits are an inadequate solution to the problem of consumer and worker safety is not apparent to the new orthodox theorists. In 1982, the Federal Trade Commission considered negotiations with a manufacturer of "survival suits" used by sailors, deep sea oil rig workers, and others facing the possibility of being plunged into cold ocean waters. The Coast Guard had found that about 90% of the suits produced by the manufacturer were defective, but could be fixed through installation of a 10 cent part. An economist at the FTC, faithful to the new orthodox creed, temporarily blocked the negotiations, on the grounds that lawsuits by affected parties or their survivors were a more cost-effective way of handling the problem than government regulation.

Someone at the FTC leaked this to Congress, and the FTC Chairman James C. Miller III, a new orthodox theorist himself, had to appear before Congress on the matter. When Congressman Albert Gore, Jr., asked Miller whether it was appropriate for lawsuits by widows and orphans to supplant FTC regulation, Miller responded, "It depends on the circumstances." As it turned out, in this circumstance the publicity and political pressure forced a regulatory response rather than relying on lawsuits, with the FTC ultimately taking action on the matter.[8]

The new orthodox claim that the failures of unregulated markets can be effectively corrected by a combination of competition and lawsuits is as fanciful as the initial assumptions of the case for the unregulated market. Were this not the case, regulation would never have developed in the first place. Past regulatory efforts have indeed been flawed. But regulation seems to be the only reasonable way to deal with the failures of markets in certain industries.

Critics of the deregulation position can point to various regulated industries that seemed to work reasonably well. The U.S. telephone service seemed to be about the best in the world. The U.S. banking system had been much more stable under close regulation than previously. But other regulated industries did not seem to perform so well, with railroads and airlines among the most frequently criticized. And who could say that performance would not be even better without regulation?

After a decade of deregulation, it is now possible to offer at least a preliminary assessment. Has deregulation lived up to its advance promotional billing? To get some idea of the relation between promise and performance, we will now examine the record of one of the industries swept by deregulation fever—banking.

The Bank Regulatory System and Its Problems

The banking system in the U.S. was only loosely regulated prior to the 1930s. The financial system was quite unstable, and waves of bank failures and financial panics were not uncommon. When the Great Depression struck in the 1930s, the banking system collapsed; almost half of all U.S. banks failed between 1929 and 1933. This collapse caused enormous hardship, as millions of families lost their savings. The collapse is also credited with making the Depression more severe and long-lasting than it might otherwise have been.

Banking regulation was introduced in the 1930s in response to this experience. This regulation had five main parts. First, the Federal Deposit Insurance Corporation (FDIC) was created to insure bank deposits. Second, interest rate ceilings were imposed on bank savings deposits, with no interest allowed on demand (checking) deposits. Third, the trend toward conglomerate financial institutions, offering all major services, was stopped by requiring that commercial banks, investment banks, insurance companies, and investment companies each keep to their original type of business. (This type of regulation is known as "product regulation," since it limits the "products" that a given financial institution is allowed to offer.) Fourth, close supervision of the financial condition and business practices of banks was established.

The fifth part of this system involved a new role for the Federal Reserve System, which itself had been in operation since 1913. It was understood that now the Fed would provide strong backing for the banking system whenever it came under strain, by pumping funds into the banks at such times.

The regulatory system which emerged from the 1930s had a sixth part which predated the 1930s. The old system of geographic limitations on bank operations, created and enforced by the states, was left intact. This system varied from state to state, but in most states it limited the establishment of multiple branches by banks within the state. And interstate banking was completely forbidden.

This new regulatory system reflected the view that banking is not just an ordinary industry, but rather the basis of the nation's monetary system, the guardian of people's savings, and a major source of funds for the entire business sector. The 1930s regulations tried to:

(1) assure stability. The regulations tried to prevent bank failures through FDIC deposit insurance, intended to make bank runs impossible, and by the Fed backing the banks. Furthermore, both interest rate regulations and the close supervision of banking practices were intended to limit competition between banks, thus increasing the safety and stability of banks;

(2) avoid conflicts of interest. The product regulations were intended to avoid a whole set of conflicts of interest which emerged with the earlier trend toward conglomerate financial institutions. Commercial banks with large loans out to a troubled company, for example, had sometimes sold bonds of the troubled company to unsuspecting customers, with the proceeds used to repay the bank loans. In such cases, regulations that prohibited transactions involving conflicts of interest also protected the stability of the financial system.

(3) limit concentration of financial resources. Fear of concentrated financial power has a long history in U.S. politics dating back to Thomas Jefferson's opposition to a national bank. This fear has its roots in the concern on the part of small farmers and small businesspeople that a highly concentrated financial system would not only wield unaccountable power but in addition would make it difficult for them to obtain the credit which they need for survival at an affordable cost. Both geographic limits and product limits had the effect of greatly reducing the concentration of the financial sector;

(4) channel credit into socially desirable activities and promote ways of life—such as family farming—thought to be worthy of support. Credit was intended to encourage homebuilding and homeownership, partly through the system of product limits (which protected the thrift institutions and required them to mainly finance

homebuilding) and the interest rate regulations (which kept mortgage rates down).

This regulatory system was very effective at stabilizing the banking system. An average of only five banks failed each year between 1946 and 1975, and no real financial panic occurred during those years. It also produced a banking system far less concentrated than that of other industrialized capitalist countries. And it succeeded in financing a huge wave of homebuilding and homeownership during the post-World War II period. By the 1970s, however, growing problems were evident.

Rising inflation in the 1970s led to rising interest rates, which caused problems for the system of interest rate ceilings. As market interest rates rose above the ceilings permitted on savings deposits at banks and thrift institutions, savers withdrew their deposits and put them instead in the higher interest unregulated money market mutual funds. And the homebuilding industry, which was supposed to be favored by the system, was denied funds as thrifts lost resources.

New communications technologies made it possible for funds to be shifted around more rapidly in search of the highest interest rate. This enabled various nonbank institutions, such as brokerage firms and money market mutual funds, to draw funds away from banks with interests rate ceilings.

Foreign banks increasingly entered U.S. markets. Since foreign banks were not subject to all U.S. bank regulations (such as the requirement that part of a bank's funds be kept in reserves, which do not receive any interest), they had a competitive advantage over U.S. banks. And most nonbank financial institutions, also less regulated than banks, began to compete more heavily with banks for funds. The banks complained that they were competing under a handicap.

The Financial Deregulation Movement

Not surprisingly, many banks, particularly the large ones, pushed for fewer regulations by the mid-1970s. They were joined by the increasingly influential new orthodox economists, who provided an intellectual rationale for bank deregulation.

The new orthodox theorists asserted that banking, like other industries, was hurt more than it was helped by regulation. The natural process of competition, it was claimed, could be relied on to assure optimal outcomes in the banking industry.

They claimed that stability could be assured without regulation. Deposit insurance could be offered by private insurance companies to banks that wished to purchase it. Supervision of banks' financial condition and management practices was unnecessary because depositors could decide for themselves whether any given bank had the degree of safety desired. And in any event, the new orthodox economists claimed, banks that are unsuccessful should be allowed to fail.

These theorists also believed that product regulations were unnecessary because conflicts of interest could be prevented through the threat of lawsuits by affected parties. Consumers would know what was being done to them, since the market would assure that sufficient information was available.

These theorists asserted that geographic restrictions were also unnecessary because rivalry among existing banks and the threat of entry by new banks would prevent the accumulation of monopoly power. They argued that geographic restrictions actually reduced competition, by protecting local monopolies held by small town banks.

Regulations encouraging credit for particular uses were also viewed as counterproductive in the orthodox view. The free market will always direct credit to its most productive uses, they said. And these uses are always the most profitable—hence able to pay the highest interest rates.

Seizing the populist mantle, the new orthodox theorists even complained that the existing regulatory system really favored the banks and the rich, by limiting competition among banks and by preventing small depositors from getting the higher market interest rates available to big investors.[9]

While new orthodox economists provided the big intellectual push toward bank deregulation, the more traditional liberal economists did not oppose the idea. Although liberal economists did not accept the view that a fully unregulated banking system would be sufficiently stable, they too had a strong faith in the efficiency of market forces, and generally argued that some loosening of bank regulation was desirable.[10] In particular, the liberals favored eliminating geographic restrictions, but advocated caution about reducing other bank regulations.

With the larger banks and the new orthodox economists pressing for deregulation in the mid-1970s, while liberal economists showed moderate approval, the process of bank deregulation began. Small banks and insurance companies, fearing competition from the large banks, opposed deregulation, but they lacked the power to stop the process.

In the 1970s, banks and thrifts were allowed to begin issuing money market certificates and thrifts in some states were allowed to offer interest-bearing checking accounts. Major deregulation steps came in 1980, with the passage of the Depository Institutions Deregulation and Monetary Control Act and in 1982 with the passage of the Garn-St. Germaine Bill.

Under these bills interest rates were gradually deregulated, and checking accounts allowed to pay interest. Thrifts were also allowed to make some commercial loans. While the new legislation weakened interest rate and product regulations, the Fed also weakened geographic regulations as it began to encourage some forms of interstate banking. In some respects these acts also extended regulation; for example, reserve requirements were applied to, and Fed services made available to, nonbank depository institutions. But the major impact, beginning in 1980, was to make financial deregulation the official policy of Congress.

By the mid-1980s, only three forms of bank regulation were left intact: federal deposit insurance, bank supervision, and the Fed's backup role *vis-a-vis* the banks. Product and geographic regulations were weaker but still present and interest rate regulations were essentially gone. The forces of competition could now take on a significant role in banking.

The Experience of Financial Deregulation

Like the free market orthodoxy as a whole, the theory of banking deregulation has been knocked around by the facts of economic life.

First the problem of external effects has become too important to ignore. While banks do not pollute the air or water, they can create equally serious spillovers.

A bank which makes a series of bad loans, in a deregulated environment, can fail and bankrupt third parties: the bank's depositors. Furthermore, a peculiarity of banking is that even a bank that has made no bad loans can become vulnerable if depositors come to believe there is danger and withdraw their funds in a state of panic.

The problem of imperfect information is also particularly severe in banking. The claim that depositors know something about the quality of the bank's loans is ludicrous. In fact, information possessed by the bank about the condition of debtor companies is confidential and can not legally be revealed to depositors.

While bank deregulation is still new, it is possible to make some evaluation of its effects so far. These effects do not seem to agree with the promises of its promoters. Problems with bank performance have already appeared in four dimensions: stability; allocation of credit; provision of bank services; and concentration.

1. Stability

Within two years of the passage of the 1980 Depository Institutions Deregulation Act, bank failures began to increase sharply (see Figure 10.1). The 1984 figure of 79 bank failures was the highest since 1938.

And there were 52 bank failures in the first half of 1985 alone.[11] By contrast, during the years 1946-78, the largest number of failures in any one year was 17 (in 1976).

The FDIC's list of "problem banks" reached a record number of 817 by the end of 1984 and was rumored to include some major banks. The previous postwar record was 380 in 1976.[12] By mid-1985 the number of problem banks included nearly 8% of the nation's banks.[13]

Several factors are responsible for this rising trend of bank failures. One is the general stagnation of the U.S. and world economies, together with the associated problems of the agriculture and energy sectors. However, the economy, expanding since the beginning of 1983, should have eased the condition of the banks.

Policies followed by the Fed since 1979, which produced high and unstable interest rates, also put pressure on many banks. But interest rates were lower in 1982-84 than they were in 1980 and 1981, while the bank failure rate accelerated after 1981.

Financial deregulation appears to be a major cause of the growing rate of bank failures because deregulation of interest rates, products, and geographic areas increased competition among financial institutions. And an enduring feature of competition is that it produces losers as well as winners. Thus, some of the weaker banks have failed, as the environment became more competitive.

Figure 10.1
Financial Instability

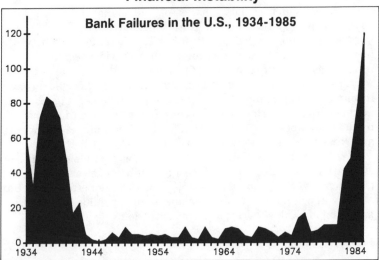

Source: Federal Deposit Insurance, **Annual Report,** various years. The figure for 1985 is an estimate reported in Nathaniel Nash, "Failures of Banks Reach 100," **New York Times,** November 9, 1985, p 37. As of November 8, 1985, 100 banks had failed in 1985.

This could turn out to be only a temporary problem. Perhaps as the environment shifts from a regulated to a deregulated one, weak banks that survived because of regulation will be weeded out, and a stronger banking industry will emerge once the transition is over.

While there are some benefits to be reaped by eliminating high cost banks, deregulation may also have a long-run negative effect on the stability of the banking system. Deregulation is goading the banks to adopt a more aggressive profit orientation. This makes it more difficult to pass up bigger profits that can come from high-risk loans and investments—if they are repaid. The process has happened before: in the 1920s, growing competition among banks led many to jump into risky, speculative loans and investments and helped precipitate the banking collapse of the early 1930s.

The presence of federal deposit insurance and Fed backing of the banks actually has a perverse effect on banks' willingness to accept high-risk loans. These safeguards make failure less costly, and for large banks, virtually impossible, as the Continental Illinois case showed.

Furthermore, the growing bank use of uninsured liabilities, such as certificates of deposit, and volatile brokered deposits, means that FDIC insurance does not necessarily guard against a run, as the Continental experience demonstrated.

Between 1946 and 1972, no bank with assets over $100 million failed. In 1973 and 1974 two very large banks failed (U.S. National Bank of San Diego and Franklin National Bank of New York). The FDIC's handling of such large failures made it apparent that even large depositors would lose no money when a large bank failed. The fact that regulatory authorities now provide greater security to the depositors of large banks than small ones has created an even greater incentive for large banks to take excessive risks. A recent study found that the average failed bank during 1973-84 was significantly larger, relative to the average size bank, than in the half-century from 1921 to 1972.[14] Large bank failures pose a particularly serious threat to the financial system.

The problem of the perverse effect of FDIC and Fed backing could easily be solved by eliminating such backing, as some extreme new orthodox theorists have suggested (or rather, had suggested, before Continental Illinois). But this move would make possible an old-style financial panic and wave of bank failures. This move is highly unlikely unless complete insanity, and historical amnesia, come to prevail at high levels. And as long as the FDIC and Fed are there, the rising trend of bank failures is unlikely to lead to a financial panic or general banking collapse.

But growing bank instability has high costs nevertheless. We are likely to see a growing number of failures among smaller banks and bailouts of large ones. And taxpayers will end up paying the cost of such bailouts.

The Fed's role as protector of the banking system requires it to flood the system with more money when big banks run into trouble. This can raise havoc with other economic policies. If the economy ever resumes a sustained expansion, such Fed moves could stir up the dormant fires of inflation.

The most likely result of the translation of orthodox economic theory into national economic policy is not an effective and lean (if mean) banking industry. Rather, the public will end up footing the bill for the failures of banking deregulation.

2. Allocation of Credit

The old system of bank regulation sought to steer credit in particular directions, such as housing construction. Since deregulation, however, the market has propelled the financing of mergers and other speculative but lucrative credit allocation.

Since 1981 a massive wave of corporate mergers has gripped the economy. By 1984, the dollar value of mergers reached the unprecedented level of $122 billion, exceeding the total amount of net investment by business on new plants and equipment.[15] Funds spent on these giant mergers do not yield any appreciable social gain in the form of greater output or efficiency. But such mergers can be very profitable for the companies concerned.

The banks have eagerly provided huge sums of money to finance these profitable, yet unproductive, activities. Standard Oil of California obtained what is believed to be the biggest private loan in history to finance its takeover of Gulf Oil in 1984: a $14 billion dollar loan from a large group of banks.[16] Nearly 20% of the dollar volume of new bank lending in the U.S. went to finance mergers and acquisitions during the first quarter of 1984.[17]

Bank willingness over the past five years to finance anything that is profitable has also fueled a wave of speculative investment in commodities futures, currencies, and anything else that can be bought and sold. A little-noticed indicator of such growing speculative activity is the rapid increase in the value of checks written during a year, relative to the value of GNP. If check value grows relative to GNP, this suggests that an increasing amount of money is going for nonproductive and speculative purchases. From 1979 to 1984, the value of checks grew at nearly two and half times the rate that GNP grew. For the major New york banks believed to be deeply involved in speculative activities, the value of checks written grew more than three times as fast as GNP during those years.[18]

The scope of speculative activity is also well-illustrated by a 1984 incident between T. Boone Pickens, the Texas stock speculator, and Gulf Oil Corporation. Pickens threatened a takeover, spending $968 million to acquire Gulf stock. His well-publicized campaign led to a big increase in Gulf's stock value. The bluff worked and Pickens sold his stock for $1760 million, realizing a profit of $792 million for his efforts—over 80% of his investment.[19]

Such mundane activities as producing food, clothing, and housing cannot make such astronomical profit rates; they naturally become the second class citizens in the domain of finance. Home-building has fared particularly poorly under the regime of market allocated credit. There were fewer than 1.5 million yearly new housing starts between 1979 and 1984, less than during the previous two home-building cycles of 1973-78 and 1969-72. Total spending on non-farm residential construction averaged less than $50 billion in constant dollars, which was also below the levels of the two previous home-building cycles.[20]

From the standpoint of either equity or economic growth, the experience to date with how a deregulated banking industry allocates credit does not seem favorable.

3. Services to Consumers

The proponents of deregulation had claimed that letting the chips fall where they may would benefit small depositors. It has not happened that way. Instead, big depositors have benefited at the expense of the majority of bank depositors.

Initially—in the early 1980s—interest rate deregulation meant that small depositors could get higher interest payments, and people could get interest on their checking account balance. But growing competition led the banks to charge fees for services that previously had no fee or only a token fee. Fees for checks, deposits, etc., have grown rapidly. For large depositors, the higher interest income outweighs the higher fees, but for small depositors, the reverse is true. Thus, the new structure emerging from deregulation entails a net transfer of benefits from small depositors to large depositors.

This inequitable result was confirmed by a 1985 study of consumer banking services offered by 100 banks and savings institutions in 10 cities. The study compared annual interest received with annual service fees for different size bank accounts. It found that a person maintaining an $8000 average daily balance would, on average, *earn* $461 on the account over the year, while someone with a $1700 balance would *pay* about $35 for the account. A person with an average balance of $600 would pay almost $95 a year for the privilege of having a checking account.[21]

Deregulation has hurt the average household by increasing interest rates charged on loans. As banks lost their legally guaranteed source of free funds in demand deposits, and as interest rate ceilings were lifted, some upward movement of the general level of rates resulted. While other factors, such as tight monetary policy, explain the major part of the giant increase in interest rates in the 1980s, deregulation does account for part of the increase.[22]

The great majority of households in the U.S. are net debtors—their debts, in the form of mortgage and consumer loans, exceed their financial assets (bank balances, securities, etc.). To the extent that deregulation raised interest rates, the majority of net debtors lost more in higher interest obligations than they gained in higher interest income. The wealthy minority of net creditors gained at the expense of the majority of net debtors.

On the other hand, some benefits have accrued to the general public. The rapid spread of automatic teller machines—which is an important convenience for many—is probably partly due to the competitive pressures released by deregulation. But whatever increases in efficiency result from deregulation will tend to disproportionately benefit the rich, as competition increasingly leads the banks to focus their attention on meeting the financial needs of the rich, since the biggest profits can be made by banks in serving those with the largest financial resources.

4. Concentration

About 40,000 diverse depository institutions, including almost 15,000 banks, are in operation today in this country. Most banks are relatively small; two-thirds of them have less than $50 million in assets. Together these small banks hold only 10% of all bank assets. At the other end of the scale are 447 banks with over $500 million apiece in assets. These banks represent only 3% of the total number of banks but held almost two-thirds of all bank assets in 1983. And at the top of the pyramid are 20 giant banks, a miniscule less than one-tenth of 1% of all banks, which hold 46.2% of all domestic bank assets.[23] In the market for very large corporate loans, only a handful of giant banks can put together the consortium required for making such loans. At the other end of the scale, in many small towns a local bank exercises significant monopoly power.

While the banking system already has a significant degree of financial concentration, additional bank deregulation is bound to bring even greater concentration at the national level. Stephen A. Rhoades, a staff economist at the Fed specializing in financial structure, remarked, "I expect we will see a pretty substantial rise in national concentration in banking as geographic restrictions are loosened." The reason is simple: the old geographic restrictions prevented the giant banks in New York, Chicago, and other money centers from entering other state banking markets. Now giant banks are poised to enter other state markets, and if the gate is finally lifted, they will sharply increase their share of U.S. bank deposits by acquiring banks across the country.

Eliminating geographic barriers is not the only part of deregulation that would increase concentration. If product regulations are abolished, as the deregulationists urge, major banks will be able to establish strong positions in other financial services, such as securities dealing and insurance. This would increase the concentration of assets in the financial sector as a whole.

Apart from any particular aspect of bank deregulation, the overall impact of the process is to increase competition within the financial sector. It may seem paradoxical that more competition can lead to more concentration, but that is indeed what will happen. The underlying reason is that more intense competition will create winners and losers. Studies indicate that banks with less than $50 to $100 million in assets suffer from a cost disadvantage relative to large institutions.[24] Thus, as banking grows more competitive, small banks will have increasing difficulty surviving the challenge of bigger banks. However, some small local banks which maintain close ties with businesses and households in their communities may be able to overcome the cost disadvantage relative to big banks because many customers might prefer to patronize a small, locally-oriented bank.

As deregulation loosens the strictures against bank mergers, the big banks' drive to grow larger should produce a growing volume of bank mergers. The experienc of states like California, which have long permitted state-wide banking, suggests that the giant banks will go after, not the small local banks, but the medium-sized banks.

Deregulation thus is likely to lead to a major transformation of the structure of American banking. One or two dozen giant financial conglomerates are likely to emerge in a dominant position in the financial sector, with a fringe of one or two thousand small, locally oriented institutions playing a marginal role.[25]

While it is too early in the bank deregulation process to see the full effects on concentration, the data do show changes in direction. Bank mergers increased sharply after 1980, with the number of mergers in 1983 more than double the average annual rate between 1970 and 1979 (see Figure 10.2). The share of all domestic bank deposits held by the largest banks also rose during 1980-83, having declined somewhat from 1970-1980 (see Figure 10.3).

Comparisons of different countries' banking systems reinforce the impression that deregulation leads to banking concentration. While all major industrialized countries regulate their banking systems, other countries do not have the strict geographic and product regulations found in the U.S. The banking systems of Canada, the U.K., and West Germany are far more concentrated than the U.S. system. Japan, which maintains some barriers against setting up multiple branches of a bank, has a concentration ratio in between that of the U.S. and the other three countries (see Figure 10.4).

Nations without strict geographic or product regulations have fewer banks. In 1980, the year that deregulation became official U.S.

Figure 10.2
Bank Merger Mania

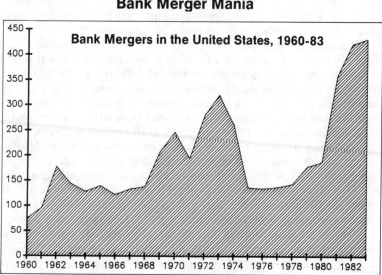

Bank Mergers in the United States, 1960-83

Source: Stephen A. Rhoades, "Mergers and Acquisitions by Commercial Banks, 1960-83," Staff Study Number 142, Board of Governors of Federal Reserve System, Washington DC, January 1985, pp 12, 13, 30.

Figure 10.3
Big Banks Get Bigger

U.S. National Banking Concentration, 1970-83		
Year	Percent of Bank Deposits Held by:	
	50 Largest Banks	100 Largest Banks
1970	38.9	48.1
1975	38.7	48.2
1980	37.0	46.8
1983	37.9	48.9

Source: Stephen A. Rhoades, "National and Local Market Banking Concentration in an Era of Interstate Banking," *Issues in Bank Regulation*, Spring 1985, p. 30. These concentration ratios are for domestic deposits only and are not strictly comparable to the other concentration ratios cited in the text.

policy, there were over 40,000 depository institutions in the U.S. That same year, West Germany, England, and Canada with a combined GNP of half the U.S. together had only 1,125 depository institutions.[26]

One can also compare the concentration of banking resources between states permitting state-wide branching by banks and states which do not. In 1982, the five top banks in each state permitting state-wide branching held an average of 75% of all bank deposits. In non-branching states each state's top five held only 41% of all bank deposits.[27] This strongly suggests eliminating geographic restrictions in the country as a whole would lead to a big increase in the national concentration rate in banking.

A major increase in financial sector concentration could undoubtedly have some beneficial consequences. Some economies of scale would be realized, as very small banks decline in numbers. In some small towns, the local monopoly held by one or two local banks might be challenged by the entry of out of town banks.

Figure 10.4
U.S. Bank Concentration in World Perspective

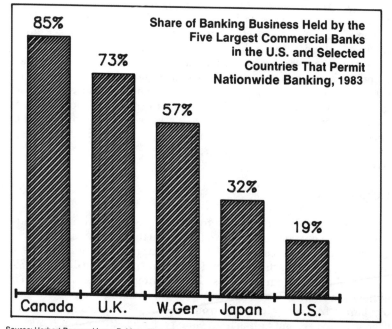

Source: Herbert Baer and Larry R. Mote, "The Effects of Nationwide Banking on Concentration: Evidence from Abroad," **Federal Reserve Bank of Chicago Economic Perspectives**, January-February, 1985, p 6, Table 1. For West Germany, Japan, and the U.S.A. the data are for bank deposits: for Canada and the U.K. the data are for lending.

Most experts believe deregulation will not increase the already high concentration of bank deposits within individual local banking markets.[28] But as the same one or two dozen giant conglomerate banks come to face each other in local markets across the country, the likelihood of collusive, monopolistic behavior could increase. One study of over 2000 local banking markets in the U.S. found that about 13% of bank profits resulted from the exercise of monopoly power in local markets.[29] Any further increase in bank monopoly power in local markets could give still greater excess profits to banks at the expense of bank customers.

But growing national bank concentration threatens small and medium-size businesses. Typically these companies, unable to tap bond and equity markets, are very dependent on bank credit for their survival and well-being. In the past, such businesses have had to rely mainly on small and medium size banks for credit, since larger banks prefer to lend to larger corporations. As deregulation reduces the numbers of small and medium size banks, it will become increasingly difficult for smaller businesses to survive. A recent study documented this danger, finding that "the credit needs of small businesses are less likely to be met in states that permit wider geographic activities [of banks]," which are the states with fewer small banks.[30]

Giant financial institutions, holding tens and even hundreds of billions of dollars in assets, have a great deal of economic and political power. The financial sector has the funds which are essential to business activity throughout the economy. Greater concentration would confer even greater economic power upon large financial conglomerates, whose decisions would largely determine which industries and companies would grow and which would wither. And greater economic power would surely lead to greater political power. If past history is any guide, the large banks would use such power to encourage monopolistic collusion among, and to aid and promote mergers among, nonfinancial corporations.[31]

Conclusion

Partly as a result of its failure to deliver on its promises, the bank deregulation process sputtered and stalled in the mid-1980s. Consumer groups, small businesses, and smaller financial institutions have loudly pointed to the problems and have had an effect. In June of 1985, the U.S. Supreme Court dealt a setback to interstate banking, when it upheld the right of states to form regional banking compacts which bar banks from certain states from entering.[32] Such compacts have been used to keep out banks from New York and other major banking centers.

It is still possible, however, that the deregulationists will regain the momentum they had earlier. If this happens, it is likely that problems encountered so far will grow more severe. And full success for the deregulation movement would lead us into a severely unstable world, similar in some respects to the 1920s.

It would be better to reform today's financial regulatory system. The reform should assure wide access to credit at a reasonable cost, while safeguarding the stability of the financial system. Financial institutions should offer services in an efficient and equitable manner, and should contribute to the goals of full employment, productivity growth, the survival of stable neighborhood communities, technical and social innovation and other valued social objectives.

The first step in this reform proposal should be to end pork barrel politics of regulation and make regulators accountable to the general public rather than to closed circles of influential industrialists. The Fed and other institutions that oversee the financial system should not be insulated from popular pressures and oversight, and their actions should not be shrouded in secrecy. Federal financial institutions should be run by people who are democratically accountable to the broad public which is affected by their decisions.

Such a move would not only be politically desirable; it would also be economically effective. The central problem with past regulation has been the attempt to carry it out through quasi-independent boards or commissions of so-called experts. Such experts tend to be sympathetic to the industry being regulated. And it is not difficult for the regulated industry to gain substantial influence over a small group of overseers who are not directly responsible to a broader constituency. The waste and socially irrational priorities of the defense contracting and nuclear power industries offer good case studies of the negative results of "in-house" regulation.

Regulators, democratically chosen and democratically replaceable, would be more difficult targets for industrial lobbyists. And the re-election incentive should encourage regulatory decisions that favor the majority. Most important, inefficient and wasteful policies are rarely in the interest of a majority. A small group usually promotes policies which enlarge its slice, but shrink the whole pie.

This first step would go a long way toward accomplishing an important second step in regulatory reform: the maintenance of reasonable interest rates, not the punishingly high rates of recent years. Low interest rates would have beneficial effects both for equity and growth.

Since the unregulated market will not allocate credit to the most productive and the most socially important uses, the newly democratic regulatory institutions should establish a system of credit allocation. That is, broad priorities should be set for the allocation of credit among different types of users. Such a system could be enforced through the regulatory institutions.

The basic difficulty in creating an effective regulatory system is that the regulations tend to clash with the regulated institutions' profit motive. The problems of excessive risk-taking, high concentration, growing service charges, and an undesirable allocation of credit all stem from the banks' pursuit of profits at the expense of the public interest. If banks are to perform their critical functions in a manner that serves the public interest, there must be an internal restructuring of bank incentives. Otherwise, the best conceived regulatory system will fail to operate effectively.

Some types of financial institutions have long been structured to pursue aims other than profits. Examples include cooperative credit unions and mutual life insurance companies. Banks should be restructured along lines similar to such institutions. Bank profits would be retained in the bank or distributed to depositors, rather than belonging to outside shareholders. Public representatives should be added to bank boards of directors. Such internal restructuring would move banks away from a single-minded pursuit of profits and toward a direct concern with the effective provision of financial services to the public.

With a reformed internal structure for banks and a democratic structure for the regulatory institutions, it should be possible to have a banking system that achieves the aims of stability, wide access to credit at a reasonable cost, and efficient and equitable provision of services. Replacing the profit motive with other aims should serve to direct institutional behavior away from monopolistic pursuits and the arbitrary exercise of private power in the economic and political sphere. The public credit allocation procedure mentioned above would help to steer credit in socially desirable directions. The regulators could require that a certain percentage of each bank's loan funds be allocated to smaller business loans, including new forms such as cooperatives. This would help deal with the problem of the concentrated banking industry's unequal treatment of small and big business. And a reduced role for the profit motive should help solve the problem of excessive risk-taking in an environment in which institutional failure has been, and should be, practically ruled out for large institutions.

Footnotes

1. *The New York Times*, May 21, 1984, p. 1, and May 17, 1984, p. 1.
2. *The New York Times*, May 20, 1984, p. F1, F8.
3. *The New York Times*, "U.S. Begins Deregulation Review on Rights and Ecology Guidelines," August 13, 1981.
4. These figures are for 1980 through the first half of 1984. U.S. Bureau of Labor Statistics, *Employment, Hours, and Earnings, United States, 1909-84*, vol. II, p. 647 and Vol. I, p. 6. The data are for SIC 421 and 432, Trucking and Trucking Terminals.
5. Leading conservative economics thinkers include Milton Friedman, George Stigler, and in the area of deregulation, Murray Weidenbaum.
6. *Wall Street Journal*, January 7, 1985, p. 50.
7. *The New York Times*, January 24, 1984, Section IV, p. 1.
8. *FTC:Watch*, "Miller Says Private Litigation by Heirs Preferable to Government Action in Some Hazardous Product Defect Cases," December 1982.
9. A thorough presentation of the new orthodox position on deregulation of banking is found in George J. Benston, "Federal Regulation of Banking: Analysis and Policy Recommendations," *Journal of Bank Research*, Winter 1983, pp. 211-244.
10. Liberal economists generally agree that the government must regulate the overall level of production and employment but that only limited intervention, at most, is needed for particular industries.
11. *The New York Times*, August 15, 1985, p. D7.
12. *The New York Times*, December 27, 1984, p. D1.
13. *The New York Times*, August 15, 1985, p.D7.
14. Eugene D. Short, "FDIC Settlement Practices and the Size of Failed Banks," *Federal Reserve Bank of Dallas Economic Review*, March 1985, p. 12-20.
15. *Economic Report of the President*, 1985, Table B-1, p. 232, and Table B-19, p. 254. 1984 figures are preliminary.
16. *The New York Times*, March 7, 1984, p. 31.
17. Richard Medley, "High Interest Rates: It's Not Just the Deficit," *Economic Policy Institute Briefing Paper*, June 1985, p. 9.
18. *Statistical Abstract of the U.S.*, 1985, p. 502, Table 843; and *Economic Report of the President*, 1985, Table B-1, p. 232.
19. *The New York Times*, March 7, 1984, p. D23 and March 8, 1984, p. D4.
20. *Economic Report of the President*, 1985, Table B-47, p. 286 and Table B-2, p. 234.
21. *Consumer Reports*, September 1985, pp. 508-9.

22. Lawrence Chimerine of Chase Econometrics estimated that deregulation of interest rates paid to depositors raised the long-term inflation-corrected rate of interest in the U.S. by about 1.5%. Reported in Kenneth H. Bacon, "Flexible Interest Rates May Add to Stability," *Wall Street Journal*, November 7, 1983.

23. Data are for 1983. *Statistical Abstract of the U.S.*, 1985, p. 491, Table 817; and William A. Lovett, Testimony before the House Committee on Banking, Finance and Urban Affairs, 11 April 1984, Table 1.

24. William A. Lovett, "The Revolution in U.S. Banking," *Challenge*, 27(5), November-December 1984, pp. 41-46.

25. See George Kaufman, Larry Mote, and Harvey Rosenblum, "Implications of Deregulation for Product Lines and Geographical Markets of Financial Institutions," *Journal of Bank Research*, Spring 1983, pp. 17-19.

26. *Savings and Loan News*, September 1980, p. 37. Germany had 800, England 225 and Canada 100.

27. Herbert Baer and Larry R. Mote, "The Effects of Nationwide banking on Concentration: Evidence from Abroad," *Federal Reserve Bank of Chicago Economic Perspectives*, January-February 1985, p. 4.

28. A study of 209 metropolitan area banking markets and 104 non-metropolitan county banking markets across the U.S. in 1981 found that the 3 largest banks held two-thirds of the bank deposits in the average metropolitan market and four-fifths of the bank deposits in the average non metropolitan county market. From Stephen Rhoades, "National and Local Market Banking Concentration in an Era of Interstate Banking," *Issues in Bank Regulation*, Spring 1985, p. 33.

29. S.A. Rhoades, "Welfare Loss, Redistribution Effect, and Restriction of Output Due to Monopoly in Banking," *Journal of Monetary Economics*, 9, 1982, pp. 375-87.

30. Peter L. Struck and Lewis Mandell, "The Effect of Bank Deregulation on Small Business: A Note," *Journal of Finance*, 38(3), June 1983, p. 1030.

31. See David Kotz, *Bank Control of Large Corporations in the United States*, University of California Press, Berkeley, 1978.

32. *The New York Times*, June 11, 1985, p. D1.

11 Long Shadow of Global Debt

Brazil will not pay its foreign debt with recession, nor with unemployment, nor with hunger. We believe that in settling this account at such high social and economic costs we would then have to surrender our freedom, for a debt paid for with poverty is an account paid for with democracy.
— Jose Sarney, President of Brazil[1]
United, Nations, September 23, 1985

...The Foreign debt cannot be paid off by any of our countries...It is either debt or democracy. This is the crux of the current Latin American situation and we must decide which road to take.
— Alan Garcia, President of Peru[2]
United Nations, September 23, 1985

I certainly didn't borrow the money.
— Baby sitter in Nezahuacoyotl, Mexico[3]

Conservative economics, by raising interest rates and the value of the dollar, has sent U.S. exports of goods plunging. But the export of conservative economics itself, under the guise of "austerity" and "stabilization," has mushroomed, partly in response to the very problems it has generated.

The monetarist tightening of 1979-82 drove not just the U.S. but the rest of the world economy into the most profound downturn since the 1930s. Declining demand in the industrialized economies led to falling export revenues for the primary commodity producers of the Third World. At the same time, the high interest rates associated with the conservative strategy drove up interest payments on debt. Squeezed from both sides, the bubble finally burst. By late 1982, a full-fledged debt crisis threatened the stability of the international financial system. It has not abated since.

Into the chaos has stepped the International Monetary Fund (IMF), an institution closely associated with the U.S. and international bankers. Its strategy for managing the debt problem parallels the conservative approach adopted domestically by the Federal Reserve System. To sustain bank profitability and avoid the financial collapse that would come from acknowledging "bad" loans, the IMF has insisted that debtor countries maintain their payments to international creditors. Meanwhile, workers and peasants have seen their living standards eroded by IMF mandated austerity measures: high levels of unemployment, cuts in social services, runaway inflation in food and other necessities and rapidly falling real incomes.

This conservative approach on a global scale is not only as unfair, inefficient, and wasteful as it is domestically; it also undermines the likelihood that the debt crisis can ever be resolved. The belt-tightening, contractionary policies pushed by the IMF mean that bankers seek ever-larger slices out of ever-shrinking pies. Such austerity sharpens conflicts between haves and have nots, with ballooning debts undermining dictatorships and democracies alike. In the long run additional repression of democratic rights may be resorted to as governments enforce the always-unpopular regime of financial austerity.

Why a Crisis?

The international banks have made many foolish loans and now we can only pray they will make some more of them.
        —Arthur Burns, Former chair of the Federal Reserve[4]

Question: The banks seem to be very worried about the level of Third World debt and they are facing some serious losses, aren't they?

Answer: Not at all. The banks are making a killing off the debt crisis, just as the oil companies did in the 1974 oil crisis.
        —international financial consultant[5]

The origins of the debt crisis are rooted in the structure of the post-war international financial system and in the processes of Third World development. Aggravated by the 1973 oil price increase, the 1974-1975 recession, and declining terms of trade, the Third World's trade deficits led to increased borrowing. The target of the banks' lending were most often those countries willing to move to a strategy of export promotion and misery-led growth. Unfortunately for the banks, it is precisely the authoritarian economic wonders of the 1970s that became the problem debtors of the 1980s.

Recent IMF estimates have placed the 1985 debt for all indebted developing countries at $865.3 billion—almost 40% of their annual output in the same year.[6] In nominal terms, this figure represents more than a sixfold increase from the external debt of 1973; in real terms—in actual Third World resources claimed by foreign creditors—the debt has almost tripled.[7]

Latin America and the Caribbean hold $357.1 billion or about 40% of the developing world's debt. This translates into $4,000 of debt per household in the region. Within Latin America, the debt is even more concentrated: Mexico, Brazil, and Argentina, hold more than 60% of the region's total.[8]

The loaning side of the debt is also highly concentrated. In 1981, for example, twenty-four U.S. banks held 80% of all U.S. private loans to non-oil developing countries (NODC's).[9] The nine largest U.S. banks held 60% of the loans; for these nine banks, loans to NODC's amounted to 221% of their capital (assets minus liabilities).[10] For one major bank, Citicorp, loans to Brazil alone represented 93.7% of capital.[11]

From the bankers' point of view, extensive bank exposure and high concentration of borrowers and lenders give rise to fears that a major debtor might refuse to honor its debt obligations and default. Such a failure to pay could wipe out individual banks and severely damage the international financial system. The point of view from the other side of the credit window is exactly reversed: continuing to pay is retarding economic growth and threatening social stability. It is this conflict of views and interests that has put the banks on a collision course with democracy in the Third World.

How did such a dangerous situation develop? Why did the banks loan? And why did the debtor nations borrow?

Why the Banks Loaned

The reasons for the increased bank exposure in the Third World are, in part, rooted in the international financial system that prevailed throughout the 1950s and 1960s. Labelled the 'Bretton Woods System' after the 1944 conference in Bretton Woods, New Hampshire which set it up, the post-war international financial order codified the dominant presence of the U.S. by making the U.S. dollar the *key* international currency. As the key currency, the U.S. dollar was backed by gold and could serve as a means of payment for the international transactions of any nation. U.S. dollars, therefore, lubricated trade not just between the U.S. and its trading partners but also between those trading partners themselves.

This role of the dollar as *the* international currency allowed the U.S. to run persistent balance of payments deficits, i.e., spend more dollars abroad on imports and foreign investment than were returned to the U.S. to purchase exports and invest here. These deficits were aggravated by the extensive worldwide military establishment and involvement in the Vietnam War necessitated by the U.S.'s responsibility as international policeman. Any other country would have had to take action to correct such payments deficits; however, the role of the dollar as the international currency meant that other nations were willing to accept dollars despite having no plans to purchase U.S. products.[12] The result was a vast expansion of international dollar holdings.[13]

Meanwhile, the long post-war boom encouraged an ethic of "go-go" banking. With corporate profit rates high in the mid-1960s and growth proceeding apace, new resources were constantly being generated to pay back bank credit. Eager to cash in on the profits and growth, U.S. bank officers sought to expand their domestic loans. And with the world awash in dollars, both U.S. banks and their European counterparts also began to aggressively market dollar-denominated loans abroad. This new ethic of international "go-go" banking and the prior expansion of international dollar holdings were the backdrop to an event that marked the beginning of the debt explosion in the Third World: the 1973 "oil crisis."

The quadrupling of oil prices in 1973 put strains on both the real and financial sectors of the world economy. The increase in the price of such an important input naturally added to inflation in the oil-importing bills of both developed and developing economies. Responding to these new inflationary pressures, as well as to the threat that rising wages posed for corporate profitability, Western governments, especially the United States, adopted the time-honored conservative deflationary strategy: repressing total demand for goods and services. The result was a global recession.

The effects of these two events—the oil price increase and the recession in the industrialized North—were severe for Third World trade and payments balances. The oil bill for the non-oil developing countries (NODC's) rose from $7 billion in 1973 to $24 billion in 1974.[14]

Meanwhile, growth in export volume collapsed as world recession reduced markets for Third World exports. The Third World's terms of trade—the price of NODC exports relative to the price of their imports—fell dramatically in both 1974 and 1975. As a result, real export earnings—what countries could actually purchase with their exports—fell and the NODC trade deficit rose four-fold in just two years, from $10.8 billion in 1973 to $40.2 billion in 1975.[15]

The effects of the "oil shock" on production levels, trade balances, and the terms of trade were accompanied by a unique financial phenomenon. As dollars flowed from Western and Third World hands to OPEC coffers, bankers, and economists worried that the drain of funds from the West would cause a credit shortage in the advanced capitalist nations. The worry was short-lived; like any smart investor, the OPEC nations begin salting away a large percentage of their dollar holdings in the safe havens of European and U.S. banks.

This created a new problem: "recycling" of the petrodollars. With recession in the Western nations, loan demand was insufficient to absorb or recycle the OPEC surpluses. International bankers turned to Third World borrowers and their gaping current account deficits (the current account includes trade in both goods and services). Facing rising oil bills and eager to take advantage of newly available credit lines, Third World countries borrowed heavily. This solution— borrowing recycled petrodollars to finance both oil purchases and development—was viewed by bankers as a rousing success. As late as 1981, Citibank's president Walter Wriston was insisting that "...those of us who believed the market would work [were] proved correct."[16] By late 1982, when many of the major borrowers proved unable to meet debt payments, bankers would sound a great deal less confident about their earlier lending practices.

Why the Third World Borrowed

In the process of their own historical evolution, many now advanced capitalist nations borrowed from abroad to finance economic development; much of the U.S. railroad construction, for example, was financed by English capital. The Third World has also sought financing for what might be labeled a "structural deficit" integral to the development process.

Growth in developing economies often requires the import of capital equipment and materials necessary for new and ongoing industries. If export revenues are insufficient to cover import bills, continued economic growth requires that this structural deficit be made up with foreign capital inflows. These financial inflows basically take three forms: aid, borrowing from banks or multilateral institutions (like the World Bank), or foreign investment.

The similar need for foreign capital inflows in the development process masks important differences between the Third World and the now advanced capitalist nations. The Third World reality is not merely a page from the past of the developed nations. Third World economic and social structures are profoundly different and are indeed intertwined with the development of the advanced capitalist world. Often colonized and developed by foreign powers as primary commodity producers, the Third World remains quite dependent on the exports of these products. The problem is that the prices of these commodities are very volatile, fluctuating dramatically with swings in the world business cycle. This makes export revenues also volatile; a recession in the advanced capitalist world can stretch a small structural deficit into a gaping trade imbalance. In such a situation, the short-term alternatives are equally distasteful. Addressing the trade imbalance through import reduction will reduce growth; financing the imbalance through borrowing will increase debt.

Worse yet, the price of Third World exports relative to their imports—the terms of trade—have been on a steady decline in the last twenty years. For the non-oil developing countries (NODC's), the terms of trade have fallen by more than 30% between 1965 and 1984, with the vast majority of that decline occurring between 1977 and 1982.[17]

Such a fall implies two things. First, the benefits of any increase in Third World productivity and the resulting economic surplus are being siphoned off to the advanced capitalist nations. To see this, consider that even if the increase in the productivity growth of an average Third World worker exceeds Western productivity growth by 30%—at the increasingly unfavorable terms of trade—this productivity growth is merely sufficient to purchase the *same* product from the U.S. or Europe. Second, the long-term decline in the terms of trade implies that the structural deficit is widening. And since foreign aid has been on the decline (dropping from .5% of developed countries' GNP in 1960 to .3% in 1983),[18] addressing this problem has increasingly required more borrowing or more encouragement of foreign investment.

For the Third World, however, foreign investment has its problems. Besides increasing foreign control of their economies, the profit outflow to foreign investors, like the declining terms of trade, implies a transfer of the surplus Third World economies produce. Borrowing presents the same problem; interest payments to creditors must be financed out of a surplus created from a productive local investment of the borrowed capital. And both the profit and interest payments add to the structural deficit. They, too, require an outflow of resources that may be unmatched by export revenues.

It was pressure from these structural deficits that led to a wave of Third World balance of payments problems in the mid- to late 1960s.[19] Dealing with the problems involved fresh waves of borrowing. In turn, creditors—both private banks and particularly official institutions like the International Monetary Fund—made new credit contingent upon adoption of a new conservative development strategy.

This strategy represented a rejection of the earlier nationalist economic policies of import-substitution, which aimed to industrialize by protecting local manufacturers from imports. Labeled "outward-looking," the new conservative approach to development called for lowering tariff barriers, promoting exports, and encouraging foreign investment. Wages were to be kept low to keep exports competitive and to attract multinational investment. Authoritarian regimes which repressed trade unions and workers' movements were often part of the package.

This package of policies had its contradictions. While conservatives claimed that export promotion would alleviate the structural deficit, increased exports also increased reliance on the volatile swings of the world market. The expanded presence of multinationals left countries vulnerable to a peculiar form of "blackmail"—the threat to move operations to other developing countries unless wages and tax burdens were kept low. On a social level, the low-wage, high-repression, strategy gave the deceptive appearance of calm while underlying social tensions simmered. Nonetheless, this strategy did promote (for example, in Brazil) what we might term "misery-led growth"—a growth pattern that highly rewards local elites and foreign investors while delivering few, if any, benefits to Third World workers and peasants. And this economic growth was fuelled by increasing loans from the private bankers who had faith in the conservative strategy.

The pattern of huge loans in the 1970s to repressive export-oriented regimes is striking. Brazil became a darling of the banking community, with its debt soaring from $13.8 billion in 1973 to $88.2 billion in 1982 (all increases in this paragraph are in current dollars). South Korea, a strategic U.S. ally and a prime example of the authoritarian export strategy, increased its debt almost eightfold over the same period. The monetarist "free market" experiment of the Pinochet dictatorship in Chile—which drastically lowered real wages and doubled the unemployment rate—was rewarded with a fourfold increase in loans between 1975 and 1982. The 1976 military coup in Argentina was labeled the "coup of credit": slashing real wages by over 30% and pursuing "free trade" led to an inflow of almost $30 billion in new loans between 1976 and 1982, a quadrupling of the external debt in six short years. The exceptions to this pattern were resource-rich countries like Mexico. Borrowing on the basis of oil reserves and not simply repression, Mexico also quadrupled its debt between 1976 and 1982.[20]

What Was Done With the Loans?

As in the case of the growing indebtedness of the U.S. economy, much of the increased borrowing did not go to productive investments that would promote economic development and support the long-run ability to repay. The authoritarian model implied an increased role for the military; they used their enhanced role to squander significant amounts of national resources on imported armaments. One study reports that for the twenty countries with the largest foreign debt "arms imports between 1976 and 1980 were equivalent to 20% of the increase in debt."[21] In addition, capital flight mounted as Third World elites often siphoned away the new loans from productive purposes at home and deposited the money in their own high interest-paying foreign accounts.

Following the dictates of the conservative "free market" approach, the new Third World borrowers had removed restrictions and allowed the easy outflow of currency; where restrictions existed, inventive elites found ways to circumvent regulations. According to one account, $30 billion—half of the new debt incurred between 1976 and 1982—was spirited out of Mexico and into foreign banks.[22] William Cline, an economist at the Institute for International Economics, has conservatively estimated that "recent capital flight has contributed nearly one-third of total debt in both Venezuela and Argentina."[23] A similarly large outflow occurred elsewhere and was aggravated in the early 1980s by the high interest rates that attracted capital to the U.S.

Thus, while workers and peasants tighten their belts to pay the banks, the banks return portions of this via interest payments to Third World elites. In the debt crisis, not only are Third World nations in conflict with Western banks; Third World workers and farmers are in conflict with their local elites.

The Crisis is Triggered

> *[The debt crisis] is like a neutron bomb in which men and women remain alive, but all that generates wealth is destroyed. It is as though madness has taken over the financial centers.*
> —Argentine President Raul Alfonsin[24]

> *The fact is that Latin America cannot pay, and it cannot continue postponing development.*
> —Peruvian President Alan Garcia[25]

In 1979, the world economy was subjected to two major changes. The first, often blamed for subsequent economic difficulties, was the second wave of oil price increases. In one year, the price of a barrel of crude rose from $14 to over $30, adding to inflationary pressures that were already present in Western and developing economies.[26]

The second change in 1979 was more severe and would have longer lasting effects: the beginning of the new conservative strategy in the U.S. The falling value of the dollar and rising U.S. inflation in the 1970s rankled the international bankers; both trends implied that their dollar-denominated loans were rapidly losing real value. The tight money policies adopted by the Fed in 1979 restored the dominance of the U.S. dollar at the cost of unemployment for U.S. workers and world economic recession. These tight money policies also triggered the Third World debt crisis as the effects of conservative economics in the U.S. spilled into financial and trade markets to the rest of the world.

With the downturn in the industrialized world, demand collapsed for the primary products of the Third World. Both the volume of trade and prices for Third World exports dropped. For the NODC's, the growth in export volume went from 8.7% in 1980 to 1.8% in 1982, far below the 1967-76 annual average of 6.7%. Meanwhile, the prices of NODC non-oil commodities fell by 15.2% in 1981 and 13.4% in 1982, again diverging from the 1967-76 average of a 7.3% annual *increase*. For the developing countries as a whole, export revenues—which had increased 19.7% annually over the same 1967-76 period—fell by 1% in 1981 and by another 12% in 1982.[27]

Added to this drop in export revenue was a rising outflow of debt payments. Roughly two thirds of the Third World debt was contracted with variable interest rates—rates that vary according to changes in the London Interbank Offer Rate (LIBOR).[28] LIBOR is the benchmark interest rate for dollar-denominated loans in European financial markets. Since what lenders are really concerned with is the real rate of interest—the nominal interest rate minus the rate of inflation—these variable rates allow the banks to protect their earnings by raising interest charges to keep pace with inflation.

Given the increasing interconnectedness of world financial markets, the U.S. monetarist approach raised the nominal level of both the U.S. prime rate and LIBOR; at the same time, the induced recession lowered inflation. From the U.S. banker's view, the combination meant that real interest rates—the LIBOR rate minus U.S. wholesale price inflation—rose from an average of -.8% between 1971-80 (or 1.66% from 1961-80) to 7.5% in 1981 and 11.0% in 1982.[29] According to the IMF, the real interest rate from the view of the indebted Third World—the nominal rate in money markets minus price changes in their exports—reached almost 20% in 1982.[30]

The results of these two trends—stagnant exports and rising interest rates—were disastrous. In 1982, nominal export revenues for the indebted developing countries had dipped *below* the 1980 figure; meanwhile the nominal value of interest payments had risen almost 60% over the same period. By 1982, the debt service ratio—the proportion of export earnings that go to pay both interest and amortization—had reached 24.6% for the indebted Third World. For Latin America and the Caribbean, more than 50% of export earnings were finding their way to the international lenders. For Argentina, debt service had risen to an unsustainable 102.9% of exports![31]

The first country to get cut up in the scissors of falling inflows and rising outflows was Mexico. With an oil boom pushing economic growth, the Mexican government and Mexican companies had borrowed $60 billion—almost $1,000 for each man, woman and child in Mexico—between 1976 and 1982.[32] As the world recession lowered both oil and other export revenues, Mexico suspended principal payments on its debt and approached its international creditors for a rescheduling, i.e., a postponement of current payments and an infusion of new loans. Argentina, battered by its defeat in the Malvinas/Falklands and the conservative economic policies of its military rulers, fell behind on payments and requested rescheduling as well. These events sent shock waves through the international banking community. The debt crisis was on.

It was worsened by the response of the banks themselves. Frightened by the Mexican suspension, the banks sharply curtailed the flow of new funds to developing countries.[33] As a result, countries like Brazil and Yugoslavia that had counted on new funds to meet old debt obligations ran into problems.

Having helped to create the problem of overindebtedness, the banks now wanted to bail out of the Third World—but continue to receive their profits. When eventually forced to reschedule old loans and extend new credits to avoid defaults, they raised the so-called "spread"—what banks charge borrowers above the LIBOR rate at which banks loan to each other. The effect in Mexico's case was to double the profit potential of the loans on paper and add to the long-term problem by increasing the overall outflow of interest payments.[34]

The conservative economic strategy launched in 1979 by Volcker's Fed had two pronounced goals: reducing inflation and protecting the dollar and thereby, it was argued, increasing the stability of the international financial system. U.S. inflation was indeed reduced but at the cost of depressing the world economy. For the developing world, growth rates plummeted from their 6% average in the period 1967-76 to around 1.5% in 1982 and 1983.[35] For Latin America and the Caribbean, the fall from its 1967-76 growth trend meant the loss of a tremendous amount of potential output. Our most conservative estimate of this lost output in the years 1980-83 is $327 billion (in 1984 dollars)—almost enough to pay off the entire Latin American debt![36]

The economic costs of the conservative strategy can also be estimated in terms of their effects on the debt itself. William Cline has estimated that for 1981-82 the combined effects of abnormally high interest rates, terms of trade deterioration, and export volume reduction added $141 billion to the debt of the NODC's.[37] The 27.5% increase in the real value of the dollar over the same period had the effect of inflating by about one-quarter the Third World resources claimed by the dollar-denominated debt. It was as though $131 billion had been added to the 1980 debt without a single trip to the bank.[38]

Given both the output loss and the debt increase attributable to the conservative strategy, it is hard to claim that conservative economics accomplished its second goal—protecting the stability of the international economy. While the high-interest policies raised the value of the dollar, the international financial system as a whole has been wracked by the strains of the growing debt crisis.

Dealing With the Crisis

For the IMF, it's OK that there is hunger, that there is unemployment, that governments fall.

—Economist in Ecuador[39]

While the Third World debt problem is rooted in the long-term processes of economic development and the declining terms of trade, it became a "crisis" when the banker-promoted conservative strategy of tight money transformed the structural development deficit into an uncontrollable hemorrhaging of Third World resources. To deal with the crisis, bankers turned to an institution long associated with a conservative economic approach: the International Monetary Fund (IMF).

The IMF's official role is to provide credit to countries having difficulties with their balance of payments—the inflows and outflows of currency associated with trade and capital flows. In keeping with the precepts of a capitalist economy, votes on IMF policies are determined by wealth; those countries who have the most currency in the Fund have the most decision-making power. The U.S., for example, has less than 1% of the total population of IMF member countries, but exercises one-fifth of the voting power, enough to veto a series of major Fund decisions that require an 85% "special majority."[40]

The inability of developing countries to make shrinking export revenues meet rising debt obligations—to cope with a worsening deficit—is precisely a balance of payments problem. Stepping into the debt crisis, the IMF has both provided funds to meet obligations and coordinated debt renegotiations with private banks. In return for these favors, the Fund insists that countries agree to a conservative set of policy measures, a so-called stabilization program.

IMF stabilization programs generally consist of three major measures. The first involves devaluation of the local currency. The theory here is that lowering the currency's value should encourage exports by lowering their price; likewise, the increased local price of imports should lead to their reduction. If the theory works, the increase in export production should offset the decrease in imports, both closing the trade deficit and promoting growth.

In the stagnant world markets of the 1980s, increasing exports has been difficult. Instead, Third World nations have been forced to reduce deficits through import reduction. The problem is that most Third World imports, particularly imported capital and intermediate goods, are critical for investment and production; for example, in a sample of seven Latin debtors, capital goods and intermediates accounted for almost 65% of imports in 1983.[41] Slashing imports has therefore reduced both local investment and GDP growth. In Ghana, for example, it is estimated that shortages of some imported intermediates mean that some industries can operate at only 20% capacity.[42]

The second standard IMF measure involves cutting back government spending, particularly by cutting back social services and consumer price subsidies. The latter measure cuts significantly into the living standards of working people since in many developing countries price subsidies are used to keep the price of basic foodstuffs (such as tortillas and beans in Mexico) within the reach of the ordinary consumer.

In the IMF's conservative theory, these drastic cuts reduce government deficits and the inflation they can induce. According to this view, any reduction in output due to cuts in government and consumer spending should be offset by the devaluation-prompted export increase. However, as noted above, export increases have been minimal and thus the reduction in government expenditures has *reduced* growth rates. Moreover, the combination of devaluation, cuts in subsidies, and reductions in national growth rates (which can create scarcities and also reduce tax revenues, adding to deficits) have actually *fuelled* the inflation the Fund purports to stop.[43] In Latin America, where almost every country is operating under IMF guidelines, the inflation rate has more than doubled since 1980.[44]

The third major IMF measure is often the least discussed. The Fund generally requires that governments hold a tough line on increases in money wages; with inflation and reductions in basic price subsidies, this implies a reduction in the real purchasing power of a worker's pay. Indeed, our own research has found that the single most significant and consistent change associated with IMF programs in Latin America through the late 1960s and 1970s was a reduction in the wage share of national income.[45] It is little wonder that labor unions, like the Argentine General Confederation of Workers (CGT), often greet the adoption of an IMF agreement with protests and calls for general strikes.

The IMF rationale for such regressive redistribution is simple conservative theory: lower wages will reduce consumption, make exports more competitive, and increase profits and investment. Unfortunately for the theory and for the people of the developing world, lower wages have performed few wonders beyond reducing consumption. Starving workers for a temporary export cost advantage cannot overcome the stagnation of world trade. New investment will not occur when both foreign and domestic markets look weak. Indeed, in Latin America, gross domestic investment fell by 13% in 1982 and by another 15.6% in 1983.[46] Even foreign investment—which the IMF's programs claim to encourage—has collapsed; for the major debtors, new foreign direct investment is down from $6.3 billion in 1981-1982 to $2.7 billion in 1983-1984.[47] As one U.S. banker in Sao Paolo put it, "Business people are simply paralyzed. No one is prepared to take any risks."[48]

The IMF's "trickle-down" economics of reduced government services and lower wages may be more appropriately labeled "squeeze-up"—squeeze the poorest so that the wealthy may benefit. Such an approach has done little for the continuing problems of low growth rates and high unemployment in the Third World; even optimistic IMF projections do not see growth rates in the latter part of the decade recovering to their 1967-76 average.[49] This baseline scenario relies on continued growth and no increase in trade protection in the industrial economies coupled with the reduction of fiscal deficits in the U.S. and the Third World. All these events seem increasingly unlikely. The costs of such low growth for the Third World are severe. In Africa, for example, the World Bank's best scenario sees a decline in real per capita earnings until 1995.[50] In Latin America, real per capita income for 1984 was 14% lower than in 1981.[51]

The reaction to IMF austerity and redistribution has been social unrest. Riots broke out after an IMF program was imposed in the Dominican Republic, killing 60, wounding 200, leading to 4300 arrests.[52] The pattern of strikes and riots in response to IMF imposed measures has been repeated through Latin America and Africa. Third World politicians are clearly worried. In subsequently rejecting the IMF program that prompted the violence, the Dominican Planning Minister noted that "It is not that we are unwilling to put our own house in order. It is that we want to keep our house and not let it go up in flames."[53]

The IMF's squeeze-up strategy in individual countries has been paralleled by a redistribution of income and wealth at a global level. In one recent study, the Inter-American Development Bank (IDB) calculated the net transfer of resources due to the debt by subtracting interest payments from net disbursements of debt (new debt minus the amortization of old debt). From a net financial resource inflow of $18 billion in 1981, Latin America had moved to a resource outflow of almost the same amount in 1983. Under one projection, this outflow will approach $40 billion annually by the end of the decade. Even under the most optimistic—and unlikely—projections of high growth rates and a rapid increase in new loans, the net outflow of financial resources caused by the debt will continue until 1989.[54]

This outflow of resources is accruing to a combination of Western banks and official creditors (governments and multilateral institutions). While we in the U.S. retain the image of the Western world aiding Third World development, the debt crisis has made the current picture quite the reverse. The countries of Latin America are now financing Western development and not the other way around.

The only way the Third World can maintain this monetary transfer to the West is ultimately through transferring real resources. The real counterpart of a net financial outflow (net of new loan disbursements and foreign investment) involves a trade surplus—

shipping other countries more of our own goods than we take in of theirs.

To pay the debt, then, Latin America has taken the modest trade deficits of the late 1970s and transformed them into large surpluses. As noted before, this has been achieved not so much by expanding exports as by drastically reducing imports. The resulting trade surpluses have allowed interest payments to be maintained but have worsened the U.S. trade deficit by reducing developing country imports of U.S. products. Indeed, *Business Week* estimates that the reduction of exports to the Third World cost more than a million U.S. jobs between 1980 and 1984.[55] Paying the banks is lengthening unemployment lines in both the advanced capitalist and developing worlds.

Finally, the Third World's burden of debt payments can be measured in more human terms. Like feudal serfs required to spend part of their year working on the lord's estate, Latin Americans now devote an average of nearly a month each year laboring to generate the resources required for debt repayment.[56] Coupled with the wastefulness produced by the global application of conservative economics and the specific country-level austerity policies of the IMF, the Third World is being condemned to underdevelopment and social upheaval. The limits to this strategy were noted in a May 1984 statement by four Latin American presidents which read: "(Our) people's yearning for development, the progress of democracy in (the) region and the economic security of (the) continent are seriously jeopardized... Our nations cannot indefinitely accept these hazards."[57]

Prospects and Solutions

> *...It is not good to squeeze the debtor. Dead men don't pay debts.*
> —Andres Townsend, Peruvian congressman and
> secretary-general of the Latin American Parliament[58]

There are, in general, two basic strategies for getting a debtor to pay his/her debts. The first involves a stick: coercion and intimidation are used to insist that the debtor hand over part of his/her existing resources as repayment. This policy follows the zero-sum logic of conservative economics—my gain must be your loss—and threatens both economic growth and political democracy. Unfortunately, it has served so far as the basis of the U.S. and IMF approach to the debt crisis.

The second strategy for debt repayment involves a carrot: let the debtor work and produce—indeed, promote production—and hope to be repaid from the new resources generated. This latter approach follows the pro-growth logic of democratic economics. It recognizes that the Third World's loss has *not* been our economic gain and demands that U.S. commitment to democracy be extended to its policies toward its global neighbors.

Until now, the debt crisis has actually been associated with a wave of democratization in Latin America, in part because the debt problems of the early 1980s made clear the economic mismanagement of military regimes. Already under attack for human rights violations, the authoritarians lost what little legitimacy they had when they could no longer boast of economic growth. In Brazil, Argentina, and Uruguay military governments handed over both political power and economic crisis to democratically elected leaders.

The increasing danger, however, is that bank pressure for repayment may force these governments to maintain unpopular policies and so promote the reemergence of authoritarianism to enforce and manage the austerity programs. With the economic costs of the IMF-sponsored approach apparent and the threat to new democracies clear, it is time for a new approach to the debt crisis.

The need for new policies is acute in light of the short-term prospects for the U.S. and global economies. Many analysts are now predicting an economic slowdown in the U.S. At the same time, record U.S. trade deficits are leading to protectionist pressures. Slowing growth and rising protection will cut off the avenue the IMF has pushed for resolving the debt crisis: expanding Third World exports. As it is, the strategy has been largely unsuccessful. While there has been some increase in export revenues in 1984 and 1985, Third World exports have barely recovered the purchasing power they had in 1980 and trade balance improvement has been achieved largely through import restraint.[59] A collapse in export revenues will further weaken growth and aggravate the debt crisis.

Even some bankers and traditional politicians have recognized the limits to the current strategy. Ex-Secretary of State Henry Kissinger, has proposed a "Marshall Plan" for Latin America. While vague in his formulations, Kissinger suggests that the U.S. and other Western nations establish a new lending institution with the power to give long-term loans at low interest rates.

Felix Rohatyn and other investment bankers have been more specific. Seeking to duplicate the scheme he designed to "bail-out" New York City—where the power over city budgeting was removed from the voters and put in the hands of New York's creditors—Rohatyn has suggested the development of a new international institution that would buy up bank loans to the Third World.[60] In a three day closed conference sponsored by the Fed, this basic idea attracted support from some private bankers; their only concern was that the loans be purchased at face value (rather than discounted by, say, 10%).[61] Meanwhile, other bankers, including Fed Chair Paul Volcker at one point, have suggested placing a cap on interest rates. Any "excess" interest would be added to the principal and repaid at a later date.[62] Some individual banks have converted debt owed by private Third World concerns into equity positions in those companies; some have suggested employing this technique as a global strategy.

These suggestions have two things in common. First, they are designed to rescue the banks and not the people of the Third World. No real change is proposed in the current austerity measures conservative economics deems appropriate for Third World debtors. Meanwhile, in a negation of the logic of the free market in which they profess belief, banks get to avoid the costs of their own lending errors. Second, these schemes all propose that U.S. taxpayers foot the bill to buy back the loans and rescue the bankers. In return, the banks, the IMF, and other "pillars of democracy" would guide and oversee the new international loan agency. This is apparently the sort of socialization of resources that the free marketeers understand.

A different approach has emerged from the developing world. In Africa, former Tanzanian President Julius Nyerere has argued that African nations should unite to demand better terms from their creditors. In Latin America, there has been growing talk of debtors' cartels and debt moratorium.

Efforts to avoid payment have already been made. Attempts by Argentine President Raul Alfonsin to buck both the IMF and the international banks caused shivers in the banking community. While Alfonsin's government implemented an IMF "shock treatment" program in June 1985, the possibility of not paying continues to be discussed in Argentine circles. Bolivia has quietly avoided paying its debt for two years; banks make little fuss, afraid to publicize the Bolivian example and aware that Bolivia's economic problems leave little room for debt service. Meanwhile, Latin American eyes have turned to the new President of Peru, Alan Garcia. Having claimed that "my government's first debt will be to the masses, not to foreign banks," Garcia used his inaugural address to announce that Peru would use no more than 10% of its export revenues to meet debt obligations.[63] This new strategy amounts to what international banks have feared for years: a unilateral rescheduling of debt payments.

Even as Garcia's notion of linking exports and debt payments gains adherents in Latin America, a new, more radical approach is being suggested by Cuba's Fidel Castro. In several important interviews and at a widely publicized debtors' conference in Havana, Castro has argued that financial transfers from Latin America to Western creditors over the next ten years will amount to twenty times (in nominal terms) what John Kennedy proposed be transferred as aid to Latin America under the Alliance for Progress program.[64] Rejecting the anti-development implications of this transfer, he proposes that Latin America stop paying and instead use the $40 billion annual outflow in interest payments to finance new development and reverse the growth crisis of the last few years.

What will happen to Western banks and the international financial system if the debt is cancelled? Castro is not so far from the bankers in suggesting that the debt be assumed by Western governments. However, Castro claims to spare the taxpayer any new burdens, noting that interest and amortization on the assumed debt could be paid by cutting military expenditures by 12%. In an interview with U.S. Congressman Mervyn Dymally and Professor Jeffrey Eliot, the Cuban President argued that if Western states[65]

> consider themselves capable of dreaming up and waging 'star wars' while giving barely a thought to the risks involved in a thermonuclear conflict that would in the first minute destroy a hundred times more than what is due their banks—in short, if the idea of universal suicide doesn't scare them, why should they be afraid of something as simple as the cancellation of the Third World's debt?

The growing Third World talk of debt moratoriums and debtor cartels has prompted the U.S. to adopt a much-publicized "new approach" to the debt crisis. As outlined by U.S. Treasury Secretary James Baker at the annual IMF and World Bank meetings in October, 1985, the new approach has three components. First, the World Bank would join the IMF in overseeing stabilization programs and would make available $9 billion in new loans. Second, the commercial banks would increase their exposure with a fresh $20 billion in additional lending. Third, developing countries would be required to move even further toward the model of promoting exports and encouraging foreign investment.[66]

The new U.S. plan is being draped in the logic of a conservative brand of growth economics: increased capital flows and "better" Third World policies will allow the Third World to grow its way out of the debt problem. But will growth occur? And what kind of growth?

Despite the "pro-growth" ballyhoo, the resources offered are paltry. As *Business Week* notes, "the entire $29 billion offer would barely exceed the annual debt service of Mexico and Brazil alone."[67] Moreover, the growth model is more of the same: increased reliance on a fluctuating external market and domination by foreign investors. The resulting pressure from this scheme would conspire to keep Third World wages low. Even if, as in Brazil in the 1970s, the model *can* promote growth, it will be dependent and inequitable growth. Moreover, it is this misery-led export-dependent strategy that drove the Third World into the debt crisis. Why should it be the strategy to take it out?

A democratic economic approach must reject the conservative strategies that helped trigger and worsen the global debt crisis of the Third World. It must also reject the Rohatyn-style proposal of displacing the burdens of bank mistakes onto U.S. taxpayers. Finally, it must reject the simple "pro-growth" strategy of the latest U.S. initiative on the debt problem.

Instead, a democratic approach would recognize the structural roots of the Third World's debt problems and seek to promote strategies that provide immediate relief in the short-run and encourage equitable growth and democracy in the Third World in the long-run (see Chapter 13 for our proposals).

Of course, it would be arrogant to assume that changes in our policies alone will resolve the Third World's problems. No amount of Western capital flow can suffice when the capital flight of local Third World elites means that the wealth produced by their people is diverted to the coffers of Western banks. No international reforms can replace the commitment of local workers and peasants that comes with democratic politics and equity-oriented economics. Growth alone is not a panacea; a high rate of growth that delivers benefits to elites who need them least will not meet the needs of the bulk of the Third World's population. A transformation toward democratic economics should also be on the internal agendas of our neighbors. But we can promote this move to domestic equity by pushing for international equity.

Democratic solutions spring from an understanding that the conservative strategy has been both unfair and ineffective. The costs have been astronomical in terms of output lost and output misallocated to an unproductive military sector. In addition, the resulting debt crisis has destabilized the international financial system. Economic repression and continuing debt service have strained Third World democracies. Meanwhile, aggressive U.S. foreign policy and an expensive arms race have hardly promoted a more secure environment. For both the U.S. and our global neighbors, a new direction is needed, one which places the cost of debt losses squarely on the shoulders of the banks, and which promotes economic development, democracy, and equity in both the U.S. and Third World. Anything less is not in our own interest.

Footnotes

1. "Address By His Excellency Jose Sarney...to the XL Session of the General Assembly of the United Nations," Brazilian Mission to the United Nations, September 23, 1985.

2. "Address by H. E. Alan Garcia to the Fortieth Session of the General Assembly," Peruvian Mission to the United Nations, September 23, 1985.

3. The baby sitter is quoted in Dan Williams, "Hardship Trickles Down to Mexico's Poorest Areas," *Los Angeles Times*, September 16, 1985, p. A1.

4. Reported in Adam Smith, "Unconventional Wisdom: How Banks Got in Trouble." in Christopher A. Kojm, *The Problem of International Debt*, (H.W. Wilson, 1984), p. 38.

5. Reported in Robert H. Girling, *Multinational Institutions and the Third World*, Praeger Press, New York, 1985, p. 59. The argument that banks are benefitting is based on the higher interest rates and service fees on debt renegotiation.

6. The figures on debt and the ratio of debt to output (Gross Domestic Product) are from the International Monetary Fund, *World Economic Outlook*, International Monetary Fund, Washington, D.C., 1985, pp. 262 & 266. The reference is to indebted developing countries. Throughout this chapter we will refer to both indebted developing countries and the non-oil developing countries (NODC's). These are slightly different groupings, the former analytical category having emerged as a result of the debt problems themselves. The indebted developing countries include all developing countries that are members of the International Monetary Fund (IMF) except for eight Middle East oil exporters (excluded for lack of debt data or because of a very small external debt). The NODC's include all developing countries except for twelve major oil exporters (including Venezuela); a number of net oil exporters (such as Mexico, Ecuador, Egypt and several others) are included under the NODC rubric. For more details, see International Monetary Fund, *op. cit.*, pp. 197-201.

7. The sixfold increase is calculated for the debt of non-oil developing countries (NODC's) using William P. Cline, *International Debt and the Stability of the World Economy*, Institute for International Economics, Washington, D.C., 1983, p. 14 and International Monetary Fund, *op. cit.*, p. 265. The real increase in debt was calculated using the nominal figures noted above deflated by the U.S. producer price index (taken from the *Economic Report of the President, 1985*, p. 297; the 1985 producer price index was calculated from the 1984 figure using the IMF's estimate of 3.8% for inflation in the GNP deflator). The result was that the 1985 real debt was 2.5 times greater than the 1973 real debt.

8. The total debt figure is from International Monetary Fund, *op. cit.*, p. 262. The concentration figure is from Inter-American Development Bank, *External Debt and Economic Development in Latin America*, Washington, D.C., 1984), p. 11. The per-household debt was calculated by dividing the total debt by the projected 1985 population for Latin America of 400.551 millions reported in the *1983 Statistical Yearbook for Latin America*, Economic Commission for Latin America, June 1984. This figure includes Cuba but excludes other countries included in the IMF's definition of Latin America. The per-capita debt was then multiplied by an assumed household size of 4.5. This figure was a conservative determination based on the household size figures reported in the same source. For a 1970 survey, only six of the twenty-four Latin countries covered had an average household size *below* 4.5 persons; the larger countries like Brazil and Mexico were above this figure. The actual household size in 1985 is likely greater than 4.5.

9. Michael Moffit, *The World's Money*, Simon and Schuster, New York, 1983, p. 104.

10. Cline, *op. cit.*, pp. 32 and 78.

11. Arthur MacEwan, "International Debt and Banking: Rising Instability Within the General Crisis," Mimeo, Economics Department, University of Massachusetts, Boston, 1985, p. 5.

12. See Fred L. Block, *The Origins of International Economic Disorder*, University of California Press, Berkeley, 1977.

13. For example, between 1969 and 1972, "foreign dollar claims on the U.S. government and on the foreign branches of U.S. banks doubled." MacEwan, *op. cit.*, p. 10.

14. Moffit, *op. cit.*, p. 100. The NODC grouping covers most of developing countries; only twelve oil exporters are excluded and many countries are included that were or became net exporters of oil, i.e., Mexico, Ecuador, Egypt, etc.

15. International Monetary Fund, *World Economic Outlook, 1980*, Washington, D.C., 1980, pp. 91 & 97.

16. Moffit, *op. cit.*, p. 108.

17. Michael Todaro, *Economic Development in the Third World*, Longman Press, New York, 1985, p. 372.

18. *Ibid.*, p. 443.

19. See Cheryl Payer, *The Debt Trap*, Monthly Review Press, New York, 1974.

20. The data on debt increases for Brazil, Argentina, Mexico, and South Korea come from Cline, *op. cit.*, p. 130. The data on Chilean debt is from IDB (1984), p. 92. The data on wages and unemployment for Argentina and Chile comes from Alejandro Foxley, *Latin American Experiments in Neo-Conservative Economics*, University of California Press, Berkeley, 1983, p. 121-122. In Argentina, both real wages in industry and real wages in the public sector fell by almost 50% between 1975 and 1977; average industrial real wages fell by around

30% in the same period. The Chilean unemployment rate is for Santiago.

21. From Ruth Leger Sivard, *World Military and Social Expenditures, 1983*, World Priorities, Washington, D.C., 1984; reported in *From Debt to Development*, Institute for Policy Studies, Washington, D.C., 1986.

22. Data on Mexican capital flight from Steve Frazier, "Mexico Tries to Revive Private Capital Markets to Spur Growth, Help End Financial Crisis," *Wall Street Journal*, November 1, 1984, p. 34.

23. Cline, *op. cit.*, p. 27.

24. Quote from Edward Schumacher, "Alfonsin Says Rate Rises in U.S. Imperil Argentina's 'Social Peace,'" *The New York Times*, May 11, 1984, p. A1.

25. S. Sri-Kumar, "The Americas," *Wall Street Journal*, May 10, 1985.

26. The price increase of oil is reported in Editors of the Foreign Policy Association, "International Debt Crisis: Borrowers, Banks, and the IMF," in Christopher A. Kojm, *The Problem of International Debt*, H. W. Wilson Co., 1984, p. 14.

27. Data from International Monetary Fund, *op. cit.*, pp. 228, 230, and 235.

28. Cline, *op. cit.*, pp. 15-16.

29. Cline, *op. cit.*, p. 23.

30. International Monetary Fund, *op. cit.*, pp. 188 and 245.

31. Data on Argentine debt service from Cline, *op. cit.*, pp. 130-131. The rest of the data on debt service is from International Monetary Fund, *op. cit.*, p. 268.

32. The per-capita increase is based on the 73.1 million Mexican population figure reported in the World Bank's *World Development Report, 1984*, Oxford University Press, 1984, p. 219.

33. Between June 1982 and December 1982, U.S. bank loans to Latin America increased by only $1.2 billion, a sharp decline from the $7.3 billion increase over the same months in 1981; Cline, *op. cit.*, p. 30. The figures exclude loans to Latin OPEC members. The International Monetary Fund reports that net external borrowing for the indebted developing countries went from $120.1 billion to $65.7 billion between 1981 and 1983; over the same period, net external borrowing for the Western Hemisphere developing countries went from $62.2 billion to $18.6 billion. International Monetary Fund, *op. cit.*

34. Cline, *op. cit.*, p. 83, reports that the average interest on Mexican loans was 0.9 percent points above LIBOR in 1978-80 and that the loans rescheduled in 1982 had a spread of 1 7/8 percentage points. New borrowings had a spread of 2.5 percentage points. As Cline notes, "an increase spread from 0.9 percentage points to 1.87 points doubles the profit potential to the lender, as represented by the spread above

LIBOR, considering that the lender is highly leveraged and lending on the basis of borrowed funds."

35. International Monetary Fund, *op. cit.*, p. 210.

36. See Appendix for details on the calculation.

37. See Cline, *op. cit.*, pp. 22-26 for his derivation.

38. The 27.5% rise in the real value of the dollar over 1980-82 was obtained by using the real multilateral trade-weighted index given in the *Economic Report of the President*, 1985, p. 351. The $131 billion was derived by multiplying the total external debt figure for NODC's reported in Cline, *op. cit.*, p. 14 by the 27.5% increase.

39. From a private conversation.

40. Using the World Bank's (1984) estimate of total world population and subtracting the socialist non-members of the IMF, we estimate the U.S. has less than 1% of the IMF membership population. For details on Fund decisions, see Joseph Gold, *Voting Majorities in the Fund*, IMF, Washington, D.C., 1977.

41. Inter-Development Bank, *op. cit.*, p. 43. Including oil would raise the percentage of imports necessary for production to 80%.

42. *South*, July 1985, p. 38.

43. One study by Center for Popular Economics staff economist Manuel Pastor ("The Effects of IMF Programs in the Third World: Debate and Evidence From Latin America," Mimeo, Economics department, Occidental College, 1985) found no significant statistical association of IMF programs with reductions in the inflation rate in Latin America. Indeed, there were grounds to believe that IMF programs were instead associated with dramatic *increases* in inflation. Similar results are reported in a review of empirical work by Tony Killick, "The Impact of IMF Stabilisation Programmes" in Killick, Ed. *The Quest for Economic Stabilization: The IMF and the Third World*, St. Martin's Press, New York, 1984, pp. 240-242.

44. Using an inflation rate for the developing Western hemisphere, with country inflation rates weighted by relative GDP, the International Monetary Fund reports price increases of 54.0% in 1980 and 113.7% in 1985. International Monetary Fund, *op. cit.*, p. 215.

45. See Pastor, *op. cit.* The period studied was 1965-1981.

46. Inter-Development Bank, *op. cit.*, p. 26.

47. John W. Sewall, "U.S. Deals in World Debt: Solvency or Small Change?" Los Angeles *Times*, October 20, 1983.

48. Quote is reported in Art Pine, "Brazil Struggles Under Its Unwieldly Debt Load," *Wall Street Journal*, May 6, 1983.

49. For 1987-90, the IMF's baseline scenario projects 4.8% annual GNP growth for the indebted developing countries while the 1967-76 average was 5.5% (figures from International Monetary Fund, *op. cit.*).

50. *South*, July 1985, p. 35.

51. Calculations from Pedro-Pablo Kuczynski, "Latin Debt: Room for Optimism," *Los Angeles Times*, August 14, 1985, p. ii-5.

52. Figures from Carole Collins, "IMF Decision Provokes Dominican Riot," *National Impact*, June 1984.

53. Quote is from "Verbatim: Rebuffing the IMF," *The New York Times*, June 3, 1984.

54. The resource outflow for 1983 is reported in Inter-Development Bank, *op. cit.*, p. 19. The projections are from Inter-Development Bank, p. 6.

55. *Business Week*, "Solving the Third World's Growth Crisis," p. 36.

56. See Appendix for calculations.

57. Reported in Schumacher, "4 Latin Chiefs Ask Easing on Debts," *The New York Times*, May 21, 1984, p. D1.

58. Quoted in Peter T. Kilborn, "Borrowers and Lenders Hunt Solution to Latin Debt Crisis," *The New York Times*, May 14, 1984, p. A1.

59. For all developing countries, the International Monetary Fund reports declines in the real purchasing power of exports (export earnings deflated by import prices) of 2.8% in 1981, 8.8% in 1982, and 1.3% in 1983. Increases of 8.4% in 1984 and the International Monetary Fund's optimistic prediction of a 4.6% increase in 1985 will have just about brought real purchasing power back to the 1980 level. International Monetary Fund, *op. cit.*, p. 228.

60. Felix Rohatyn, "A Plan for Stretching Out Global Debt," *Business Week*, February 28, 1983, p. 15-16.

61. Reported in Leonard Silk, "The Dangers in the Debt Crisis," *The New York Times*, May 4, 1984, p. D2.

62. From Kilborn, *op. cit.*, and Robert D. Hershey Jr., "Volcker Suggests Limit on Interest for Third World," *The New York Times*, May 13, 1984, p. A1.

63. Quote is from *Business Week*, "Latin American Debtors are Spoiling for a Fight," May 27, 1985, p. 53.

64. *South*, July 1985, p. 21.

65. Reported in "There's No Other Choice: The Cancellation of the Debt or the Political Death of the Democratic Processes in Latin America," from the cited interview, Editora Politica, Habana, p. 18.

66. Details from *Business Week*, "Facing Realities on Latin Debt," October 21, 1985; and Art Pine, "U.S. Proposal on World Debt Face Hurdles," *Wall Street Journal*, October 8, 1985.

67. *Business Week*, "Facing Realities on Latin Debt," October 21, 1985, p. 37.

Part IV

The Economics of Democracy

Preface

Six years under the tutelage of conservative economics has left the U.S. a socially divided and financially indebted nation. Its trickle-down precepts and its penchant for playing hardball with the American people and with our global neighbors alike share a common flaw: conservative economics leaves people out of the equation. The omission is not only mean-spirited and politically dangerous; it is costly, for it invites an escalation of the costs of containing and managing the hardship and conflicts which are brought on by the failure of its own false promises.

Many of the costs of conservative economics result from leaving the needs, dreams, and self-respect of ordinary people out of the picture. Conservative economics is wasteful because it is an unfair and arrogant imposition which invites resistance and promotes social conflict.

We can do better. We can rid the U.S. of the suffering of unemployment without promoting a burst of inflation. We can divide up the pie more fairly while making it bigger. We can eliminate racial and sexual discrimination, which is an economic and moral necessity, not a luxury to be postponed until better times.

The main obstacles to an economic program which places people at its center are not technical and economic but political. Can those who would benefit from a democratic alternative to the reign of greed unify around an effective program? Can those who gain from the costly errors of conservative economics be isolated?

Our ideas concerning an alternative economic program have grown out of seven years of discussion of economic alternatives with thousands of activists from unions, women's groups, neighborhood organizations, peace groups, and many others who have been participants in programs of the Center for Popular Economics. We present these proposals here to join with others as part of the on-going process of building a broad-based political movement which can challenge and ultimately unseat the ruling economic orthodoxy.

12 A New Democratic Order

In the depths of the Great Depression, economists preached forebearance, balanced budgets, and the virtues of a free market. The failure of these policies spawned a new economic theory, developed by John Maynard Keynes and his circle of young followers, which held that the economy was suffering from an insufficiency of demand for goods and services. According to Keynes, there was too little purchasing power in the hands of those who would spend it—middle and low income groups. The solution was a redistribution of purchasing power and increased government spending.

Accompanying this theory was a new political logic. Orthodox economists had stressed "excessive wages," highlighting the conflict between firms and workers. Keynes, by contrast, implied that redistribution toward workers would help profits, and laid the basis for an alliance between labor and some business groups.

Like the 1930s, the stagnation of the 1970s and 80s suggests the need for a new logic. But this time, the economy is suffering not so much from a dampening of demand due to the maldistribution of income as from an outmoded, conflict-ridden and ineffective top-down approach to economic management. This approach, which pervades the U.S. economy from the Oval Office to the board room and from Wall Street to Main Street, relies almost exclusively on the pursuit of corporate profits as a guide to economic decisions. The profit-centered, hierarchical approach has been tried—and it has failed.

The solution today requires not only the Keynesian prescription of redistributing purchasing power, but the redistribution of power itself. We need to break the stranglehold of large corporations and the singleminded pursuit of corporate profit by granting civil and participatory economic rights to workers, communities, consumers and citizens. We need a new political logic, one in which the less powerful come together to build a more democratic and fair society.

This report has shown that conservative economics is costly. The poor, people of color, farmers, women, Third World debtors, unions and the unemployed are paying its bitter price. The manufacturing sector is being decimated by an overvalued dollar. Our future is being mortgaged—ensuring future indebtedness and slow productivity growth.

What are the alternatives to current policies? While the press has focused on right-wing debates between supply-siders and monetarists, the most likely alternative to conservative economics comes from another quarter—a loosely defined group which we call the "new mercantilists." They are the heirs of eighteenth-century economists who argued for trade surpluses, the creation of monopolies by the crown, and government intervention in the economy.

The new mercantilism is represented by Democrats like Felix Rohaytn, the investment banker, and Republicans such as Congressman Jack Kemp and writer Kevin Phillips. They advocate national economic planning, government subsidies to promote international competitiveness, and austerity—increased business investment at the expense of wages and government benefits.

But the new mercantilism is deeply flawed. While it has correctly targeted the importance of the global economy and the irrationality of laissez-faire, its solutions are inadequate.

New mercantilists have failed to place international competitiveness in perspective, forgetting that it is important only as a means to higher living standards, greater leisure time, or other goals. To some, competitiveness is a political goal, aimed at restoring U.S. global power at the expense of people in other countries, or increasing corporate power at the expense of workers. What they call "economic" or "business nationalism" is at times little more than pin-stripe jingoism.

The new mercantilism export-oriented strategy would also leave the people of the U.S. vulnerable to instability in world demand, overproduction in world supply, and downward pressure on living standards. It entails a loss of democratic control over domestic economic policy, by forcing us to conform to the policies of our trading partners.

The new mercantilists advocate government intervention—under the control of business and other elites. They favor undemocratic, invisible institutions such as the Federal Reserve Board, the Synthetic Fuels Corporation, and the Municipal Assistance Corporation (Big Mac) of New York City. They apparently believe, as Bertolt Brecht put it, that "ruling is too difficult for ordinary men [sic]."[1]

Such institutions not only offend democratic sensibilties; they promote irrational and inefficient policies. If history is any guide, their "blue ribbon industrial policies" will be a *carte blanche* for corporate boondoggling, similar to the military contracting system or the multibillion dollar subsidies to the misbegotten nuclear power industry.

Finally, like conservative economics, the new mercantilist program would encounter widespread resistance and correspondingly high enforcement costs. It proposes that we need to consume less in order to invest more, and it orchestrates the belt tightening operation through top-down institutions. By itself, either austerity or authoritarianism is feasible: austerity with democracy may work or authoritarianism with prosperity. But austerity plus authoritarianism is likely to provoke serious political resistance.

Toward a Garrison Economy?

The mercantilist alternative shares with conservative economics the prospect of an escalation of social conflict and division. This is not only an ugly vision for a future United States; it is a strategy which would accelerate a long-term trend toward the proliferation of costly strategies for the containment of conflict. These range from the booming sales of double and triple locks on doors and the mushrooming market for exotic security devices, to corporate strategies of union busting, to the national strategy of arms buildup.

A comprehensive measure of the resulting costs is no doubt impossible, but a sense of the magnitude of enforcement costs in the U.S. economy today may be gained by considering the amount of "guard labor" in the U.S. economy. As in any economy, a significant number of people in the U.S. do not produce goods or services directly but rather enforce the rules—formal and informal, domestic and international—that govern economic life. We term these activities guard labor. Those performing guard labor include security personnel, prison guards, foremen, and others. Many, such as supervisory employees, do both, at once directing the work process and controlling the pace of work.

The presence of guard labor in an economy is hardly an indictment of an economic system: it is a fact of life that rules are necessary and that they do not enforce themselves. But some rules are harder to enforce than others. Ways of doing business which people regard as fair and types of work which people find rewarding and fairly paid tend to need little enforcement. Correspondingly, economic policies which go against the grain of what people think is reasonable, decent and fair often incur substantial costs. These enforcement costs stem from the resistance and lack of commitment which people feel towards the resulting economic activities. In the workplace, for example, it takes large expenditures on surveillance and security personnel to enforce rules which workers perceive to be invasive, unfair, or oppressive.

While necessary to uphold a given set of rules, guard labor is a drag on the economy. Supervisors who are controlling the pace of work of others are not themselves productive; security guards and people in the armed services—however necessary—are not producing goods or services that may be consumed or invested.

Stick strategies are based on the spectre of punishment. They tend to raise enforcement costs, particularly where citizens enjoy sufficient democratic rights to make their displeasure heard. Carrot strategies, on the other hand, tend to lower them.

In the international arena, the cost of a stick strategy depends on the balance of power. When one nation is clearly dominant, as England was throughout much of the 19th century and as the U.S. was immediately following World War II, the costs of maintaining a particular political, military and economic regime may be low. But following an aggressive and unilateral stick strategy in a world of more nearly equal nation-states is likely to be not only dangerous, but ineffective and costly.

The amount of guard labor in the U.S. economy today can hardly be estimated with precision. But a reasonable measure might include the following:[2]

— the unemployed, whose joblessness disciplines the work effort of those fortunate enough to have a job, as well as moderates their demands for better wages and working conditions. Counting those who would be working if jobs were readily available, the unemployed total 11.7 million in 1984;[3]

— some portion of the foremen, supervisors, managers, and others in the corporate and governmental hierarchies of command. Based on detailed occupational descriptions we estimate this figure to be 8.5 million;

— the uniformed and civilian employees of the armed forces and those producing military goods, or 4.9 million;

— employees of police departments, prisons, and courts, as well as prisoners—whose incarceration encourages respect for the law— private detectives, and security personnel, or 2.2 million.

According to this count, guard labor accounted for 27.4 million people in the U.S. in 1984.

The measure is arbitrary in some respects: lawyers are not included, nor are teachers, who are also employed in rule enforcement; not all police work is law enforcement; and so on. But the order of magnitude is indicative: *well over one in nine people—counting all ages—is a guard worker.* By a considerable margin, guard workers outnumber production workers in non-military manufacturing, mining, and construction combined.[4]

By contrast, at the height of the Vietnam War in 1969, guard labor accounted for less than one person in thirteen. And the growth of guard labor seems to be accelerating: between 1965 and 1969, the population grew by 7 million, while guard labor grew by less than half a million, or one sixteenth the amount of population growth; between 1969 and 1979 the population grew by 24 million, while guard labor grew by one quarter of that amount or 6 million. From 1979 to 1984, the heyday of economic orthodoxy, the increase in guard labor was well over half the growth in population (see Figure 12.1).

Figure 12.1
The Mounting Costs of Enforcing the Rules of the Game
Guard Labor in the U.S. Economy, 1969-1984

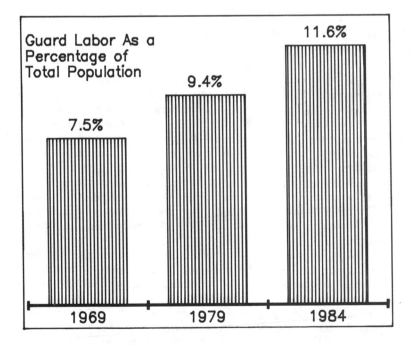

Guard Labor As a Percentage of Total Population

7.5% 1969

9.4% 1979

11.6% 1984

Source: text and appendix.

Not all of the proliferation of guard labor can be blamed on conservative economics. but some of it can be. And it is reasonable to assess any economic strategy in terms of its effect of what percentage of the population will as a result be engaged—wittingly and willingly or not—in enforcing the rules.

We believe that the social tensions engendered by the mounting inequality and the dog-eat-dog logic of conservative economics will continue to fuel the escalation of guard labor. The neo-mercantilist alternative would most likely offer a different menu of tensions. But it would not abate them, because new mercantilism is incapable of addressing the underlying conflict concerning whether the U.S. economy is to be run in the interests of the few or the many. It also ignores the question of whether the world economy should rest on reciprocal and respectful relations between sovereign nations, or on the escalation of conflicting gameplans made in Washington, Moscow, and other major centers of power.

The Economic Logic of a Democratic Alternative

If neither conservative economics nor the new mercantilism is the answer, then what is? Is it possible to construct an economy around the principle of democracy? Could it promote equality and participation and still be efficient and dynamic? We think so.

A democratic economy is built on widespread social participation and basic economic rights, such as the right to a job. It is guided, not by large corporations' search for profits, but by the values and goals of the majority. It would reduce the power of multinational corporations and increase their accountability to workers, consumers, and citizens.

Democratic economics is not merely another name for existing economic systems, such as centrally-planned socialism, or Social Democracy. While it would contain features of both, it is an attempt to build something new, based on American democratic traditions and values. Echoing Thomas Jefferson's belief that economic dependency makes a mockery of freedom, it carries the best of our political tradition into the economy itself, and thereby aims to overcome both the wastefulness of conservative economics and its intolerance for democracy.

The challenge of democratic economics is to construct a "working" economy on the basis of rights and participation. A "working" economy is one which provides economic security to all, increasing realms of choice and free time, and rising living standards.

The idea underlying a democratic economy is that it works precisely because it is democratic and fair. A greater popular sense of fairness and belonging would obviate the inefficiency generated by conservative economics. It would facilitate innovation, particularly in the public sector, and create new public programs which are not possible now because entrenched powers oppose them.

We could share our wealth more fairly, and thereby reduce the substantial racial and sexual divisions among us—divisions which threaten our ability to be a free and democratic society. And this program could facilitate our own perpetuation as a society, by respecting both the value of the next generation—our children—and the earth on which we live.

Our program is primarily a series of structural reforms, such as raising minimum wages, guaranteeing jobs, and controlling inflation through incomes policies. What are the conditions under which structural reforms like this can work? The key to their success is the creation of broad-based, representative institutions, such as democratic trade unions, community development bodies, and popular control over policy agencies such as the Federal Reserve Board. Without popular institutions, and without a well-informed and politically mobilized population, economic policies will satisfy the demands of narrow interests and will be wasteful from the point of view of society as a whole.

Public institutions enhance the possibility for both technical and political innovation. Conservative economists contend, for example, that we should abandon traditional industries in the face of international competition, arguing that to do so serves the general interest. But the burdens of adjustment fall almost completely on the people in those industries who justifiably resist being sacrificial lambs on the altar of "international competition." If workers and communities had a voice in trade policies and were assured of gaining new employment, and if firms were aided in moving into new products and markets, the economy could respond to changing circumstances in a humane and efficient way. As it is, workers and communities are pitted against each other in "beside-the-point" debates about free trade and protectionism.

The experience of some Western European economies in the postwar period illustrates the point. Those with more broadly based representative institutions, particularly for workers, and more of an emphasis on democratic consensus, such as Austria and Sweden, have responded well to the economic challenges of the last decade. They created less unemployment and more growth, and suffered less erosion in living standards than in the United States.[5]

The Political Logic of Democratic Economics

Little progress can be made in this direction until we change the rules of the economic game we are playing. But how can a successful challenge to the power of entrenched interests be mounted, particularly now, when trade unionists, feminists, environmentalists, civil rights groups, and liberal Democrats are so much on the defensive? Can a democratic and fair a program win enough adherents to become reality? Can it do so in the face of hostile reaction from business, who can pack up shop and move away?

Ultimately, business may be willing to go along with a program of democratic economics, for pragmatic reasons. In the face of the widespread mobilization which would be necessary to enact this program, business may conclude that they should acquiesce in substantial changes, as they eventually did during the New Deal, and as their counterparts in many Western European countries have done. Social Democratic or New Deal capitalism, they reckoned, is better than no capitalism at all.

But U.S. capitalists are ideological and may shun the pragmatic response. Their answer may be plant closures, refusal to invest, capital flight, and heavy-handed political measures—often called "capital strike."

A successful response to capital strike is not impossible. It requires being ready—if business should decide to jump ship—to move forward along the road to a democratic economy, not backward, to a "pro-business" climate. Elements of such a response include worker takeovers or buyouts of abandoned plants, expanded public sector employment, strict restrictions on the outflow of financial capital, and government production in critical industries.

The problem of capital strike is more political than economic. Corporations cannot take our natural resources, our labor, or in most cases, the capital stock out of the country. They can take their money, but that is secondary to the real inputs for production.

Which brings us to the hard part—organizing ourselves and reaffirming the belief that change is possible. We need to design programs which promote general interests, such as full employment or social security. These policies create commonalities and reduce divisions. The people of the U.S. are now deeply divided by inequalites of income, wealth, race, gender, occupational status, and opportunity. Given the rules of the economic game today and the prevailing ideology, our immediate dollars-and-cents interests often pit us against one another as workers and consumers, men and women, taxpayers and public employees, blacks and whites.

The program in the next chapter addresses these disparate interests. Even in the short run, it promises economic and social benefits for the great majority of individuals, as a result of reduced waste and higher wages. It does not proclaim a false necessity of austerity and deprivation. And even as it promotes the interests of particular groups, thereby encouraging their support, it reaffirms and creates common interests, through economic structures which unify us and reduce our divisions.

Conservative economics increases these painful social divisions. A democratic economic program can do just the opposite: its success will depend on its ability to bring Americans together.

Footnotes

1. Bertolt Brecht, "Those Who Take the Meat From the Table," in *Selected Poems*, Harcourt Brace Jovanovich, New York, 1947.

2. The estimates which follow are from the U.S. Census Bureau, the *Statistical Abstract of the United States, 1985*, and other sources. The calculations are presented in an Appendix.

3. This figure includes an estimate of the number of workers who are not officially counted as unemployed because they are not actively seeking work, but who would be looking for work if there were jobs to be found. We have conservatively selected the official U.S. Department of Labor estimate of the number of these so-called "discouraged workers." Our own estimate—the details of which are described in chapter 8 and in an appendix—is based on an econometric projection of how large the labor force would be if the nation had achieved a 3% unemployment rate over the previous three years.

4. *Economic Report of the President*, 1985, p. 275.

5. See Robert Kuttner, *The Economic Illusion*, Houghton Mifflin, Boston, 1984.

13 Expanding Democracy

There are three distinctive features of what we term a democratic approach to the economy: fairness through the redistribution of work, rather than welfare; a greater material abundance and more free time through raising wages and ending discrimination; and structural reforms which pay for themselves because they eliminate waste.[1]

All economic programs embody a logic of redistribution, whether egalitarian or trickle-down. Many progressive programs, in their concern for fairness and equity, propose remedies which would essentially slice up the same pie in a different way. They advocate expansion of the welfare state, redirection of government spending from military to human services, and tax reform.

We support these objectives, but the thrust of our proposals is different. As they are normally conceived, proposals for redistributing income are divisive. They tend to pit one group against another—taxpayers against welfare recipients, workers in defense industries against those in human services. Many accept the conservative view that the economy is a zero-sum game—more for some means less for others. But the zero-sum straight jacket is a myth. Our economy is capable of delivering much more, raising living standards and enriching the free time of the vast majority of Americans. But breaking out of the divisive zero-sum bind can only be done if we make some changes in the rules of the game.

Our view is that we should redistribute and revalue *work itself*. People want decent jobs which pay living wages, rather than unemployment or life on the dole. Mothers want their childrearing labor to be highly valued and paid accordingly and many fathers want the chance to jointly raise their children. Our program therefore guarantees everyone the right to a job. It makes part-time jobs more desirable, provides day care, and raises benefits for single parents raising children at home. And of course, the redistribution of work, now so unequally divided and unequally rewarded, will carry in its wake a fundamental redistribution of income as well.

The politics of work redistribution are not divisive. We are not limited in our ability to create jobs, in the way that we are limited by the amount of income generated by an existing economy.

The second distinctive feature of the ten-step program is wage-led growth. We propose raising the minimum wage to $8 an hour. This will increase wages all around, force firms to innovate, and shift both labor and capital to high productivity sectors. It will result in high levels of purchasing power, thereby encouraging investment and employment. By eliminating low-wage labor, it will reduce racial and sexual discrimination.

But higher wages will also lead some low productivity firms to lay workers off or to encounter difficulty selling their goods, particularly abroad. Therefore, it is only feasible if it is enacted along with a guaranteed right to a job.

The importance of the right to a job suggests a crucial aspect of our program. Our economy is an integrated system; carrying out one major reform without others can spell disaster. While there are aspects of this program which can stand alone, it is not a shopping list from which one can pick and choose. It is a unified program which operates on the economy as a whole and radically transforms the way it functions (see Figure 13.1).

Figure 13.1

Ten Steps to a Democratic Economy

1. The Right to a Job
2. Raise Minimum Wages
        —Promote Economic Flexibility
3. Reforming the Money System
4. Control Over Our International
        Economic Relations
5. Family Policy
6. End Discrimination
7. Environmental Sustainability
8. Democratic Labor Relations
9. Government Accountability
10. Expanding Democracy

Its primary logic is that the expansion of democracy and fairness will reduce waste. For example, it compresses inequalities among us, by raising low wages and weakening industrial loyalties. This enhances productivity and economic flexibility. It reduces waste, whether it is caused by discrimination, environmental carelessness, unemployment, or rigidity in public policy. And it encourages innovation—by firms and governments.

Finally, this program is inexpensive. In fact, it yields a surplus of $85 billion compared to the current government budget. This is because it is not a spending spree, but a series of structural reforms, which can be shown to increase democracy, fairness and efficiency by reducing the waste of a game with unequal players.

Steps I and II, the guaranteed right to a job and higher wages, will raise productivity and utilize idle labor and factories. Reforms of the financial and international systems (Steps III and IV) are necessary both to reign in rampant economic instability and to allow Steps I and II to work. The proposals on family policy, discrimination and environmental sustainability (Steps V, VI and VII) reduce social costs, talent waste, and occupational inefficiency caused by gender and race discrimination. The last three steps, on labor unions, government accountability and democracy (Steps VIII, IX and X) will help create democratic institutions and therefore move economic policy towards meeting the needs of the majority rather than maximizing profits.

In the pages which follow, we outline one road to a democratic economy. Our proposals are not a detailed blueprint but are painted with a broad brush, at various levels of generality—from specific reforms of the unemployment insurance system to a call for more planning in international trade. This diversity is intended to demonstrate the wide range of changes we can contemplate. Throughout, the logic is based on an integrated set of structural reforms necessary for transforming a complex economic system. While we recognize that we have omitted or inadequately treated important areas, it is our hope that this program is read in the spirit with which it is written—as an attempt to project a vision which gives us a real alternative to conservative economics.

I. The Right to a Job

The right to a job is the centerpiece of a successful democratic economy. Technological progress, structural change, anti-discrimination efforts and environmental protection are more possible when job rights are secure; without job rights, such efforts threaten segments of the population and lead us into fights among ourselves. Here are a number of steps which will lead to full employment.[2]

Reduce Interest Rates

Real interest rates (interest rates corrected for inflation) remain at unprecedented levels. High rates put a damper on consumer spending and business investment. They serve as a magnet for foreign capital, thereby raising the value of the dollar. This leads to unemployment, by reducing the demand for domestically-produced goods, and encouraging U.S. businesses to produce abroad, where labor and resources are cheaper.

An important cause of high rates is tight monetary policy by the Federal Reserve Board, which we believe should immediately take steps to reduce interest rates.

Interest rate reduction will not only stimulate employment but will simultaneously help alleviate the problems of farmers and Third World debtors. It will also ease the financial constraints for small businesses, and reduce the rising barriers to home ownership. Indeed, lower interest rates will benefit just about everyone except bankers.[3]

Free Time and Flexibility in Work Hours

Remarkably, despite enormous increases in productivity, the modern worker spends no less time in the workplace than did European peasants during the Middle Ages.[4] This is in part because capitalist economies have a bias toward cashing in their productivity increases for more goods and services, rather than for more free time. But we could have more choice about how to reap the fruits of innovation and more flexible patterns of work and leisure, both over our lifetimes and on a weekly and monthly basis. Discretion over time spent at home or on the job is particularly important for joint parenting and gender equality.

—Reform of Unemployment Insurance System

Among the most irrational aspects of U.S. employment policy is its bias in favor of layoffs rather than work-sharing. Layoffs place the burden of slack demand on a small group of workers, rather than sharing it equitably. The unemployment insurance system is a barrier to work-sharing because in most cases benefits are only available to workers who are wholly unemployed, and not to those involuntarily working fewer hours.

A modification of the system would compensate workers whose hours have been cut due to slack demand, at a replacement rate of 80% of the hourly wage.[5]

—Reduction of the Standard Workweek

The standard workweek, beyond which employers must pay overtime, has stood at 40 hours for nearly four decades, despite tremendous productivity advances which make hours reduction feasible. We propose lowering the standard workweek to 35 hours.

—Benefits for Part-Time Workers

Part-time workers are often denied medical and other benefits, which has at least two adverse effects: it encourages employers to hire part-time workers, which results in involuntary "underemployment," and it discourages couples from voluntarily taking part-time work in order to share childrearing responsibilities.

One remedy is legislation making it illegal for firms to discriminate against part-time workers in terms of benefits. This implies that part-time jobs should carry with them pro-rated medical, disability, and pension benefits.

Guaranteed Right to a Job

The above steps by themselves will not guarantee jobs for all. Some unemployment is the result of discrimination and some is geographically concentrated. We need to tackle these problems head-on.

And like any other right, the right to a job will not be secure unless it carries with it specific guarantees. One simple provision is that state, local, and national governments institute employment programs. Every citizen will be guaranteed the right to participate in a public sector jobs program, which pays a living wage. Evidence shows[6] that these programs have been highly effective in reducing unemployment, particularly for low-wage workers.[7]

We suggest four programs. The first is employment in human services, such as hospitals, schools, and day care centers, which are currently understaffed and underfunded. The second is an infrastructure program devoted to repairing the nation's crumbling bridges, roads, and other public works. The third is a program for inner-city youth, who are experiencing devastating levels of unemployment. The final example is a local initiatives program. Locally-elected boards, particularly in depressed areas, could be allocated monies for projects proposed by non-profit organizations, businesses, and government agencies.

As these proposals suggest, the obstacles to full employment are political rather than structural. Indeed, the level of employment is in large part a political decision. The unemployment rate in Sweden averaged less than 2% over the post-World War II period, and even over the first half of the 1980s averaged less than 3%.[8] The U.S. economy operated at full employment during the Second World War, and at near-full employment in the late 1960s.

II. Raise Minimum Wages—Promote Economic Flexibility

There are two paths to economic growth. One, export-led growth, is based on low wages, abundant supplies of labor, and relatively low productivity. Because low wages and high unemployment inhibit domestic demand, rapidly growing world markets for exports are necessary for this strategy to succeed. Also characteristic is a "dualistic" structure, in which the export sector is more prosperous than the remainder of the economy, which remains poor and backward.

The alternative is wage-led growth. This has been the U.S. model for 200 years, and is the secret of our prosperity. Limited supplies of labor and workers' ability to migrate to the frontier kept U.S. wages unusually high. High wages led firms to shift from low to high productivity sectors and forced them to choose efficient technologies. On the demand side, well-paid workers became a lucrative and stable domestic market.

The wage-led growth strategy has the advantage of producing high living standards, low unemployment, and less reliance on an unpredictable world market. In addition to the U.S., the richer countries of Western Europe, such as Germany and Belgium, have successfully followed this model.

Conservative economics bids us to choose the low-wage path. It advocates lower minimum wages, worker concessions, regressive redistribution through the tax and transfer systems, and policies which will keep unemployment high. The payoff is supposedly more international competitiveness and investment.

But this strategy is irrational when viewed over the longer term. Why destroy a well-developed domestic market and a valuable capital stock? Why choose policies that reduce our living standards? Why— when we could instead follow a high-productivity, high-wage path, which reproduces the conditions of our past economic success.

Raise the Minimum Wage to $8 Per Hour and Index It to Inflation

Along with policies to ensure full employment, a higher minimum wage, phased in gradually, will raise productivity and demand, lift millions out of poverty, and reduce inequality. How would this work? Many businesses in the U.S. survive only because they have access to cheap labor. Raising the minimum wage would force these companies to improve productivity, by driving them into productive sectors and out of backward ones, and by leading them to add capital equipment and reorganize inefficient production methods. Those who failed to do so would face bankruptcy. Businesses which cannot provide a living wage for their workers are a dubious blessing in an economy where there are many other productive and prosperous firms. Workers who lose their jobs in these backward firms can be readily reemployed, either in private firms or public sector employment.

It may be argued that higher minimum wages will price U.S. goods out of world markets. This is unlikely to be the case, for two reasons. First, competitiveness depends on productivity, as well as wages. Higher wages will raise productivity, both for the reasons cited above and because they reduce labor turnover and raise effort. Second, many of our low-wage firms are in services or other areas which are not traded internationally.

Raising the minimum wage will promote racial and gender equality, because women and racial minorities are disproportionately employed in low productivity firms and industries. It will also lift full-time minimum wage workers, many of whom are women, out of poverty, since even a full-time job at the current minimum wage yields an income well below the poverty line. Indexing the minimum wage to inflation ensures that it will not deteriorate over time, as it has been allowed to do.

Economic Flexibility

A key to raising living standards is to move from low to high productivity sectors. Indeed, economic historians have found that sectoral changes, such as the shift from agriculture to industry, have been the major cause of productivity advance.

Such advances require that people sometimes change jobs. However, the orthodox prescription for sectoral flexibility is that workers bear the costs through geographic relocation. But this is irrational, as it often destroys communities which already possess developed infrastructure, family networks and social institutions. In many cases it makes more sense—when all the costs are added up—for the people to be immobile and the jobs to move.

Declining communities should be revitalized by relocating investment and production in them. Direct subsidies to high unemployment areas can be used by local governments and economic development boards to attract outside investment, or finance local investment projects.

Public Support for Research and Free Higher Education

Elsewhere in this *Report*, we have outlined the problem of public goods in a market economy (see Chapter 10). In an "information economy" these inefficiencies are magnified in importance. It costs almost nothing, for example, to reproduce a piece of computer software and make it widely or freely available. But private producers prefer to charge a high price and spend valuable dollars trying to protect their "private property."

Many goods are "underproduced" if the criterion for production is private profitability. As a result, we are less able to innovate and advance technologically, because the free diffusion of information and technology is inhibited. Despite the rapid growth of information, economic logic suggests that it is being underproduced.

The administration wants to reduce the public role even in cases where the market is widely agreed to be flawed, such as information and education. But recent cuts in government monies for education and research and development will prove costly. Instead, the government should raise its contribution to basic research and development and devote an increased percentage to non-military uses. We would also reaffirm the nation's historic commitment to education, by establishing universal free higher education at public institutions. Free higher education will reduce the great waste of talent represented by steep high school dropout rates, particularly in poor and inner-city neighborhoods.[9]

III. Reforming the Money System

For our proposed structural overhaul of the U.S. economy to succeed, financial reform is necessary. We are saddled with insolvency in major banks, a Federal Reserve Board which is unaccountable to the public, an overvalued dollar, and an international credit system which is out of control. Knowledgeable analysts believe that the possibility of worldwide financial collapse is real, and indeed a serious depression is already occurring in the farm sector, parts of Africa, and the debtor countries of Latin America.

Democratization of the Federal Reserve Board

We have proposed that the Fed lower interest rates and argued that the benefits of doing so will be felt throughout the economic system. Yet, if the benefits are so great, why are rates being kept so high? Part of the answer is fear of inflation—a real problem which we address below. But the other part is that the Fed is relatively immune from popular pressures and largely under the influence of commercial banks and other financial institutions which benefit from high rates.

This private, self-interested control of national monetary policy undermines popular sovereignty. If Congress cannot effectively control credit and interest rate conditions it is inhibited in its constitutional duty to determine taxation and expenditure policies.

To enact a low interest rate policy, structural reforms are necessary. Congressional authority over the Fed should be increased through Congressional appointment of Fed Governors, and the reduction of their terms of office from 14 to 4 years. Congress should select yearly growth, employment and inflation targets which Fed policies, in coordination with fiscal policy, must be designed to meet.

Global Debt

The global debt crisis is potentially a source of great instability. Current measures are inflicting the debt burden on the people least able to pay—the working people of the indebted countries. Prudent steps to prepare for default are not being taken.

We believe that the debt crisis can be solved by growth, not austerity. We also believe that the banks which made the loans, and who have already profited greatly from them, should be prepared to take losses. The banks' view—and Reagan policy—is that the burdens should be borne by groups who have not been party to the loans: U.S. taxpayers and the workers and peasants of the debtor countries.

Ordinarily, with potentially bad loans, banks are required to "provision," or set aside, a portion of their profits for the event of a default. U.S. banks are making extraordinarily high profits on their Third World loans, through high interest rates and rescheduling fees. But they are doing little provisioning, and instead are pursuing a strategy which keeps them in a vulnerable position. If the banks cannot afford to write off the bad loans, then the government must bail them out, out of fear of financial collapse.

We propose that the true status of outstanding loans be verified by bank regulators and that banks be required to follow standard provisioning requirements. This should be carried out in conjunction with an orderly, multi-year write-off of a substantial portion of the unpayable debt. The losses will therefore be borne by bank stockholders. The value of bank stocks will fall, but a careful write-down program will ensure that banks do not fail and financial chaos does not result.

Expansionary macro-economic policies and more openness to Third World goods in the developed countries will facilitate debt repayment. The collapse of world markets and growing protectionism have undermined the ability of indebted countries to generate export earnings. In response, the IMF and the banks impose austerity. But this approach is perverse, for it undermines the capacity to invest and ultimately to export. It increases hardship for impoverished populations and generates social tension.

In return for debt write-off, we would urge that indebted countries take steps to stem and reverse capital flight. Anticipating governmental claims on their assets, wealthy individuals and firms in indebted countries have been legally and illegally exporting capital to the U.S. and Europe. Particularly since much of the debt was privately incurred, but is now the responsibility of governments, this practice is illegitimate.

Making Financial Markets Accountable to Social Objectives

As we noted in Chapter 10, financial deregulation has brought instability and bank failures. While many earlier regulations are now anachronistic, regulation remains vital. Money and credit are social goods, whose use has effects throughout society. We would reaffirm the government's role in keeping financial markets safe, stable, and consistent with the pursuit of social objectives.

Regulations governing international financial transactions are necessary. For example, the Eurodollar market should be regulated through the extension of Fed authority in conjunction with the Central Banks of Europe. Eurodollars are under no governmental control at all, and pose a threat to the Fed's ability to control domestic credit conditions.

Reduction of the International Role of the Dollar

A major source of domestic monetary instability is the world's reliance on the U.S. dollar as the international currency. The dollar does "double duty," as both a national and an international currency. This helps large U.S. banks, who get extra business from it, but hurts almost everyone else. National economic policy can be held hostage to the requirements of maintaining an international currency: the declining value of the dollar in late 1979 was the primary factor prompting the Fed's dramatic raising of interest rates.

We support de-emphasizing the international role of the dollar. One country's currency should not do double duty. Instead, we should gradually be evolving toward an international currency unit, along the lines of Keynes' "bancor," the European currency unit (ECU), or the IMF's Special Drawing Rights (SDR). While there is not yet an international institution which can control monetary policy, its creation is probably not far off.[10] Some schemes for international money are tied to resource flows to the developing countries, such as the SDR link (a transfer of SDR purchasing power to the Third World) and World Bank issues of SDR bonds.

IV. Control Over Our International Economic Relations

Faith in free trade is pervasive. The standard dogma is that unrestricted trade between nations is always mutually beneficial, because it allows goods to be produced where conditions are most advantageous. Intervention in international trade is alleged to raise prices and harm consumers.

The strength of the free trade view is surprising. Economists who readily acknowledge that domestic markets are imperfect and cannot be left unattended fail to apply analogous logic to international markets. Even workers, when trying to protect their jobs against the ravages of international competition, often argue that "free trade is best in theory, or fine in the long run..." But it is hardly accidental that the principle of free trade has historically been advanced by the then-dominant world economic power.

The power of the free trade orthodoxy is partly based on a failure to examine the assumptions behind it. The axiom that world prices reflect "economic" conditions is particularly suspect. Even more than domestically, political factors influence international prices and market conditions. Since at least the Second World War, U.S. strategic and economic objectives have been intimately coordinated. Consider just two international prices—the price of oil and the price of the U.S. dollar. In both cases, political influences loom large. The distinction between "free" trade and "political" intervention is ill-conceived. The real issue is in whose interests and toward what ends political influence will be exercised.

But this is not the only error of orthodox free traders. With unemployment and unused productive capacity, and unequal power relations, free trade is not best. Better policies are those which fully use inputs, shelter weaker players, and protect living standards. If the market is flawed domestically, why assume it is any different internationally?

Dangers lurk behind the "world market," which must be confronted for a democratic economic program to succeed. Perhaps most important for the U.S. is the downward pressure on wages resulting from the increased internationalization of its economy. In an uncontrolled global economy there is a tendency to equalize wages around the world. Wage equality would be welcome if it came about through rising living standards in the Third World. Instead, international competition is used to gain wage concessions and reductions in domestic living standards.

A second danger is the loss of sovereignty over national macroeconomic policy. In a world economy with mobile capital, independent monetary, tax and spending policies are difficult to pursue. Low interest rates induce capital outflows; budget deficits may lead to a rising dollar, and harm exports. A country which tries to expand its economy when other countries are not so inclined finds itself subject to capital flight, inflation, and unemployment.

These examples challenge the free trade orthodoxy. But the problem is less in the "trade" than the "free." For it is the "freedom" of business to locate production around the world, to move funds in and out of countries at will, and to flood markets with job-displacing imports which threatens our well-being.

Protectionism is not the answer. Tariffs and quotas raise prices, which usually translates into higher profits for firms. Those profits are often used not to modernize or expand, but to abandon an industry. And protectionism embodies a divisive political logic, for it creates vertical alliances, by industry, between workers and management, and fosters horizontal divisions, between different types of workers, between farmers and workers, and between workers and consumers. Far better than protecting prices and profits—which may or may not save jobs—is direct protection of people's incomes and a full employment economy.

Negotiated Trading Agreements

The dichotomy between free trade and protection is ill-conceived; a more meaningful choice is between international economic relations based on corporate profit-making or democratic objectives. The problem is to find solutions which maintain pressures to innovate at the same time that they provide economic security. Trade can promote innovation in domestic firms and rapid diffusion of innovations around the globe. Coupled with a sensible macro-economic policy, innovation, not wage reduction, is the key to maintaining competitiveness.

One policy which meets these objectives is long-term negotiated trading agreements between nations. They provide the benefits of increased trade at the same time that they promote stability and cooperation.

Controlling the Globalization of Production

The threat to locate production abroad is a powerful lever for reducing wages and working conditions. The "runaway shop" leaves workers in the U.S. vulnerable to low-wage pressure from abroad. For the most part, businesses move abroad to find markets or take advantage of low costs, especially wages, rather than because production is more efficient.

Measures to reduce business's appetite for cheap labor include withdrawal of the substantial tax advantages for overseas production; an end to military support and trade preferences for regimes which deny basic workers' rights; and strong domestic plant closing legislation.

Trade gradualism

The high value of the dollar is rapidly destroying many U.S. industries, leading to unemployment and personal hardship for many. People and firms should be moved out of industries which can no longer be internationally competitive, but gradually. Otherwise, the process is extremely costly, both in human terms and in dollars and cents. Planned attrition rather than abrupt demise is appropriate. Temporary protection may be necessary for firms to innovate and adapt, but we should insist that firms give *quid pro quos* on employment, investment, and technology in return for import barriers.

A Tax on Currency Speculation

International currency speculation sabotages domestic policy by affecting the value of the dollar. It diverts firms from using their capital productively and increases international monetary instability. Currencies should trade hands to finance real economic activity, not to reap instant profits. We support macro-economist James Tobin's proposal for an internationally uniform tax on currency conversion to discourage speculation.[11]

V. Family Policy

In the Depression, the failures of the economic system led to demands for government support, culminating in the social security system. Today, we are witnessing similar failures. The traditional, one-earner nuclear family, once a primary unit of income redistribution, is no longer predominant. Governmental provision of income and services to support childrearing is therefore essential, but has not been forthcoming.

One reason is certainly our devaluation of childrearing. Done almost solely by women, and mainly in the home, this work is often invisible, and largely uncompensated. But childrearing is socially productive, indeed indispensable, and should be valued accordingly.

Day Care

Demographic and social trends, detailed in Chapters 3 and 5, have resulted in a widespread need for accessible, quality day care. But facilities are in short supply. Salaries for day care workers, nearly all of whom are women, are intolerably low, mirroring the failure to compensate women workers in the home. We suggest a large expansion in government funded, community-controlled day care, paying the workers a living wage.

Adequate Welfare Benefits

Expenditures for single women raising children have been eroded by inflation and budget cutting. The average welfare benefit is less than half the poverty line.[12] We propose raising benefits under Aid to Families with Dependent Children to 125% of the poverty line and easing eligibility requirements, to include, for example, parents who are unemployed, going to school, or enrolled in job training programs. Single men raising children should also be eligible. We oppose the imposition of workfare programs, which are punitive in nature. Instead, we prefer programs such as Massachusetts' ET Choices, which is voluntary, and emphasizes schooling, employment, and training.

We also urge a rise in the Food Stamp benefit, which currently pays for less than even the Thrifty Food Plan, an emergency food diet which is medically inadequate on a long-term basis.[13] And for persons unable to work because of disability or similar reasons, a guaranteed income is needed.

These changes, along with a guaranteed right to a job, will result in comprehensive income coverage. Each person desiring a job at going wages would be employed; single parents raising children at home would receive substantial benefit increases; and those unable to hold jobs for reasons of disability would be guaranteed a living income.

VI. End Discrimination

Conservatives advocate abandoning government efforts to redress inequality on the grounds that the market will cure discrimination. This is a cynical argument, because it is precisely the "market valuation" of women and people of color which reproduces discrimination. Discrimination is *profitable*, because it keeps wages low. But it is also wasteful, because it deprives people of economic opportunity and deprives the economy of the opportunity to make the best use of the talents of all Americans.

Legislation Ensuring Equal Pay for Work of Equal Value

Discrimination cannot be ended merely by ensuring equal pay for identical work, because the kinds of work that men and women do differ. Existing evidence reveals discrepancies in pay for jobs of comparable skill, education, responsibility and difficulty. Some local and state governments have done studies of occupational pay differentials by gender; all should do so, and compensation ought to occur for discriminatory salary structures among public employees. We also suggest the passage of national legislation mandating all firms to conduct similar studies and adjust compensation where appropriate.

Enforce Affirmative Action

Ending discrimination requires a renewed commitment to affirmative action. Existing mandates should be vigorously enforced; goals and timetables should be adhered to; and sanctions, such as withholding of Federal monies, should be applied in cases where the law is ignored.

VII. Environmental Sustainability

We are on a collision course with nature. Toxic chemicals, depletion of natural resources, and air and water pollution threaten the planet. Because firms do not pay social costs, the system is biased toward environmental degradation and laxity on occupational health and safety. Firms often knowingly maintain unsafe workplaces because they prefer to compensate workers through a socialized compensation system, as the sufferers of black, brown, and white lung can attest. Firms dump toxic wastes because they do not anticipate paying for the cleanup.

All this filth is extremely costly. Cleaning up after acid rain, nuclear waste, or occupational hazards is more expensive than preventing them in the first place, but preventive methods are not profitable to private business.

Environmental protection and higher living standards are not incompatible. Productivity growth allows us to have more material goods while using fewer inputs and provides the potential for more leisure time. Sensible policies can promote renewable energy sources, long-lived products rather than planned obsolescence, and an environmentally-sound economy.

Strengthen Environmental Protection

The Administration has tried to dismantle the government's protection of the environment. Rather than relaxation, we need stronger standards for air and water, stricter regulations on toxics, and increased resources for enforcement.

National Right-to-Know Bill for Workers and Communities

Workers and communities should have the right to know what chemicals are being used in their workplaces and neighborhoods. Twenty-three states have passed right-to-know legislation, and action is overdue at the federal level.[14]

VIII. Democratic Labor Relations

Americans are deeply concerned with the nature of work, as well as its availability.[15] In order to ensure high-quality jobs we need democratic worker organizations. But we have witnessed a decade of corporate resistance to unions (see Chapter 6).

The decline of unions, contrary to widespread myths, is detrimental to our economic well-being. Unions increase productivity.[16] Perhaps even more important, in the long run, is the role that workers' organizations can play in a democratic economy. To construct democratic and efficient national economic policies, it is necessary to have democratic worker organizations. National policies to restrain inflation or labor-displacing technical changes can be instituted equitably and accountably, with sacrifices and gains fairly distributed. But without comprehensive representation of workers, national negotiations over economic policy will not adequately incorporate workers' interests and will not win the support of most Americans. Higher levels of unionization and more democratic unions can lead to a more productive and healthy economy.

A Worker's Bill of Rights

As citizens our constitutional rights protect us from the power of the state. As workers, however, we have few rights to protect us from the power of our employers—or even of our unions. Within the factory gates, the rights of property owners take precedence over the rights of workers as persons. Basic rights of association and free speech, for example, are denied: employers can prohibit workers from distributing printed materials of a political nature or even wearing a favorite button.

We propose the establishment of a set of civil rights, independent of collective bargaining, which are guaranteed to workers. These would include, at minimum, the right not to be discharged at will; prohibition of search and seizure within the factory; freedom from sexual harassment; the right to information about chemicals used in the workplace; the right to have worker representatives present at corporate board meetings; the right to refuse unsafe work; the right of association and assembly; and the rights associated with the First Amendment (free speech).

In addition, rights of democracy within worker organizations themselves should be ensured, such as the right to elect union officials and the right to vote on contracts.

Like other rights, these should be guaranteed through the judicial process.

A New Labor Code

As it has evolved, labor law currently embodies some anti-union biases which should be removed. As part of a sweeping revision of the U.S. labor code, we propose the following:

—Expedite Union Elections

Delays between card signing and union elections are a powerful factor for maintaining the (anti-union) *status quo*. Union drives lose momentum, firms have time to mount anti-union campaigns, and the union's ability to produce results for workers is eroded. We propose that elections be held within one month after 40% of a workforce has signed union representation cards.

—Invoke Sanctions for Violations of Labor Law

Employers frequently engage in illegal tactics, such as discrimination against union supporters and sham bargaining after representation rights have been won. The National Labor Relations Board has no power to enact punitive sanctions against firms for their violations of the law. Unfair labor practices which frustrate the representation process should carry punitive sanctions.

—Repeal Taft-Hartley

The Taft-Hartley Amendment to the Wagner Act, which permits right-to-work laws and prohibits secondary boycotting, has proven to be a powerful impediment to unions. Taft-Hartley should be repealed.

IX. Government Accountability

The public supports significant changes in spending and taxation. The evidence from opinion polls, Congressional pressure, and other public channels indicates that majorities want reductions in military spending, protection of social welfare expenditures, and tax reform.[17]

The administration, however, appears to be more interested in shaping public opinion than responding to it. Indeed, the power of private lobbyists and campaign contributors, as well as corporate ability to withhold investment if government policies are not to its liking, are important factors limiting government's responsiveness to the public. But government accountability is the backbone of a democracy, in economic as well as social and political matters.

Social Needs Inventory

Ten years of economic stagnation and five years of Reaganism have taken their toll. Estimates of the homeless range up to 2 million, illiteracy or semi-illiteracy plagues 60 million, and one in twelve Americans now goes hungry.[18] Mass transit systems are starved for funds; health care is unavailable to many.

We propose a bi-yearly inventory of social needs. Modelled on the Census, it would be a comprehensive accounting and ranking of social needs, as represented by a full cross-section of the population. Local and state governments, community and environmental organizations, along with individual households could respond to a social needs census. Public hearings could be held across the country.

Congressional action in response to the findings of the inventory should be legislatively mandated.

Health Care

Relative to other countries, the U.S. spends heavily on health care, yet measures of health status, such as infant mortality and life expectancy, put us below more frugal countries.[19] Part of the problem is an inefficient health care system, controlled by the industry, which is both the demander and the supplier. Costs are excessive and public health and preventive care are under-emphasized.

Of particular concern are the growing numbers of people without health care coverage. A rapidly increasing number of workers, as well as the unemployed, have no benefits. Yet Congress has failed to pass even national health insurance, despite its popularity,[20] leaving us decades behind other industrialized nations. We need a government-funded, publicly-controlled health care system.

Reduced Military Spending

The U.S. military has multiple functions. One is to defend the country, in the case of either nuclear or conventional attack. A second is to project U.S. power and defend U.S. interests throughout the world. To accomplish the latter, the U.S. maintains huge naval, air, and land garrisons in Europe, Asia, and the Pacific and Indian Oceans, and fosters the capability to intervene militarily throughout the world.

In our view, the only legitimate functions for the U.S. military are defensive. We should be equipped to protect our territory; we should not be spending money to project power and conduct offensive operations throughout the world. Instead, our policies should promote peace and economic cooperation and respect the sovereignty of other countries. Adherence to these principles would both enrich us morally and cost less. Greater use of diplomacy and negotiations and real rather than phony arms control talks will further reduce unnecessary military spending.

Reforming the Tax System

The need to reform our tax system is widely-recognized. The triumph of special interests has produced an inefficient, complex, and unfair tax system. Recent estimates show either little progressivity or regressivity, depending on the underlying assumptions.[21] The system represents a virtual abandonment of any commitment to equity.

The tax system should be simple and fair, and should therefore rely more on a progressive income tax. Elimination of loopholes and base-broadening are steps in the right direction. In addition, the standard deduction should be raised, to free low income groups from an onerous tax burden. Base-broadening can substantially raise collections, permitting moderate rates overall.[22]

X. Expanding Democracy

Many of the problems outlined in this report can be attributed to the existence of concentrated blocs of economic and political power. Powerful corporations and individuals have the ability to make decisions which may satisfy their own interests but not those of the people around them, and we argue that an undemocratic economy is inefficient as well.

Making our economy truly democratic is a formidable task. Here we outline some general programs which would substantially enhance democratic participation in the economy. Some of the details need to be filled in, but their thrust should be clear.

Investment Accountability

Firms are free to undertake investment largely without regard to its effects on workers, consumers and communities. We propose that corporations be held accountable for investment decisions, particularly with regard to their effects on employment, prices, availability of goods, and communities. Elected worker representatives should be permitted to attend corporate board meetings and enjoy other rights of access afforded to directors. Major investment projects should be preceded by "investment impact statements," which detail the project and its likely effects on employment, output, prices, taxes paid to local communities, and profits.

Workplace Democracy

Programs in workplace democracy have overwhelmingly resulted in higher productivity, output and job satisfaction. Yet firms resist self-management, presumably because it threatens the role of managers and supervisors. Banks are reluctant to lend to worker-owned or managed enterprises.

We propose the creation of a capital fund, along the lines of the federal home mortgage or farm loan programs, for starting worker-managed firms and for worker and community buyouts of existing firms. In addition, there should be an independent center for research and technical assistance on workplace democracy, to aid workers who are trying to institute self-management.

Price Controls Through Incomes Policies

Some aspects of the foregoing program will reduce inflation, such as the emphasis on innovation, productivity growth, and full utilization of capacity (lower costs and larger supply). But others, such as high levels of demand for labor and products will lead to upward pressure on prices.

Inflation must be confronted directly. Yearly negotiations between business, labor and government over wages, prices, profits, and interest rates should determine maximum growth rates. Government should be empowered to use tax penalties and rewards for corporate compliance.

Democratic Planning

Our premise is the need for more public control over economic decisions. In large part, this program would effect that control through structural reforms rather than direct planning. Some areas of the economy, however, require more direct planning, for instance in the provision of basic social needs, or international trade. We propose the creation of democratically-elected boards. While the precise manner in which these boards operate is an open question, they will serve a vital function in a democratic economy.

Can We Pay for It?

A common objection to many economic proposals is that they sound appealing, but are too expensive. By contrast, this program pays for itself, and in fact can even save money. This is because it uses currently idle resources and shifts labor and materials from policing an unfair system to productive activities.

There are two kinds of cost calculations to be made when evaluating an economic program. One is the overall economic impact. These calculations measure the true social costs and benefits, as for example with environmental policies, or the value of increased free time. The second is the impact on the government's balance sheet—budget expenditures and outlays.

Let's begin with the government. For the sake of argument, we will make conservative assumptions about the indirect effects of the program and assume that it succeeds in getting us to full employment in two years, cuts interest rates in half, and does not lower productivity growth. On the revenue side, there are three major items.[23] If we reduce unemployment to 3% in the first year, by the standard rule of thumb, Okun's Law, this will produce an additional 12% GNP. With no tax increases, this yields a revenue increase of $88.2 billion. If tax reform returned us to the pre-Reagan tax yield, there would be an additional $96.6 billion in the government coffers.

Second is reduced military spending. Weapons analysts from the World Policy Institute's Security Project have estimated that a military commitment of $1.25 trillion dollars over a period of five years is sufficient to meet genuinely defensive goals.[24] Compared with the administration's proposals, this represents a budgetary savings of $94 billion per year. Third, lower interest rates will reduce net interest payments on the debt, which are running at $130.4 billion per year. If interest rates are halved, we could have saved $65.2 billion in 1985.

These savings total $255.8 billion for 1985 alone. As Everett Dirksen once remarked, "A billion here, a billion there. Pretty soon it starts to add up to real money."

What about the costs? Many of the reforms are not costly to the government, such as increased minimum wages in the private sector, anti-discrimination measures, workplace democracy, and lower interest rates. Only Steps IX and X (Government Accountability and Toward a Democratic Economy) propose large expenditures, although there are also some other spending proposals, for example a jobs program, increased welfare benefits, day care, free higher education and pay equity. How far could $255.8 billion go towards these goals?

Here are a few examples to get an idea of the magnitude of these programs. Increasing the welfare benefit to 125% of the poverty line would cost roughly an additional $37 billion per year.[25] Free higher education would cost roughly $10 billion;[26] doubling federal expenditures for science and technology and the environment would be $8.7 billion and $11.4 billion, respectively. Adding all these expenditures, plus raising spending on health by $20 billion would cost a total of $87.1 billion.

If the government hired 2 million workers in job programs at $15,000 per year, it would cost $30 billion. Add to that a one-time allocation of $10 billion for a worker's bank,[27] $10 billion for day care, and $10 billion in investment subsidies.

The only other significant expenditure we've proposed is for pay equity. If half the existing gender pay gap (a 20% reduction) were eliminated, and on a full-time equivalency, women are 40% of the workforce, then pay equity will cost an estimated 8% of the government's wage bill or roughly $23.5 billion.[28]

This leaves $85.2 billion, which we could use to fund a resource transfer to the Third World, provide free day care for everyone, or reduce the deficit.

What about the overall economic costs? The picture is even more striking. For here we will reap the benefits of the expanded government programs and the structural reforms. The program will yield lower future costs for environmental decay, a healthier population, and less need for "guard labor" and other enforcement costs. The gains from full use of our plant and equipment and labor dwarf the costs of getting there.

Even this brief accounting suggests a simple observation. We can certainly afford this program. On economic as well as moral and political grounds we cannot afford anything less.

Footnotes

1. For related programs to reform the U.S. economy, see M. Carnoy and D. Shearer, *Economic Democracy*; G. Alperovitz and J. Faux, *Rebuilding America*; and S. Bowles, D. Gordon and T. Weisskopf, *Beyond the Wasteland*.

2. By full employment we mean jobs for all who desire them, at going wages, rather than an unemployment rate of 6 and 1/2% or more, as proposed by conservative economists. In the U.S., full employment means measured unemployment of 2% or 3%.

3. One common argument against low interest rates is that they will promote inflation. Our anti-inflation proposal is presented in Step X below.

4. See Harold Wilensky, "The Uneven Distribution of Leisure: The Impact of Economic Growth on 'Free Time'," *Social Problems*, 9(1), Summer, 1961.

5. Ten European countries and at least six states now have compensation for reduced hours. See Saul Blaustein and Isabel Craig, *An International Review of Unemployment Insurance Schemes*, W.E. Upjohn Institute, Kalamazoo, Michigan, 1977, and Steven M. Bloom and David E. Bloom, "U.S. Labor Unions: Losing Their Grip?," *Baltimore Sun*, September 1, 1985.

6. See the review by the Congressional Budget Office, *Temporary Measures to Stimulate Employment*, Washington, D.C., September, 1975.

7. The means to finance these jobs and other programs are discussed below in the section entitled, "Can We Pay For It?"

8. U.S. Bureau of Labor Statistics unpublished estimates of unemployment rates using methods comparable to U.S. data.

9. As a recent "experiment" shows, the promise of a free college education reduced dropout rates in a Harlem high school to zero. See "One Man's Gift: College for 52 in Harlem," *The New York Times*, October 19, 1985, page 1.

10. See the article by Richard Cooper in *The International Monetary System*, Conference Series #28, Federal Reserve Bank of Boston, 1984, for advocacy of a coordinated world monetary policy.

11. See James Tobin, "A Proposal for International Monetary Reform," *Eastern Economic Journal*, July/October, 1978.

12. Average monthly payment under Aid to Families with Dependent Children, July-September 1983, latest published figure, from *Social Security Bulletin*, Social Security Administration, Washington, D.C., June 1985.

13. Food Research and Action Center, "Food Prices—Fact and Fiction: Assessing the Adequacy of USDA's Thrifty Food Plan," Washington, D.C., 1985.

14. Source is private conversation with Office of Right to Know Coordinator, Massachusetts Industries and Labor Department.

15. See *Work in America Report of a Special Task Force to the Secretary of Health, Education, and Welfare*, Washington, D.C., 1973.

16. See Richard Freeman and James Medoff, *What Do Unions Do?*, Basic Books, New York, 1984.

17. See *Gallup Report*, #237, January, 1985.

18. Estimates of homelessness are from Joe Conason, "Body Count: How the Reagan Administration Hides the Homeless," *The Village Voice*, December 3, 1985. Illiteracy estimates are from Jonathon Kozol, *Illiterate America*, Doubleday and Company, New York, 1985. Hunger statistics are from the *The New York Times*, March 5, 1984.

19. Health status indicators are from *World Health Statistics Annual*, World Health Organization, Geneva, 1983.

20. For public opinion on health care, see *Gallup Report*, February, 1977 and January/February 1984.

21. Joseph A. Pechman, *Who Paid the Taxes, 1966-85*, The Brookings Institution, Washington, D.C., 1985).

22. For the impacts of various tax reform plans, see Congressional Budget Office, *Revising the Individual Income Tax*, Washington, D.C., July, 1983.

23. Throughout, we will be using 1985 estimated tax receipts and expenditures to calculate the effects of the program. These can be found in *The Budget in Brief FY 1986*, Government Printing Office, Washington, D.C.

24. First Report of the Security Project, a research project of the World Policy Institute, New York, 1984.

25. This calculation assumes 4 million recipients, whose average benefit is $4066 per year. The differential between the current benefit and 125% of the poverty line is $9247, making the total increase $37 billion. The 1985 poverty line for a family of four, slightly above the AFDC average, is $10,650. We suspect that if well-paid jobs were available, the number of people receiving AFDC payments would fall, not rise.

26. Estimate is from Bowles, Gordon, and Weisskopf, *op. cit.*

27. The bank would be self-financing from its interest income.

28. These estimates were derived from Elaine Sorensen, "Implementing Comparable Worth: A Review of Recent Job Evaluation Studies," paper presented at American Economic Association Meetings, December 1985. Government wage bill is from *Statistical Abstract of the United States, 1985,* Table 473, page 292.

Appendix

All data reported from the U.S. national income and product accounts refer to the data prior to the revision of the accounts by the Commerce Department made available at the end of 1985.

How We Calculated the Cost of Conservative Economics

To determine the cost of conservative economics, we ask: what would have happened if the government's economic policy had been different? To do this we specify a benchmark full employment alternative set of policies. We then compare the level of goods and services produced under the alternative policy with the level of goods and services produced under the policies of conservative economics. The difference between the two is the lost output due to the policies followed, or the cost of conservative economics.

Of course, it is quite difficult to estimate this cost with any certainty. Moreover, there are many costs—increased social division, escalating military waste and environmental imbalance—which we do not include in this chapter, though many of these are discussed in other chapters of this report. With these qualifications, we can describe these calculations.

As described in the text we have to calculate the effects of these alternative levels of unemployment on the production of goods and services in the economy. To do that we consider three effects of unemployment on the level of production. First, lower unemployment increases production because a larger fraction of those looking for work are finding it. Second, lower unemployment increases production because more people enter the labor force and look for work. With a greater labor force, for any measured rate of unemployment, there are more people working and producing goods. Third, lower unemployment increases production because, up to a point, factories are able to operate at a more efficient level of output, thereby increasing productivity.

These effects can be summarized in equation 1 which is *identically* true:

$$(1)\ GNP = \frac{GNP}{employed\ workers} \quad X \quad \frac{employed\ workers}{labor\ force} \quad X \quad labor\ force$$

247

Since:

(2) $$\frac{\text{employed workers}}{\text{labor force}} = (1 - \text{unemployment rate})$$

then, by substituting (2) into (1)

(3) $$\text{GNP} = \frac{\text{GNP}}{\text{employed workers}} \times (1 - \text{unemployment rate}) \times \text{labor force}$$

Equation (3) is the basic equation used to estimate the cost of conservative economics. It embodies the three factors described above. The first term represents productivity: the amount of output produced by employed workers. The second represents the measured unemployment rate. And the third represents how large the labor force is. To estimate the effects of various levels of unemployment on GNP, it is necessary to estimate the effects of unemployment on the productivity (the first term) and the labor force (the third term). And, of course, the unemployment rate enters the middle term directly.

We estimated econometrically the effect of unemployment on productivity by using historical data of the postwar period in the U.S. We found that for each one percentage point reduction in the unemployment rate, production per employee increased on average by $213. A reduction of the unemployment rate from 7.5% to 3% would increase the level of output per worker by 4.5 X 213 or about $960. In 1984, the level of output per employed worker was about $35,000 when the unemployment rate was 7.5%. If the unemployment rate had been 3% instead, by these calculations the level of output per worker would have been about $36,000 instead.

We then estimated the relationship between unemployment and the labor force. We found that each 1% (not percentage point) reduction in the unemployment rate increased the labor force by .03%. For example, a reduction of the unemployment rate from 7.5% to 3%, is 4.5 percentage points or a 4.5/7.5 = 60% reduction in the unemployment rate. This gives a 60 X .03 = 1.8% increase in the labor force. In 1984 the measured labor force was almost 114 million. So a reduction of the unemployment rate from 7.5% to 3% would bring (.018 X 114 million) = 2.6 million more workers into the labor force which would increase the labor force to 116.6 million workers.

We then plugged all of these back into equation (3). In 1984, for example, if the unemployment rate had been 3%, GNP would have been:

GNP   ($36,000) X (1 - .03) X (116,600,000) = $4,071,672,000,000

or over 4070 billion dollars. In 1984, with an unemployment rate of 7.5%, the actual GNP was 3663 billion dollars. So the cost of conservative economics by this measure is 407 billion dollars in 1984, which is similar to the figure shown in the text.[1]

An Estimate of Guard Labor

Estimates of guard labor in the U.S. economy appear in the figure below.

Guard Labor

Type	1965	1969	1979	1984
(1) Unemployed	3,366,000	2,832,000	6,137,000	8,522,900
(2) a. DOD employees	3,914,000	4,560,000	2,987,000	3,501,700
active duty	2,857,000	3,293,000	2,020,000	2,443,500
civilian	1,057,000	1,262,000	967,000	1,058,200
b. Employees in defense products industries	1,266,000	1,647,000	1,299,000	1,444,000
(3) Discouraged workers (econometric estimate)*	925,000	362,000	1,964,000	3,135,000
(4) Prisoners	351,895	350,683	493,500	715,594
(5) Supervisors**	4,101,420	4,545,120	7,079,300	8,541,600
(6) Guards	663,000	727,000	1,121,000	1,494,000
Total Guard Labor	14,487,310	15,013,803	21,080,800	27,354,794
Guard Labor/ Labor Force (Official Measure)	.196	.186	.201	.240
Guard Labor/ Population	.075	.075	.094	.116

Sources: Complete sources are available in Samuel Bowles and Hannah Roditi, "Guard Labor" mimeo 1985, available from the authors at the Department of Economics, University of Massachusetts, Amherst, MA 01004. The main sources are the U.S. **Statistical Abstract, Business Conditions Digest,** and **Employment and Earnings.**

*The number of discouraged workers is estimated using methods described in the text and in this appendix.

**Supervision generally involves both co-ordination and control. Our estimate here is one half of all supervisors (excluding those counted as DOD employees and those engaged in military goods production). Detailed information on the categories referred to as "supervisors" is presented in "Guard Labor."

1. This is not identically equal to the figure in the next table because we have slightly simplified the explanation and rounded numbers. For a complete explanation of the methods and a full presentation of the data, see J. Epstein, "The Cost of Conservative Economics" mimeo, 1985, available from the author at the Department of Economics, New School of Social Research, 66 West 12th Street, New York, N.Y. 10011.

The Burden of Conservative Economics in Latin America

There are at least two novel calculations which deserve some review in this appendix. The first is the estimate of output loss for Latin America. The second is the percentage of the year the average Latin American works to repay the debt.

We made several estimates of lost output, using data from the United Nations publication, *National Accounts Statistics, Analysis of Main Aggregates, 1982* and the International Monetary Fund, *World Economic Outlook* (Washington, D.C., 1985). Estimates of output loss using U.N. data were larger than those obtained using IMF data; we report the more conservative figures in the text.

In the reported estimate, we chose 1984 dollars as the relevant base, in keeping with other portions of the Economic Report. Using IMF (1985), we estimated 1984 current dollar GDP for Western hemisphere developing countries by dividing the reported debt figure of $351.1 billion by the debt to GDP ratio of 46.0. Using this figure, we estimated 1979-1983 GDP in 1984 dollars by successively subtracting the real growth in GDP (which was sometimes negative) from the previous year's GDP in 1984 dollars (real growth figures were taken from IMF (1985), p. 210). We then took the 1979 estimate and projected what GDP would have been if the 1967-76 growth rate of 5.9% had obtained. These figures and the resulting output loss are reported below. (All figures are in billions of 1984 dollars.)

Year	GDP	GDP (projected)	output loss
1984	763.262	979.068	215.806*
1983	745.161	922.974	177.813
1982	768.623	870.094	101.471
1981	776.348	820.243	43.895
1980	768.623	773.249	4.626
1979	728.947	728.947	--

total output lost, 1980-83 = 327.805

*1984 figure not included in the total

The percentage of the year spent working to pay the debt was determined by the debt service as a percentage of GDP. Since this was not readily available in the data, it was calculated according to the following formula:

$$\frac{\text{debt service}}{\text{GDP}} = \frac{\text{debt service}}{\text{exports}} \quad X \quad \frac{\text{exports}}{\text{debt}} \quad X \quad \frac{\text{debt}}{\text{GDP}}$$

where exports here means exports of goods and services. Using the reported 1985 figures for the indebted developing countries in the Western hemisphere from IMF (1985), pp. 266 and 168 (with the second right-hand term calculated as the inverse of the reported ratio of debt to exports), we obtain:

Debt service/GDP $= .405$ X $.371$ X $.456 = .0685$

Thus, about 7% of annual GDP— or about 25 days of a 365-day year— is surrendered in the form of debt service. If we were to use net domestic product in the calculations (arguably a better measure), the time devoted to debt servicing would likely increase.

Index